GRAMMAR OF THE
YIDDISH LANGUAGE

GRAMMAR OF THE YIDDISH LANGUAGE

by
DOVID KATZ

Duckworth

First published in 1987 by

Gerald Duckworth & Co. Ltd.

The Old Piano Factory

43 Gloucester Crescent, London NW1

British Library Cataloguing in Publication Data

Katz, Dovid

Grammar of the Yiddish language.

1. Yiddish language—Grammar

I. Title

437'.947   PJ5115

ISBN 0-7156-2161-0 (cased)

ISBN 0-7156-2162-9 (paper)

Yiddish type font designed by the author

Printed in Great Britain by

Redwood Burn Limited, Trowbridge

CONTENTS

3 GREETINGS

4 NOUNS

5 NOUN PHRASES

6 PRONOUNS

7 VERBS

8 PREFIXED VERBS

9 ANALYTIC VERBS

10 ADVERBS

11 QUESTIONS

12 NUMBERS

13 TIME

14 SYNTAX

15 SEMANTICS

16 PHRASEOLOGY

ACKNOWLEDGEMENTS

The *Grammar* has grown from materials and methodology developed at the Oxford Centre for Postgraduate Hebrew Studies between 1978 and 1986. The project was undertaken at the suggestion of Professor William J. Fishman (Queen Mary College, University of London) and Mr Colin Haycraft of Gerald Duckworth & Company (London). I am grateful to both for their support and advice.

The philosophy of Yiddish grammar implicit in the *Grammar* was largely inspired by Ber Borokhov's *Ufgabn fun der yidisher filologye* (pp. 1-22 in S. Niger's *Pinkes,* Vilna 1913). Strategies for abstracting a broadly based middle ground from variation in contemporary usage were substantially assisted by consultation with Y. Mark's *Gramatik fun der yidisher klal-shprakh* (New York 1978).

A preliminary version was published by the Oxford Centre for Postgraduate Hebrew Studies for experimental use in the elementary course at the fifth annual Oxford Summer Programme in Yiddish Language and Literature in August 1986. The course was taught by Christopher Hutton and Dov-Ber Kerler, both of whom offered valuable advice and assistance.

My sincere thanks to the colleagues and friends who took the time and trouble to read earlier drafts and offer their indispensable suggestions, many of which have been incorporated. They are Devra Asher (St Cross College, Oxford); Deborah Blake (Duckworth and Company, London); Professor Carey Crantford (Furman University, Greenville, South Carolina); David Djanogly (Arenski Gallery, London); Dr Daniel Frank (Oxford Centre for Postgraduate Hebrew Studies and Wolfson College, Oxford); Professor Christopher Hutton

(University of Texas, Austin); Menke and Rivke Katz (Bitterroot magazine, New York); Dov-Ber Kerler (Oxford Centre for Postgraduate Hebrew Studies and Lincoln College, Oxford); Michele McHugh (Middlebury College, Vermont); Professor Wolf Moskovich (Hebrew University, Jerusalem); Elinor Robinson (Columbia University, New York); David Schneider (Exeter College, Oxford).

The author alone assumes responsibility for shortcomings as well as for the opinions inherent in the presentation.

Oxford, February 1987   Dovid Katz

FOREWORD

The *Grammar* was prepared with a dual readership in mind. The first intended users are university students enrolled in Yiddish language courses. Ideally, the qualified teacher will converse extensively in Yiddish from a very early stage of the course while supplying genuine literary texts. Lessons can be chosen as necessary from various sections to suit the requirements of the course. In place of 'fill in the blanks' exercises, it is recommended that students be asked to write original sentences and compositions on the basis of a selected section. The dictionaries recommended for use alongside the *Grammar* are Bergman's at an elementary stage; Weinreich's at a more advanced stage; and Harkavy's at a still more advanced stage at which the student is reading from works of Yiddish literature on his or her own (see 'Dictionaries', p. 277). Reading may be culled from any of a number of anthologies or readers (see 'Anthologies', pp. 278–279), or better still, from original works of modern Yiddish masters selected by the instructor.

The second intended user is the more advanced student or general reader who requires a reference grammar either to help master the language or as a work to be consulted as necessary.

Suggestions for improvements in future editions may be sent to the author at the Oxford Centre for Postgraduate Hebrew Studies, 45 St Giles, Oxford OX1 3LW, England.

INTRODUCTION

Yiddish was created some thousand years ago by a Jewish minority population that had resettled from the ancient Near East to medieval Central Europe. Although it almost never enjoyed official government status, it thrived and was spoken and written by millions over a vast European territory, and gave rise to a substantial literature. Over the past century, Yiddish was carried to many parts of the world by East European Jewish immigrants and their descendants. Discovered only recently by large numbers of West European and American readers, Yiddish literature has assumed an international position, not least in consequence of its portrayals of the specifics of East European Jewish culture and the more universal implications of that culture.

Yiddish was never the language of all world Jewry. It is, rather, the traditional lingua franca of the *Ashkenazim,* the descendants of the makers of the medieval Jewish civilization that arose on Germanic-speaking territories. The name derives from the medieval Jewish term for those territories, *Ashkenaz.* With the early migrations of large numbers of Ashkenazim as far south as Italy, as far north as Holland and as far east as Russia, Yiddish spread over much of Europe, far beyond the Germanic-speaking lands.

Yiddish entails an intricate fusion between its three major components — the Semitic component deriving from the Hebrew and Aramaic of the ancient Near East that the first settlers in Ashkenaz brought with them; the Germanic component from the medieval Germanic lands where Yiddish was born; and, over the last few centuries, a Slavonic component in Eastern Europe. The two previous Jewish languages, Hebrew and Aramaic, that the first settlers had brought with them, fused with a number of local varieties of medieval German city dialects deriving from the Upper and Central German areas. Statistically speaking, the greatest part of both the vocabulary and the morphological and syntactic machinery of the language is Germanic. Nevertheless, even the Germanic component of Yiddish is not congruous with any one German dialect, while each Yiddish dialect remains systematically relatable to any other Yiddish dialect. To the historical linguist, this is evidence of a Yiddish speech community that interacted with other far-away Yiddish-speaking communities vastly more than with the neighbouring speakers of the local or national non-Jewish languages. Yiddish linguistics focuses on the unique and creative ways in which the disparate parts of Yiddish combine to form a powerfully expressive language. Its major registers feature human sensitivities, logical precision and a sense of humour emphasizing irony and satire.

The origins of Yiddish literature are still somewhat obscure. Traces of written Yiddish go back to the eleventh century. The earliest extensive manuscript bearing an explicit date is from 1382. Appropriately enough, many of the early Yiddish literary manuscripts represent interaction of the ancient but always evolving Jewish culture of the day with selected trends from contemporary Western civilization. One of the favourite early genres is the extensive epic poem. In a number of surviving Yiddish manuscripts, medieval romances such as *King Arthur* are adopted from German models. In many others, however, the European epic is the form applied to such traditional Jewish motifs as the Biblical books of Samuel and Kings. In others still, both European form and content are reworked into a highly original Yiddish masterpiece. The best known example is *Bovo d'Antona* (Bovo of

Antona), written by the great Yiddish poet (and Hebrew and Aramaic grammarian and Yiddish etymologist) Elijah Levita (1469 – c. 1549), better known in Yiddish as Elye Bokher. In this first application of the masterly Italian ottava rima (abababcc) in any Germanic language, Elye Bokher took as his immediate source *Buovo d'Antona*, an Italian romance, which is itself closely related to the English *Beve of Hampton.*

All these works were written in various forms of *Western Yiddish,* the collective name for the Yiddish dialects of Central Europe. With the advent of printing, Yiddish literature was launched for a pan-European market of readers. Largely to this end, writers and publishers consciously evolved a standard written form of Yiddish, based upon the western dialects, that would be intelligible to all readers. This standard, clearly discernible in the 1540s, when Yiddish printing really got off the ground (although a handful of prints are extant from the 1520s and 1530s), survived right up until the beginning of the nineteenth century.

By the late eighteenth century, Western Yiddish, centred in Germany, had begun to decline, largely in consequence of the demise of Western Ashkenazic culture and the linguistic assimilation to German of the Western Ashkenazim who were becoming simply 'German Jews'. In the Slavonic and Baltic lands, by contrast, *Eastern Yiddish* flourished as it never had before, and Eastern Europe remained the heartland of Yiddish until the Holocaust. Following its conscious elevation to a status of sanctity by the mystical Chassidic movement of the eighteenth century, the literary and social functions of the language expanded to suit the needs and wishes of the diversified literary, cultural and political movements of nineteenth-century Jewish Eastern Europe. The *Haskóle* (Haskalah), or enlightenment movement, and the Zionist (and Hebraist), Socialist and Yiddishist movements in all their colourful variety, made extensive literary use of Yiddish as a means of communicating their philosophies.

By the early nineteenth century, there were clear examples of the emerging new standard language, based upon the eastern dialects. Reformist writers of varying cultural persuasions did away with Western Yiddish archaisms that had long been in disuse, and evolved the modern literary standard that is based on the thriving Yiddish of Eastern Europe. Traditionally, the credit for forging a unified literary language from the dialects of East European Yiddish is assigned to the 'grandfather of Modern Yiddish literature' – Mendele Moykher Sforim (pen name of Sholem-Yankev Abramovitsh, c. 1836 – 1917). His two fellow classicists in the triumvirate of nascent modern Yiddish literature are humorist Sholem Aleichem (Sholem Rabinovitsh, 1859 – 1916) and romanticist Y. L. Peretz (1852 – 1915)

Within the European Jewish community, Yiddish was, up until the modern era, one of three Jewish languages – Hebrew, Aramaic and Yiddish – which complemented each other in a stable interrelating system of intracommunal languages. In addition, of course, all members of the community had knowledge of one or more non-Jewish coterritorial languages. The Yiddishist movement, a child of nineteenth- and twentieth-century Jewish Eastern Europe, has sought consciously to enhance the role of the everyday spoken language of Ashkenazic Jewry. For many years, pro-Yiddish sentiment was severely opposed by both assimilationists who sought to supplant Yiddish with the national languages of the countries in which Jews lived, and the Hebraists, who sought (and in Israel, succeeded) in reviving ancient Hebrew as an everyday spoken language. There are almost infinite combinations of love, hate, jealousy and ambiguous love-hate toward Yiddish. For many centuries, the three Jewish languages of Ashkenaz had lived in harmony; suddenly, two of them were proclaimed sworn enemies by their adherents. The 'language controversy', as it is usually called, burned most passionately in the waning nineteenth and the early twentieth century. The third Jewish language of Ashkenaz, Aramaic, was spared from conflict because of its lack of widespread active usage. It is the most elite of the three Jewish languages of Ashkenaz, written and studied only by the most educated, the scholars of two great branches of Jewish learning and literature created in it, the Talmud (Jewish law) and Kabbalah (Jewish mysticism).

The modern literary language, known as Standard Yiddish, has drawn upon the resources of all three major East European dialects of Yiddish: Mideastern Yiddish (popularly 'Polish'), Southeastern Yiddish ('Ukrainian') and Northeastern Yiddish ('Lithuanian'). Standard languages generally come into being as a result of sociological and geocultural factors, not via mathematical equations giving everybody an equal share. Standard Yiddish pronunciation is far closer to Northeastern Yiddish, especially as cultivated in its centuries-old cultural capital, Vilna, than to any other dialect. In grammar, the historical sources of the standard are spread rather differently among the dialects, and if anything, the standard is furthest from Northeastern usage. Hence the popular conception that Standard Yiddish is a 'compromise' between Northeastern pronunciation and Southern (i.e. Mideastern and Southeastern) grammar, while a vast oversimplification, is none the less largely accurate.

ABBREVIATIONS

adv.	adverb
cf.	compare
e.g.	for example
esp.	especially
f.	feminine
i.e.	namely; that is
inf.	infinitive
lit.	literally
m.	masculine
M.E.	Mideastern Yiddish ('Polish')
n.	noun
N.E.	Northeastern Yiddish ('Lithuanian')
pej.	pejorative
pl.	plural
sg.	singular
S.	Southern Yiddish (= Mideastern Yiddish plus Southeastern Yiddish)
S.E.	Southeastern Yiddish ('Ukrainian')
trans.	transitive
v.	verb
var.	variant form

ALPHABET CHART

Name	Printed Form	Script Form	Transcription
áləf	א		—
pásekh áləf	אַ		[a]
kómǝts áləf	אָ		[o]
beyz	בּ		[b]
veyz *	ב		[v]
giml	ג		[g]
dáləd	ד		[d]
dáləd záyin shin	דזש		[j]
hey	ה		[h]
vov	ו		[u]
tsvey vovn	וו		[v]
vov yud	וי		[oy]
záyin	ז		[z]
zayin shin	זש		[zh]
khes *	ח		[kh]
tes	ט		[t]
tes shin	טש		[tsh]
yud	י		[y] / [i]
tsvey yudn	יי		[ey]
pásǝkh tsvey yudn	ײַ		[ay]
kof *	כ		[k]
khof	כ		[kh]

lángər khof **	ך		[kh]
lámǝd	ל		[l]
mem	מ		[m]
shlósn mem **	ם		[m]
nun	נ		[n]
lángər nun **	ן		[n]
sámǝkh	ס		[s]
áyin	ע		[e] / [ǝ]
pey	פ		[p]
fey	פֿ		[f]
lángər fey **	ף		[f]
tsádik	צ		[ts]
lángər tsadik **	ץ		[ts]
kuf	ק		[k]
reysh	ר		[r]
shin	ש		[sh]
sin *	ש		[s]
tof *	ת		[t]
sof *	תּ		[s]

*   occurs in the traditional system only

** final form of preceding

1 THE ALPHABET

1.0 OVERVIEW

The Yiddish alphabet, written from right to left, is an evolved form of the ancient Semitic alphabet. Two systems of spelling coexist within it. The greatest part of the language is spelled according to the **phonetic system**, which features one-to-one correspondence between letter and sound. The minority Semitic component of Yiddish, deriving from Hebrew and Aramaic, is spelled etymologically according to the **traditional system**. A number of variations may be encountered in Yiddish spelling. The most widely used system is **modern standard orthography**. Other systems are used by certain communities.

1.1 THE YIDDISH WRITING SYSTEM

The Yiddish writing system is a variant of the Hebrew and Aramaic alphabet. Like all Semitic-derived scripts, it is written and read from right to left. Semitic alphabets are originally consonantal. Explicit letters to mark vowel sounds are absent. They are not necessary for native speakers of Semitic languages, where the three-consonant Semitic root itself signifies membership in a family of related words. Skeletal consonantal spellings are therefore perfectly comprehensible. When in the histories of these languages (not infrequently because of their demise as vernaculars and their perpetuation as liturgical or classical languages), it did become necessary for literary or educational purposes to mark vowels, this was usually accomplished by the addition of a system of diacritic marks (or 'points') below or above the line. The history of the Yiddish alphabet reveals creative reworking of an Eastern cultural phenomenon – the ancient consonantal Semitic alphabet – to match a Western reality – a European language for which the representation of vowels is crucial.

1.1.1   The phonetic system

The phonetic system of Yiddish spelling generally provides a perfect one-to-one correspondence between letter and sound. It is used for the non-Semitic parts of the language, hence for the vast majority of words. It has evolved through many intermediate stages and a few regressions. Over the past thousand years, Yiddish has increasingly made use of those letters that had lost the phonetic consonantal values they once had in Hebrew and Aramaic, especially áləf (→ §§1.2.2, 1.2.3) and áyin (→ §1.2.24) and put them to work as full-fledged vowel letters, instead of introducing sublinear or supralinear points and dots). The two vowel diacritics that are retained, kómats (= [o]) and pásəkh (= [a]) are both confined to specific letters (אָ = [o] → §1.2.3; אַ = [a] → §1.2.2 and יי = [ay] → §1.2.17); hence they too are in effect parts of vowel letters rather than free-floating vowel points that can be affixed at will to any consonant. In short, Yiddish has evolved a Western type alphabetic structure in which both consonants and vowels are marked by letters, while preserving the form and direction of the inherited Semitic alphabet.

1.1.2   The traditional system

The traditional system governs the orthography of the Semitic component within Yiddish, comprising several thousand words, nearly all of which are spelled historically, that is to say, as they are spelled in Hebrew or Aramaic. The correspondence between the traditional system and the vocabulary derived from Semitic would be perfect were it not for a handful of words of Semitic origin that have come to be spelled according to the phonetic system (e.g. טאָמער 'if; in case') – and an even smaller handful of non-Semitic component words that have realigned themselves to the traditional system (e.g. male forename קלמן [káimən]). For those who know Hebrew, mastering the traditional system poses no problem. For others, the spelling of each Semitism must be learned along with the word, although certain master patterns will become evident.

1.2   THE YIDDISH ALPHABET

The alphabet (or *áləfbeyz* as it is also known, from its name in Yiddish – אַלף־בית) derives from the classic twenty-two Semitic letters. The number of symbols in Yiddish is increased by the word-final forms of the five letters that have them (כ → word-final ך, מ → ם, נ → ן, פ → ף, צ → ץ), and the spirant counterparts of four plosives (cf. ב [b] vs. בֿ [v], כ [k] vs. כ [kh], פ [p] vs. פֿ [f], ת [t] vs. ת [s]). The number of functions is increased first by the various combinations of letters that Yiddish makes use of to effect complete coverage of the sound system of the language, and secondly by the use of one symbol for more than one function where the true function may be deduced from position in the word. The printed and script forms of each letter, and its phonetic transcription in Latin characters, are provided. The transcriptions, enclosed in square brackets [ ], represent a modified version of the transcriptional system of the Yivo Institute for Jewish Research, which was designed for English speakers. Where the transcription differs radically from accepted phonetic transcription, the international phonetic equivalent follows in parenthesis. Yiddish handwriting is frequently characterized by flamboyant strokes above and below the line for the risers and descenders (often extending higher and lower than risers and descenders in English). Where possible, the samples provided illustrate usage in initial, medial and final position.

1.2.1   áləf

Print: א   Script: ⅃k (or ⅃c)

א has no phonetic realization. It has two functions.

1.2.1.1   א to avert ambiguity

א systematically averts ambiguity by distinguishing consonantal וו (tsvey vovn = [v] → §1.2.10) before and after vocalic ו (vov = [u] → §1.2.9) and before diphthongal וי (vov yud = [oy] → §1.2.11).

SAMPLES OF א TO AVERT AMBIGUITY

וואו	‌	[vu]	'where'
פרואוון	‌	[pruvn]	'try'
וואוינען	‌	[vóynən]	'live (= dwell)'

1.2.1.2   א to mark word, syllable and stem onset

א marks the onset of words, syllables and stems that begin with the vowels

ו (vov = [u] → §1.2.9), וי (vov yud = [oy] → §1.2.11), י (yud = [i] → §1.2.15), יי (tsvey yudn = [ey] → §1.2.16), and ײַ (pásəkh tsvey yudn = [ay] → §1.2.17).

SAMPLES OF א TO MARK WORD ONSET

אוּן		[un]	'and'
אוי		[oy]	'Oh!; Oh dear!'
אין		[in]	'in'
אייביק		[éybik]	'forever'
אײַז		[ayz]	'ice'

SAMPLES OF א TO MARK SYLLABLE ONSET

אומרואיק		[úmruik]	'restless'
אַסאָציאירט		[asotsiírt]	'associated'
פֿעאיק		[féik]	'skilful; capable'
קאָנטינואום		[kontinúum]	'continuum'

SAMPLES OF א TO MARK STEM ONSET

פֿאַראייניקן		[faréynikn]	'unite (v.)'
באַאײַנפֿלוסן		[baáynflusn]	'influence (v.)'
ריבאײַזן		[ríbayzn]	'foodgrater'

Note: Word, syllable and stem onset are *not* marked by א before the vowels אַ (pásəkh áləf = [a] → §1.2.2), אָ (kómǝts áləf = [o] → §1.2.3) or ע (áyin = [e] → §1.2.24), hence:

אַוועק		[avék]	'away'
אָן		[on]	'without'
עסן		[ésn]	'eat'

6

1.2.2   pásəkh áləf

Print: אַ   Script: אַ   Realization: [a]

SAMPLES OF אַ

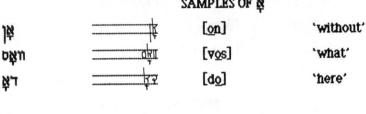

אַלע		[álə]	'all'
זאַך		[zakh]	'thing'
נאַ		[na]	'here!'

1.2.3   kóməts áləf

Print: אָ   Script: אָ   Realization: [o] (= ɔ)

SAMPLES OF אָ

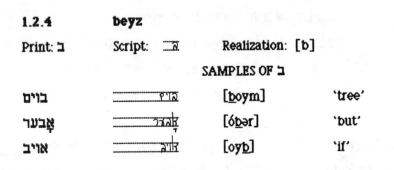

אָן		[on]	'without'
וואָס		[vos]	'what'
דאָ		[do]	'here'

1.2.4   beyz

Print: ב   Script: ב   Realization: [b]

SAMPLES OF ב

בוים		[boym]	'tree'
אָבער		[óbər]	'but'
אויב		[oyb]	'if'

1.2.5   veyz

Print: בֿ (/ב)   Script: בֿ   Realization: [v]

בֿ occurs in the traditional system only. In the phonetic system, [v] is rendered by יו (tsvey vovn = [v] → §1.2.10).

SAMPLES OF בֿ

בבל		[bóvl]	'Babylonia'
חבֿרה		[khéyrə]	'group of friends; crew'
אגבֿ		[ágəv]	'by the way'

1.2.6 giml

Print: ג. Script: Realization: [g]

SAMPLES OF ג

גוט		[gut]	'good'
באַגיסן		[bagísn]	'spill (on top of ...)'
אויג		[oyg]	'eye'

1.2.7 dáləd

Print: ד. Script: Realization: [d]

SAMPLES OF ד

דאָרטן		[dórtn]	'there'
אָדער		[ódər]	'or'
באָד		[bod]	'(Turkish) bath'

1.2.7.1 dáləd záyin shin

Print: דזש Script: Realization: [j] (= ǰ/dž)

דזש functions as a single consonant.

SAMPLES OF דזש

| דזשין | | [jin] | 'gin' |

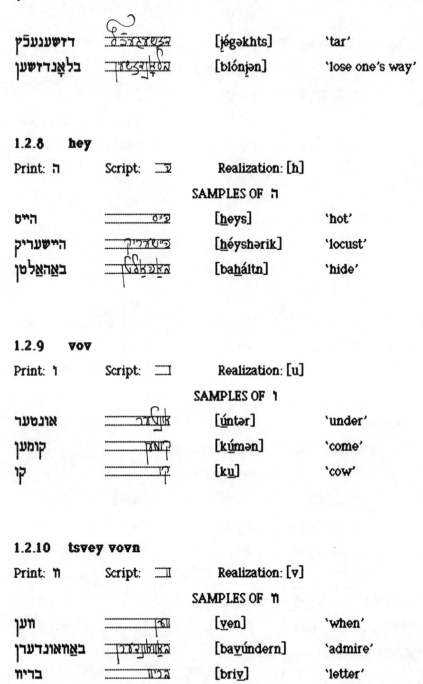

| דזשענגלק | | [jégəkhts] | 'tar' |
| בלאָנדזשען | | [blónjən] | 'lose one's way' |

1.2.8   hey

Print: ה   Script: ה̄   Realization: [h]

SAMPLES OF ה

הייס		[heys]	'hot'
היישעריק		[héyshərik]	'locust'
באַהאַלטן		[baháltn]	'hide'

1.2.9   vov

Print: ו   Script: ו   Realization: [u]

SAMPLES OF ו

אונטער		[úntər]	'under'
קומען		[kúmən]	'come'
קו		[ku]	'cow'

1.2.10   tsvey vovn

Print: וו   Script: וו   Realization: [v]

SAMPLES OF וו

ווען		[ven]	'when'
באַוואונדערן		[bavúndern]	'admire'
בריוו		[briv]	'letter'

1.2.11   vov yud

Print: יו   Script: ⊐I   Realization: [oy] (= ɔj)

SAMPLES OF יו

אויס	_____ ōīk	[o̱ys]	'finished!; it's all over!'
מויז	_____ ẕīṉ	[mo̱yz]	'mouse'
שטרוי	_____ ꞮƖⱮ	[shtro̱y]	'straw'

1.2.12   záyin

Print: ז   Script: ⊐3   Realization: [z]

SAMPLES OF ז

זאַװערולבע	_____	[z̲avərúkhe]	'blizzard'
באַזוכן	_____	[baz̲úkhn]	'visit'
גלאָז	_____	[gloz̲]	'glass'

1.2.12.1   záyin shin

Print: זש   Script: ⊠3   Realization: [zh] (= ž)

SAMPLES OF זש

זשאַבע	_____	[zhábə]	'frog'
װאַזשנע	_____	[váz̲hnə]	'impressive; classy'
שאַנטאַזש	_____	[shantáz̲h]	'blackmail'

1.2.13   khes

Print: ח   Script: ⊐Ɪ   Realization: [kh] (= x)

ח occurs in the traditional system only. In the phonetic system, [kh] is
rendered by כ (khof → §1.2.19).

SAMPLES OF ה

חלום		[khólǝm]	'dream'
בחור		[bókhǝr]	'fellow; bachelor'
כוח		[kóyǝkh]	'strength'

1.2.14   tes

Print: ט   Script: Realization: [t]

SAMPLES OF ט

טומל		[tuml]	'noise'
מאַנטל		[mántl]	'coat'
רויט		[royt]	'red'

1.2.14.1   tes shin

Print: טש   Script: Realization: [tsh] (= č/tš)

טש functions as a single consonant.

SAMPLES OF טש

טשײניק		[tsháynik]	'teakettle'
פֿאַרטײטשן		[fartáytshn]	'explain; translate'
בײטש		[baytsh]	'whip'

1.2.15   yud

Print: י   Script:

י has two realizations.

1.2.15.1   Consonantal י

י is consonantal [y] (= j) at the beginning of a syllable.

SAMPLES OF CONSONANTAL ʼ

יאָ		[y̲o]	'yes'
יאַסלעס		[y̲ásləs]	'gums'
סטאַנציע		[stántsyə]	'station'

1.2.15.2 Vocalic ʼ

ʼ is vocalic [i] at the middle or end of a syllable.

SAMPLES OF VOCALIC ʼ

בין		[bi̲n]	'bee'
וויכטיק		[ví̲khti̲k]	'important'
זי		[zi̲]	'she'

1.2.16 tsvey yudn

Print: ײ Script: Realization: [ey] (= ej)

SAMPLES OF ײ

איידעם		[é̲ydəm]	'son in law'
שיין		[she̲yn]	'pretty; beautiful'
קליי		[kle̲y]	'glue'

Note: Diphthong ײ is preceded by א at the start of a word or syllable (→ §1.2.1.2). When two ʼs occur at the beginning of a word, syllable, or stem, they represent a sequence of consonantal ʼ (= [y] → §1.2.15.1) plus vocalic ʼ (= [i] → §1.2.15.2), i.e. [yi], rather than diphthong [ey], hence:

ייד		[yi̲d]	'Jew'
ייִדיש		[yí̲dish]	'Yiddish; Jewish'
ייִנגל		[yí̲ngl]	'boy'

12

1.2.17 pásəkh tsvey yudn

Print: יִ (/יִי) Script: ⸗   Realization: [ay] (= aj)

In many texts, יִ is written יי, i.e. identically with יי = [ey] (→ §1.2.16).
Where יִ is not used, the difference must be ascertained via knowledge of
the word or checked with a dictionary.

SAMPLES OF יִ

אײַזן	⸗	[áyzn]	'iron'
בײַטן	⸗	[báytn]	'change'
געטרײַ	⸗	[gətráy]	'faithful'

1.2.18 kof

Print: כ (/ך) Script: ⸗   Realization: [k]

כ occurs in the traditional system only. In the phonetic system, [k] is
rendered by ק (kuf → §1.28).

SAMPLES OF כ

כבוד	⸗	[kóvəd]	'honour'
כלה	⸗	[kálə]	'bride'
בכוח	⸗	[bəkóyəkh]	'capable'

1.2.19 khof

Print: כ (/ך) Script: ⸗   Realization: [kh]

SAMPLES OF כ

כאליאַסטרע	⸗	[khalyástrə]	'gang'
כאפן	⸗	[khápm]	'catch'
זיכער	⸗	[zíkhər]	'certain; definite(ly)'

1.2.19.1 lánger khof

Replaces כ in word-final position.

Print: ך   Script: ڬ   Realization: [kh]

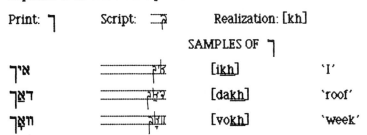

SAMPLES OF ך

איך		[i<u>kh</u>]	'I'
דאַך		[da<u>kh</u>]	'roof'
וואָך		[vo<u>kh</u>]	'week'

1.2.20 lámed

Print: ל   Script: ڷ   Realization: [l]

SAMPLES OF ל

לאָמפּ		[<u>l</u>omp]	'lamp'
ווײַלינקע		[váy<u>l</u>inkə]	'little while'
טאָל		[to<u>l</u>]	'valley'

1.2.21 mem

Print: מ   Script: ℵ   Realization: [m]

SAMPLES OF מ

מענטש		[<u>m</u>entsh]	'person'
טאָמער		[tó<u>m</u>ər]	'if; in case'
צימער		[tsí<u>m</u>ər]	'room'

1.2.21.1 shlósn mem

Replaces מ in word-final position.

Print: ם   Script: ℗   Realization: [m]

14

SAMPLES OF ס

בוידעם	מזיבזוב	[bóydəm]	'attic'
נאַראָנים	ניבאַנז	[narónim]	'fools'
שלום	שזולש	[shóləm]	'peace'

1.2.22   nun

Print: נ   Script: ꞁ   Realization: [n]

SAMPLES OF נ

נודניק	ןזינדוב	[núdnik]	'boring person; pest'
וואַנע	ןזאַוו	[vánə]	'bath'
שאַנדע	ודזאַבש	[shándə]	'disgrace'

1.2.22.1   lángər nun

Replaces נ in word-final position.

Print: ן   Script: ꞁ   Realization: [n]

SAMPLES OF ן

מאַן	ןאַמ	[man]	'man; husband'
צאָן	ןאָצ	[tson]	'tooth'
שפּין	ןיפּש	[shpin]	'spider'

1.2.23   sáməkh

Print: ס   Script: ꞓ   Realization: [s]

SAMPLES OF ס

סאַמאָוואַר	ראַוואָמאַס	[samovár]	'samovar'
בײַסן	ןסײַב	[báysn]	'bite'
שפּאַס	סאַפּש	[shpas]	'fun'

1.2.24　áyin

Print: ע　　　Script: ⌐

ע has two realizations.

1.2.24.1　Stressed ע

ע is realized as [e] (= ε) in stressed position.

SAMPLES OF STRESSED ע

עסן		[ésn]	'eat'
נעכטן		[nékhtn]	'yesterday'
זע		[zé]	'(I) see'

1.2.24.2　Unstressed ע

ע is realized as [ə]　(= i, ɪ, ə, etc.) in unstressed position.　It is sometimes called 'Reduced ע'.

SAMPLES OF UNSTRESSED ע

געזאָגט		[gəzókt]	'said'
באַנען		[bánən]	'trains'
קאַװע		[kávə]	'coffee'

1.2.25　pey

Print: פ (/פּ)　Script: ⌐　　Realization: [p]

SAMPLES OF פ

פּשוט		[póshət]	'simple'
עפּל		[épl]	'apple'
טאָפּ		[tóp]	'pot'

16

1.2.26 fey

Print: פֿ (/פ)   Script: ‗פֿ̄   Realization: [f]

SAMPLES OF פֿ

פֿאַנטאַסטיש		[fantástish]	'fantastic'
אפֿשר		[éfshər]	'maybe'
האָפֿן		[hófn]	'hope'

1.2.26.1 lángər fey

Print: ף   Script: ‗ף̄   Realization: [f]

Replaces פֿ in word final position.

SAMPLES OF ף

בלאָף		[blóf]	'bluff'
װאָלף		[vólf]	'wolf'
עלף		[elf]	'eleven'

1.2.27 tsádik

Print: צ   Script: ‗צ̄   Realization: [ts] (= c)

SAMPLES OF צ

צאַצקע		[tsátskə]	'toy'
צירק		[tsirk]	'circus'
קיצלען		[kítslən]	'tickle'

1.2.27.1 lánger tsadik

Replaces צ in word final position.

Print: ץ   Script: ‗ץ̄   Realization: [ts] (= c)

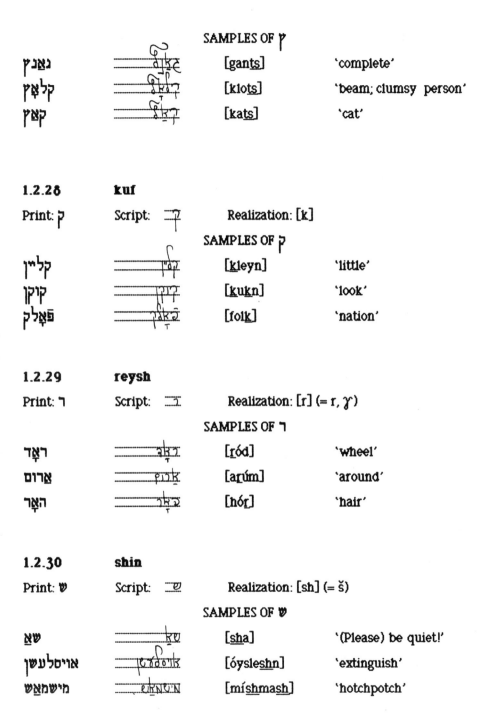

SAMPLES OF ץ

גאַנץ		[gan**ts**]	'complete'
קלאָץ		[klo**ts**]	'beam; clumsy person'
קאַץ		[ka**ts**]	'cat'

1.2.28 **kuf**

Print: ק   Script: Realization: [k]

SAMPLES OF ק

קלײן		[**k**leyn]	'little'
קוקן		[ku**k**n]	'look'
פֿאָלק		[fol**k**]	'nation'

1.2.29 **reysh**

Print: ר   Script: Realization: [r] (= r, ɣ)

SAMPLES OF ר

ראָד		[**r**ód]	'wheel'
אַרום		[a**r**úm]	'around'
האָר		[hó**r**]	'hair'

1.2.30 **shin**

Print: שׁ   Script: Realization: [sh] (= š)

SAMPLES OF שׁ

שאַ		[**sh**a]	'(Please) be quiet!'
אױסלעשן		[óysle**sh**n]	'extinguish'
מישמאַש		[mí**sh**ma**sh**]	'hotchpotch'

18

1.2.31 sin

Print: שׂ (/שׂ) Script: ⵉ⵿⵿⵿⵿ Realization: [s]

שׂ (= sin) occurs in the traditional system only. In the phonetic system, [s] is rendered by ס (sámekh → §1.2.23). In some texts, the Hebrew diacritic dot to the upper left of the letter (שׂ) is employed to distinguish it from שׁ = [sh] (→ §1.2.30).

SAMPLES OF שׂ (= sin)

שכירות	שְׂכִירוּת	[skhírəs]	'wages'
שנאה	שׂנְאָה	[sínə]	'hatred; enmity'
ארץ ישראל	אֶרֶץ יִשְׂרָ	[erəts(y)isró(ə)l]	'Land of Israel'

1.2.32 tof

Print: ת (/ת) Script: ⵉⵏ Realization: [t]

ת occurs in the traditional system only. In the phonetic system, [t] is rendered by ט (tes → §1.2.14).

SAMPLES OF ת

תאווה	תַּאֲוָה	[táyvə]	'passion; obsession'
תענוג	תַּעֲנוּג	[táynəg]	'delight'
אסתר	אֶסְתֵּר	[éstər]	'Esther'

1.2.33 sof

Print: ת (/ת) Script: ⵉ Realization: [s]

ת occurs in the traditional system only. In the phonetic system, [s] is rendered by ס (sáməkh → §1.2.23).

SAMPLES OF ת

חתונה	‏חָתֻנֶּ	[khásənə]	'wedding'
אמת	‏אמֶת	[éməs]	'true; truth'
שבת	‏שַבָּת	[shábəs]	'Saturday; Sabbath'

1.3   DELETION OF REDUNDANCIES

Note that two or even three traditional system consonants may be phonetically identical in Yiddish (although they were not, of course, in ancient Semitic). The phonetic system, adhering to its principle of one letter for one sound, selects one of the homophonous characters as follows:

Sound	Traditional system	Phonetic system
[k]	כ or ק	ק only
[kh]	ח or כ	כ only
[t]	ט or ת	ט only
[s]	ס, ש or ת	ס only
[v]	ב, ו, or וו	וו only

1.4   COEXISTENCE OF THE TWO SYSTEMS

The (majority) phonetic system and the (minority) traditional system coexist happily in Yiddish writing. The two can be joined in a single word. This occurs frequently where a Semitic component stem is incorporated into a Germanic component morphological pattern, e.g. חלומען [khóləmən] 'dream (v.)', where חלום [khóləm] 'dream (n.)' is verbalized via suffixation of infinitivizing suffix ‏(ע)‎- [(ə)n]; likewise ‏שכלדיק‎ [séykhldik] 'logical', from ‏שכל‎ [séykhl] 'logic; common sense' plus adjectivizing suffix ‏דיק‎-.

1.5 MODERN STANDARD ORTHOGRAPHY

Modern standard orthography is relatively uniform. The minor variations that are still encountered do not pose a serious problem for the student.

1.5.1 Origins of modern standard orthography

Modern standard orthography was, in its broad outlines, formulated by the pioneer of modern Yiddish studies, Ber Borokhov, in 1913, and modified by the great Yiddish scholar Zalmen Reyzen in 1920. In that year, Reyzen's final version went into effect worldwide and has been followed since by culturally conscious Yiddish writers and publishers, voluntarily, and with none of the legal compulsion that usually accompanies orthographic reform. These and a number of other leading Yiddish scholars of the early twentieth century saw the need to modernize, rationalize and standardize. They believed that the phenomenal growth of Yiddish literature, press and theatre, and the overall expansion of Yiddish culture into many spheres of twentieth-century life would be hampered by inconsistencies and by the useless cumbersome machinery of silent letters that had been incorporated several decades earlier by the Germanizing press of the late nineteenth century. The introduction of modern standard orthography was not universal. Moreover, there is some acceptable variation within modern standard orthography.

1.5.2 Press orthography

The daily Yiddish press, in contrast to literary periodicals and books, did not on the whole accept the orthographic reforms. Many have retained the silent ע‎s and ה‎s that had been 'imported' from German in the late nineteenth and early twentieth centuries (e.g. זאָגען for זאָגן 'say', יאָהר for יאָר 'year'). Some features of press orthography are not Germanisms, but rather features that were not accepted by modern standard orthography. Most notable of these is the continued use of אי rather than יי for [yi], still extensively encountered in newspaper usage, e.g. אידיש for ייִדיש 'Yiddish', אינגל for יינגל 'boy'.

1.5.3 Orthodox orthography

The most traditional religious Ashkenazic Jewish communities around the world, primarily (but not exclusively) Chassidic, make use of a system of spelling deriving largely from the nineteenth and early twentieth century. It is remarkably similar to press orthography, differing from modern standard orthography most markedly in its retention of silent letters and other features that were, paradoxically, taken from modern literary German by proponents of the anti-traditionalist Enlightenment movement and later by the (even more anti-traditionalist) revolutionary parties. It is ironic that for today's traditional communities, the Germanizing orthography of the late nineteenth century, which emanated from a conscious effort to destroy all that they cherish, is now their symbol of identity in Yiddish spelling, setting them apart from almost all 'secular cultural Yiddishists' who discarded that system in 1920 in favour of modern standard orthography. The lesson for cultural historians lies in the symbolic values which facts assume in a society, rather than the 'physical derivation' of those facts in history. In Chassidic circles, however, a number of genuine Old Yiddish traits do survive, most notably the use of ' rather than ע to mark initial and medial unstressed [ə], e.g. גידאָגט for געדאָגט 'said', the ע for [ə] being one of the features of Germanizing late-nineteenth-century spelling that was retained by modern standard orthography. In pre-World-War-II Poland, the eminent Yiddish scholar Solomon A. Birnbaum perfected a standardized version of Orthodox orthography.

1.5.4   Soviet orthography

Soviet Yiddish scholars embarked on a radical program of orthographic reform shortly after the Russian Revolution in 1917. Most of its features were in widespread use by the mid-1920s.

1.5.4.1   The phonetic system in Soviet orthography

The phonetic system within Soviet spelling eliminates the א that separates consonantal וו from vocalic ו (→ §1.2.1.1) and the א marking syllable onset, (→ §1.2.1.2) while retaining it to mark word onset. The confusion resulting from the ambiguous sequences ווו (= [vu] or [uv]) and יי (= [ey], [ii] or [yi]) is mitigated by the introduction of two Hebrew diacritics to mark the vocalic use of ו and ' in ambiguous positions (וּ for [u] and יִ for [i]), hence ווּ for וואו 'where', אַסאָצייִרט for אַסאָציאירט 'associated', העברעיִש for העברעאיש 'Hebrew'.

1.5.4.2   The traditional system in Soviet orthography

Soviet spelling eliminates the traditional system altogether, and respells the

entire Semitic component in accordance with its modified phonetic system,
e.g. עפֿשער for אפֿשר [éfshər] 'perhaps'. The aim of this radical reform was
to de-Hebraicize and de-Judaize Yiddish, goals it thought it could help achieve
by doing away with the special historical spelling conventions of the
traditional system and, indeed, by doing away with the Semitic component
itself in Soviet Yiddish. In addition to explicit anti-Hebrew and anti-tradition
sentiments expressed by the Soviet reformers of the 1920s, the argument in
favour of a unified and phonetically based system for the whole of Yiddish
was also frequently put forward, both inside and outside pro-Soviet circles,
on logical and practical grounds. Most pre-World War II versions of Soviet
spelling also did away with the five word-final forms of letters (e.g. שאָלעם
for שלום [shóləm] 'peace') although these were generally reintroduced in the
early 1960s.

1.5.5   Yivo orthography

A widely taught (but less widely used) variant of modern standard
orthography is that of the Yivo Institute for Jewish Research. The Yivo system
arose in the 1930s as a compromise between the modern standard
orthography of 1920 and the Soviet system (→ §1.5.4). Following Soviet
spelling, the Yivo system eliminated the א separating consonantal וו from
vocalic ו (→ §1.2.1.1) and the א marking syllable onset (→ §1.2.1.2); unlike
Soviet spelling, Yivo orthography did retain א to mark stem onset (→
§1.2.1.2). It followed the Soviet system in mitigating the resulting confusion
by introducing וּ for [u] and יִ for [i] in a number of positions. Both systems
mark the sequence [yi] by יִי, hence ייִדיש for ייִדיש.

1.5.6   Innovations

The *Grammar* adheres to modern standard orthography. The only innovation is a graphic one. Following the practice that has developed at Oxford in recent years, the *Grammar* reintroduces the historical horizontal bar (known as the רפֿה [rófə], or more informally as the דעכלעלע 'little roof') over the spirants כ (= [kh]) and ת (= [s]), bringing them into line with בֿ (= [v]) and פֿ (= [f]). Thus all four plosive vs. spirant oppositions (ב [b] vs. בֿ [v]; כ [k] vs. כ [kh]; פ [p] vs. פֿ [f]; and ת [t] vs. ת [s]) are consistently marked, as was the case in Yiddish from the fourteenth century onwards. From the nineteenth century to the present, a multitude of combinations, none of them internally consistent, has arisen, sometimes using the Hebrew diacritic dot in the middle of the letter to mark the plosive for one, two, three or all of the four plosives, sometimes the horizontal bar to mark the spirant for one or more of the four spirants.

2 PHONETICS

2.0 OVERVIEW

The phonetic structure of Yiddish differs appreciably from that of English, and acquaintance with its major features at the outset is advisable. Despite the differences, the sound pattern of the language can generally be mastered with far greater ease, than, say, that of French, where the base of articulation and the accentuation pattern are vastly more distant from English. Square brackets [ ] enclose the phonetic transcriptions used in this book (→ §1.2). Where these transcriptions, intended for the English-speaking student, differ substantially from accepted phonetic transcription, the appropriate international phonetic symbol follows in parenthesis ( ). The sound system of Standard Yiddish is used in the *Grammar*. The major phonetic differences between the dialects lie in the realization of the stressed vowels.

2.1 VOWELS AND DIPHTHONGS

2.1.1 Stressed vowels and diphthongs

The standard language does not distinguish long from short vowels. Stressed vowels are of roughly equal length. They are closer to the peripheral locations of the cardinal vowels in the vocal tract than their counterparts in English.

2.1.1.1 א [a]

א [a] is more peripheral (closer to the far front of the vowel space in the mouth, hence also more tense) than London *u* in 'c*u*t' or New York *o* in 'p*o*t'. Cf. 'Continental a' in French, Dutch and German.

2.1.1.2 ע [e] (= ε)

ע [e] is more peripheral than English *e* in 'p*e*n'.

2.1.1.3 י [i]

י [i] is higher and more tense than English *i* in 't*i*n' but it is not lengthened or diphthongized as English *ee* in 'thr*ee*'.

2.1.1.4 א [o] (= ɔ)

א [o] is higher and more rounded than London *o* in 'l*o*t'; more peripheral, rounded and tense than New York *u* in 'tr*u*ck'. Cf. 'Continental o'.

2.1.1.5 ו [u]

ו [u] is more tense and peripheral than English *u* in 'p*u*t' but not diphthongized as English *oo* in 'sp*oo*n'.

2.1.1.6 ײ [ay] (= aj)

ײ [ay] starts at א [a] (→ §2.1.1.1) and ends at offglide [y] (=j). The nucleus of the diphthong is shorter, more front, and more tense than English *i* in 'wr*i*te'.

2.1.1.7 ײ [ey] (= ej)

ײ [ey] starts higher than ע [e] (= ε) (→ §2.1.1.2) and ends at offglide [y]

(= j). Cf. English *ai* in 'ra<u>in</u>'.

2.1.1.8 יו [oy] (=ɔj)

יו [oy] starts at אָ [o] (= ɔ) (→ §2.1.1.4) and ends at offglide y (= j). The nucleus of the diphthong is shorter and more tense than English *oi* in 'f<u>oi</u>st'.

2.1.2 Reduced vowels

Reduced vowels occur in unstressed reduced syllables where the vowel repertoire is generally reduced. Most frequently, [ə] and [a] occur before the stress of a word, [ə] and [i] after it.

2.1.2.1 Pronunciation

The most frequent graphic representation of reduced vowels in the phonetic system is ע (→ §1.2.24.2). In the traditional system, they most often correspond with ה or א. Reduced vowels are generally transcribed [ə] in this book, but actual phonetic realization can vary according to a number of factors. Before the stressed syllable of a word, it usually approximates lax [i] (= ɪ), resembling English *i* in 'ex<u>o</u>tic', e.g. געזאָגנט [gizókt] (= gɪzɔ́kt) 'said'. After the stress it tends toward [i] before certain consonants, especially ב, e.g. בוידעם [bóyd<u>i</u>m] (= bójdɪm) 'attic'. It also tends toward [i] word-finally, e.g. קאַווע [káv<u>i</u>] (= kávɪ) 'coffee', חלה [khál<u>i</u>] (= χálɪ) 'Sabbath bread'. In the final reduced ע of the second diminutive (→ §4.33), it tends toward [ə], hence טישעלע [tishel<u>ə</u>/tishal<u>ə</u>] (= tíšələ /tíšalə) 'very little table'.

2.1.2.2 Shift to [a] before [kh]

Reduced ע may be pronounced [a] before [kh] (כ, ך or ח), e.g. כוח [kóy<u>ə</u>kh] or [kóy<u>a</u>kh] 'strength'.

28

2.1.2.3 Shift to [a] in the second diminutive

The first reduced ע in the suffix of the second diminutive, עלע- (→ §4.3.2) may be pronounced a̲, e.g. ביימעלע [béymə̲lə] or [béymə̲lə] 'very little tree'. In the plural of the second diminutive, עלעך-, the second reduced ע may be rendered [a] by assimilation to the following [kh] (→ §2.1.2.2). Vowel harmony is then applied to the first reduced ע, and both may be pronounced [a], hence [béymə̲la̲kh].

2.1.3 Vowels not corresponding with the phonetic system

There is a handful of words, all of them very frequently used items in everyday speech, in which vowel letters do not correspond with their expected phonetic correlates within the phonetic system. Note however that some speakers have come to use 'spelling pronunciations' based on the conventional orthography ([oyf] etc.). Most other instances of incongruence result from assimilations and rhythmic factors. Wherever the usual pronunciation of a word is not self-evident from the spelling, a transcription in square brackets is supplied in the *Grammar*.

אויף 'on; upon; to' (→ §15.16.5)		[af]
אויפֿן 'on the; upon the; to the' (→ §5.3.3.1)		[afn]
אויפֿ- 'up (verbal prefix)' (→ §8.2.2)		[uf]
אים 'him' (→ §§6.1.2.2, 6.1.3.2)		[em]
בײַ 'at; by' (→ §15.1)		[ba]
בײַם 'at the; by the' (→ §§5.3.3.1, 15.1)		[bam]
קוים 'barely' (→ §10.1)		[kam]
קיין 'to' (→ §15.16.3)		[kin]

2.2   CONSONANTS

2.2.1   Voicing

The consonants [b], [d], [g], [v], [z], and [zh] (= ž) are fully voiced in all positions, including word-finally (except when processed by assimilation → §2.2.2. − §2.2.4), e.g.

שרײַב '(I) write'	[shray<u>b</u>]
רעד '(I) speak'	[ré<u>d</u>]
וואָג 'weight'	[vo<u>g</u>]
אײַז 'ice'	[ay<u>z</u>]
שאַנטאַזש 'blackmail'	[shantá<u>zh</u>]

2.2.2   Devoicing assimilation

Voiced consonants [b], [d], [g], [v], [z], and [zh] (= ž) usually undergo devoicing as follows − [b] → [p;] [d] → [t]; [g] → [k]; [v] → [f]; [z] → [s]; [zh] (= ž) → [sh] (= š) before any of the voiceless consonants [f], [k], [kh], [p], [s], [sh], [t] and [ts]. The devoicing by assimilation of [b] and [d] is the most consistent.

SAMPLES OF CONSONANTS PROCESSED BY DEVOICING ASSIMILATION

שרײַב [shray<u>b</u>] '(I) write'	→	שרײַבסט [shráyp̱st] 'you (familiar) write'
רעד [red] '(I) speak'	→	רעדסט [rétst] 'you (familiar) speak'
וואָג [vog] 'weight'	→	וואָגשאָל [vók̲shol] 'scale'
בריוו [briv̲] 'letter'	→	בריוװטרעגער [bríf̱tregər] 'mailman'
אײַז [ayz] 'ice'	→	אײַזקאַסטן [ays̲kastn] 'ice box'
שאַנטאַזש [shantázh]	→	שאַנטאַזש־שטיק [shantás̲h shtik]
'blackmail'		'blackmailing tactics'

30

Devoicing assimilation may occur across word boundaries. Cf. קלוג [klug]
'clever' vs. אַ קלוג קינד [a klug/kluk kind] 'a clever child'.

2.2.3 Voicing assimilation

Voiceless consonants [f], [k], [kh] [p], [s], [sh], [t] and [ts] may undergo
voicing as follows – [f] → [v]; [k] → [g]; [kh] (= x) → [gh] (= γ); [p] →
[b]; [s] → [z]; [sh] (= š) → [zh] (= ž); [t] → [d]; [ts] (= c) → [dz] before
any of the voiced consonants [b], [g], [d], [v], [z] and [zh] (= ž). Voicing
assimilation is less consistent than devoicing assimilation, but it is frequently
heard in natural speech. The consonant transcribed [gh] (= γ) is the voiced
counterpart of [kh] (= x), which has no independent status in the language. It
also serves as one of the possible realizations of ר (→ §2.2.11.1).

SAMPLES OF CONSONANTS PROCESSED BY VOICING ASSIMILATION

אויפֿ- [uf] 'up (v. prefix)' → אויפֿחעקן [úvvekn] 'wake up'

באַק [bak] 'cheek' → באַקביין [bágbeyn] 'cheekbone'

בוך [bukh] 'book' → בוך־געשעפֿט [búghgəsheft] 'bookstore'

קאָפ [kop] 'head' → קאָפוויײַטיק [kóbveytik] 'headache'

זיס [zis] 'sweet' → זיסוואַרג [zízvarg] 'candy products'

רעש [rá(ə)sh] 'noise' → רעשדיק [rá(ə)zhdik] 'noisy'

ווײַט [vayt] 'far' → ווײַטזעעוודיק [váydzeəvdik] 'farsighted'

שוויצן [shvítsn] 'sweat (v.)' → שוויצבאָד [shvídzbod] 'steambath'

Voicing assimilation may occur across word boundaries. Cf. קוש [kush] 'kiss'
vs. אַ קוש געבן [a kúzh gebm] 'give a kiss'.

2.2.4 Chain assimilation

In both devoicing and voicing assimilation, it is the last of a series of consonants that affects its predecessor either to devoice or to voice. Where three or more consonants occur sequentially, the last may mutate them all. Thus, ערשט [ersht] 'just' followed by געשען [gəshén] 'happened' yields ערשט געשען [érzhd gəshén] via chain assimilation. There are a few cases when assimilation is progressive rather than regressive, and a consonant's voicing status affects the following consonant (→ §7.3).

2.2.5   Aspiration

Plosives b (ב), d (ד), g (ג), k (ק, כ), p (פ), t (ט, ת) are never aspirated. To perfect pronunciation, utter each of these in word final position, holding a mirror a short distance from the mouth, until oral discharge is eliminated.

לויב 'praise'		[loy<u>b</u>]
קלייד 'dress (n.)'		[kley<u>d</u>]
קלוג 'clever'		[klu<u>g</u>]
האַק 'hatchet'		[ha<u>k</u>]
זופ 'sip'		[zu<u>p</u>]
נאַכט 'night'		[nakht]

2.2.6   Pronunciation of כ [kh] (=x)

English speakers unfamiliar with [kh] (ח and כ) may begin from its corresponding velar plosive [k] and proceed to spirantize. Cf. *ch* in the German 'ach Laut', Scottish *ch* in 'lo<u>ch</u>'.

2.2.7   Pronunciation of ל

Many older speakers born in Eastern Europe still distinguish a 'hard' from a

32

'soft' (= palatalized) לּ. The distinction, common in the Slavonic environment, is rapidly losing ground in modern spoken Yiddish. 'Soft l' is heard most often before ', e.g. קליאַמקע [klyámkə] 'doorknob'.

2.2.8   Syllabic לּ [l] (= ḷ)

לּ functions as a 'vowel' when it follows a consonant in an unstressed syllable. It is not preceded by a shewa vowel in speech or ע in writing, but carries syllabicity on its own, e.g. גאָפּל [gópḷ] (= gópḷ) 'fork', לעפל [léfḷ] (= léfḷ) 'spoon'.

2.2.9   Syllabic נ [n] (= ṇ)

נ (or ן) [n] too, can function as a 'vowel' when it follows a consonant in a reduced syllable. It is not preceded by a shewa vowel in speech or ע in writing, but carries syllabicity all on its own.

SAMPLES OF SYLLABIC נ

וואָגן 'wagon'	[vógṇ]
טאַנצנדיק 'while dancing'	[tántsṇdik]
מאַכן 'make'	[mákhṇ]
מענטשן 'people'	[méntshṇ]

But, unlike לּ which is always syllabic when it follows a consonant in a reduced syllable, נ is not syllabic when the preceding consonant is מ [m], נ [n], any stressed vowel or diphthong, or one of the following three sequences: נג [ng] (= ŋg), נק [nk] (= ŋk), or consonant plus לּ [l]. In these cases, a shewa vowel is heard and ע appears.

קוימען 'chimney'	[kóymən]
באַנען 'trains (n.)'	[banən]

עסײַען 'essays' [eséyən]

פֿאַנגען 'capture (v.)' [fángən]

זינקען 'sink (v.)' [zínkən]

גאָפּלען 'forks' [góplən]

Note however that adjectives ending in [ng] and [nk] do exceptionally retain syllabic [n] both in speech and writing, when inflection to an objective case (→ §§5.5.2 – 5.5.4) results in one of the sequences [ng] + [n] or [nk] + [n], e.g. לאַנגן [lángn̩] 'long', פֿלינקן [flínkn̩] 'agile'.

2.2.10 Bilabial assimilation

Syllabic נ (or ן) is pronounced [m] rather than [n] via assimilation following bilabials ב [b] and פ [p], e.g. אויסקלײַבן 'choose' [óysklaybm̩], האָבן 'have' [hóbm̩], ליפּן 'lips' [lípm̩].

2.2.11 Pronunciation of ר [r]

There are three acceptable realizations of ר.

2.2.11.1 Fricative [r]

Fricative [r] (=ɣ) is produced at the velum. It is the spirantized counterpart of [g], and the voiced counterpart of [kh]. Most English speakers master this realization most successfully. The target sound may be approached from [g], [k] or [kh] (→§2.2.6).

2.2.11.2 Lingual [r]

Lingual [r] is produced at the upper gums by tongue vibration.

2.2.11.3　Uvular [r]

Uvular [r] is produced by vibrating the uvula.

2.2.12　Pronunciation of　צ [ts] (= c)

Affricate צ [ts] resembles the English sequence *t* + *s* in 'cut̲s̲' but it functions as a single sound unit and is consequently pronounced in a shorter timespace than its English counterpart.

2.3　RHYTHM

2.3.1　Syllables

There are four syllable types.

2.3.1.1　High syllables

High syllables have primary stress (marked by ´ over the vowel nucleus of the syllable), e.g. [mé] in [paméləkh] פּאַמעלעך 'slowly'. High syllables are loud, long and intoned and can have as their nucleus any of the repertoire of stressed vowels and diphthongs.

2.3.1.2　Low syllables

Low syllables are never stressed, and have a very limited number of vowel nuclei (usually [ə] or [a] before the word stress and [ə] or [i], or syllabic [l] or [n], after it) e.g. [pa] and [ləkh] in פּאַמעלעך. Low syllables are far less loud than high ones, and they are short and unintoned.

2.3.1.3 Middle syllables

Middle syllables have secondary stress (marked by ˋ over its vowel nucleus),
e.g. [kàyt] in [pamélekhkàyt] פּאַמעלעכקײט 'slowness'. In a more detailed
treatment, nonprimary stress would be further analyzed into secondary,
tertiary etc.

2.3.1.4 Lowered syllables

Like the high syllables from which they derive (→ §2.3.1.1), lowered syllables
may have any nucleus vowel. They may have secondary stress (like middle
syllables → §2.3.1.3) or none at all (like low syllables →§ 2.3.1.2). A lowered
syllable is a syllable that declines from high to middle or low, or from middle
to low in normal continuous speech, in deference to the master rhythmic
pattern (→ §2.3.4), e.g. [me] in איך בין נעכטן פּאַמעלעך אַהײמגעגאַנגען
[(i)khbin nèkhtn pamèləkh ahéymgəgangən] 'I walked home slowly
yesterday', although [me] would of course remain high if the speaker
wished to emphasize the slowness of the journey.

2.3.2 Word stress

Word stress (usually high in isolation) is bound to the root syllable, which is
most frequently the first. No matter how many syllables are added in
inflections or derivations, the same syllable, while it may be reduced to
secondary stress in consequence of contextual reduction, retains its full vowel
and, relationally speaking, retains its stress vis à vis any low syllables, e.g.
לעב [léb] '(I) live', לעבן [lébm] 'life', לעבעדיק [lébədik] 'alive',
לעבעדיקערהייט [lèbədikərhéyt] 'while living'. While lowered from high to
middle in this last word, [le] always remains stressed vis à vis [bə].

2.3.2.1   Semitic component word stress

In the Semitic component, stress is generally assigned to the penultimate syllable. The consequence is that upon suffixation, stress jumps to the new penultimate syllable, e.g. חֲבֵר [khávər] 'friend' vs. חֲבֵרִים [khavéyrim] 'friends'. The low [ər] of [kháver] emerges as the high [éy] of [khavéyrim].

2.3.3   Word rhythm

The most common word rhythm is a trochee pattern of ´ (high) followed by __ (low), e.g. בעקער [bék__ər__] 'baker', אפֿשר [éf__shər__] 'perhaps', נודניק [núd__nik__] 'boring person; pest; poor conversationalist'. If there is an unstressed syllable before the stress, the amphibrach __ ´ __ results, e.g. געגאַנגען [__gə__gáng__ən__] 'went', עקשנות [__ak__shó__nəs__] 'stubbornness', כֿאַליאַסטרע [__khal__yás__trə__] 'gang'. Both types share penultimate stress which is the most common type in the language. Many thousands of Yiddish words were incorporated into the language in the nineteenth and twentieth centuries, largely from the lexicon of internationalisms that have permeated Western languages generally. These frequently preserve full vowels in unstressed syllables (e.g. אָרגאַניזאַציע [organizátsyə] 'organization'), iambic stress pattern (e.g. אַטאָם [atóm] 'atom'), or both (e.g. קאַפּאַציטעט [kapatsitét] 'capacity; big-shot'). They have, in effect, evolved a new pattern that coexists with the old. In rapid speech, however, some reduction of unstressed syllables to [ə] does occur (e.g. [erəplán] for [eroplán] ער-אָפּלאַן 'airplane').

2.3.4 The master rhythmic pattern

The master rhythmic pattern entails highs at roughly equal intervals, interlaced with a far greater number of middles, lows and lowereds. The result is a starkly contrasting 'mountain range' pattern, with roughly equidistant peaks. Each rhythmic unit (e.g. phrase, sentence) has one and only one high. Reduction (the lowering of highs to middle or low and of middles to low) is roughly in direct proportion to the rhythmic requirement that stresses be kept equally apart.

2.3.5 Sentence rhythm

Phrases and sentences in everyday speech tend to follow the same metrical structures as words, e.g. איך װייס ניט 'I don't know', comprising [ikh], [veys] and [nit] is realized as amphibrach [$_{ikh}$véys$_{nit}$] in moderate speech, and trochee [khvéys$_{nit}$], with only two syllables, in more rapid speech. The Yiddish rhythm pattern extends word rhythm over phrases and sentences, so that each sentence, like the word, has a single stressed syllable, which may or may not be surrounded by many reduced syllables (some of which retain some secondary stress). The actual stress pattern can vary depending on message and emphasis. The major constraint is that the high stress be selected from a syllable that can bear word stress when that word is uttered in isolation. Those syllables stressed in isolation will of course lose stress when they are not selected for sentence stress. They are relegated to reduced syllable status in lowness and shortness, but the repertoire of vowels need not be reduced as in a word uttered in isolation. The underlying principle is the presence of a single climactic stress somewhere along the line. Hence

אַיך חייס ניט װאָס ער פּלאַפּלט, sequentially [ikh veys nit vos er plaplt] can be realized [(i)khvéysnitvoserplàplt] 'I don't know what he's babbling about' or [(i)khvèysnitvoserpláplt] 'I don't know what he's *babbling* about'. A series of reduced syllables tends to be packed into the same timespan accorded a single stressed syllable.

2.4   DIALECT VARIATION

There are many differences between the spoken varieties of Yiddish in morphology, lexicon and grammar (e.g. → §§4.1.4, 6.1.4, 7.3.5). The best-known and most salient features distinguishing the three major modern Yiddish dialects are the systems of stressed vowels. The standard language, used throughout the *Grammar,* enjoys nearly perfect one-to-one correspondence between symbol and sound, at least in the phonetic system governing the largest part of the language (→ §2.1.3 for exceptions). It is very close to the stressed vowel system of Northeastern ('Lithuanian') Yiddish. The only major difference is that part of the series of words in the standard language with [oy] has [ej] in Lithuanian; hence װאוינן [voyn] 'live; dwell' and װײן [veyn] 'cry' are both [veyn] in Northeastern Yiddish. The other two dialects, Mideastern ('Polish') and Southeastern ('Ukranian') Yiddish have rather more vowels and therefore exhibit a one-to-two or one-to-three relationship between symbol and sound. The student learning the language as a beginner is best advised to master Standard Yiddish in the first instance, and to investigate dialectal variation at a later stage. The student who has a native dialect, on the other hand, is best advised to adhere to his or her native variety. All the native dialects are nonstandard insofar as none is identical with the standard. None of the dialects are substandard and use and preservation of genuine dialect is encouraged. The following are the major stressed vowel correspondences of the three dialects. Long vowels are marked by a macron above the vowel letter (ā, ē, ī, ō, ū). Note that the [u] and [ū] realizations for וֹ in Mideastern and Southeastern dialects occur only in nineteenth- and twentieth-century borrowings. The words themselves entered these dialects long after the sound change [u] → [i] had been completed, and they were therefore unaffected. Assorted consonantal differences may be noted from the examples cited.

Standard	Northeastern	Mideastern	Southeastern
2.4.1 אַ=[a]	[a]	[a]	[o] or [a]
הַאַנט 'hand'	[hant]	[hant]	[ont]
שוואַך 'weak'	[shvakh]	[shvakh]	[shvakh]
2.4.2 ע=[e]	[e]	[e] or [ey]	[e] or [ey / i]
בעט 'bed'	[bet]	[bet]	[bet]
בעטן 'ask'	[betn]	[beytn]	[beytn / bitn]
2.4.3 י=[i]	[i]	[i] or [ī]	[i] or [ī]
ליפ 'lip'	[lip]	[lip]	[lip]
ליב 'love'	[lib]	[līp]	[līb]
2.4.4 אָ=[o]	[o]	[o], [u] or [ū]	[o] or [u]
גאָט 'God'	[got]	[got]	[got]

40

זאָגן 'say'	[zogn]	[zugn]	[zugn]
פֿאָרן 'ride; go'	[forn]	[fūrn]	[furn]

2.4.5 ו=[u]   [u]   [u], [ū], [i] or [ī]   [u] or [i] or [ī]

קולטור 'culture'	[kultúr]	[kultúr]	[kultúr]
זון 'sun'	[zun]	[zin]	[zin]
זון 'son'	[zun]	[zīn]	[zīn]

2.4.6 ײ=[ay]   [ay]   [ā]   [a] or [ay]

זײַן 'be'	[zayn]	[zān]	[zan]
כדאי 'worthwhile'	[kədáy]	[kədā́]	[kədáy]

2.4.7 יי=[ey]   [ey]   [ay]   [ey]

שײן 'beautiful'	[sheyn]	[shayn]	[sheyn]

2.4.8 וי=[oy]   [ey] or [oy]   [oy] or [ōu]   [oy] or [ou / u]

טויב 'deaf'	[teyb]	[toyp]	[toyb]
טויב 'pigeon'	[toyb]	[tōup]	[toub / tub]

3 GREETINGS

3.0 OVERVIEW

The sampling offered provides time-related and more general greetings. A number of greetings have familiar and formal variants (→ §§6.1.6.1, 7.5.1).

3.1 TIME-RELATED GREETINGS

3.1.1 Morning

(אַ) גוט מאָרגן! [(a)gut mórgn] 'Good morning'.
Response:
אַ גוט יאָר! [agut yór] 'Good morning to you' (lit. 'A good year').

3.1.2 Evening (upon meeting)

(אַ) גוטן אָװנט! [(a)gut nóvnt] 'Good evening'.
Response:
(אַ) גוטן אָװנט! 'Good evening to you'.

3.1.3 Evening / night (upon parting / going to bed)

אַ גוטע נאַכט! [a gútə nákht] 'Good night'.

42

Responses:

א גוטע נאַכט! 'Good night to you'.

שלאָף געזונט! 'Sleep well (familiar)'.

שלאָפֿט געזונט! 'Sleep well (formal)'.

זיסע חלומות! [zísə khalóyməs] 'Sweet dreams'.

3.1.4 On Friday (upon parting) or Saturday before sundown (upon meeting or parting)

(אַ) גוט שבת! [a gut shábəs] 'Have a Good Sabbath'. When used upon parting on Friday, (אַ) גוט שבת may have the sense of 'Have a good weekend'. A 'secular' alternative, specific to the whole of the weekend, is

אַ גוטן סוף־װאָך! [a gutn sòvvókh] 'Have a good weekend'.
Response:
(אַ) גוט שבת! 'Good Sabbath / weekend to you'.

3.1.5 On Saturday evening (after sundown)

אַ גוטע װאָך! / גוט־װאָך! [gudvókh / a gútə vókh] 'Have a good week'.
Response:
אַ גוטע װאָך! / גוט־װאָך! 'A good week to you'.

3.1.6 On the eve of a traditional holiday or on the holiday

(אַ) גוט יום טוב! [(a)gut yóntəf] 'Good holiday'.
Responses:
(אַ) גוט יום טוב! 'Good holiday to you'.

אַ גוט יום טוב דיר! [(a)gut yóntəf dír] 'Good holiday to you (familiar)'.

אַ גוט יום טוב אײַך! [(a)gut yóntəf áykh] 'Good holiday to you (formal)'.

3.2   GENERAL GREETINGS

3.2.1   Upon meeting

‏װאָס מאַכסטו? [vos mákhstə?] 'How are you? (familiar)'.

‏װאָס מאַכט איר? [vos mákhtir?] 'How are you? (formal)'.

‏װאָס הערט זיך? [vos (h)értsakh? / vos (h)érdzakh?] 'What's new?'.

‏װאָס הערט זיך עפעס? [vos (h)értsakh épəs? / vos (h)érdzakh épəs?] 'So what's new?'.

‏װאָס הערט זיך עפעס גוטס? [vos (h)értsakh epəs gúts? / vos (h)érdzakh epəs gúts?] 'What's the good news?'.

‏װאָס מאַכט אַ ייד? [vos makht a yíd?] 'How are you doing?' (lit. 'How is a Jew?').

Possible Responses:

‏ברוך השם [borkhashém] 'Fine' (lit. 'Blessed is God').

‏גאָט צו דאַנקען [gòt tsə dánkən] 'Fine' (lit. 'Thank God').

‏אַ דאַנק [adánk] '(Fine) thank you'.

‏גאַנץ גוט [gándz gút] 'Pretty good'.

‏נישקשה [nishkóshə] 'Not too bad'.

‏אַזױ [āzóy] 'So so' (with lengthening of both vowels; often accompanied by horizontal wagging of fingers of one or both hands and inclining of head).

‏ס׳קען אַלעמאָל זײַן בעסער [sken àləmol zayn bésər] 'Could always be better'.

‏ס׳קען אַלעמאָל זײַן ערגער [sken àləmol zayn érgər] 'Could always be worse'.

‏װאָס זאָל איך מאַכן? [vozl ikh mákhn?] 'What do you expect?' (lit. 'How should I be?').

44

וואָס מאַכסטו? [vos makhstú?] 'How are *you?* (familiar)'.

וואָס מאַכט איר? [vos makht ír?] 'How are *you?* (formal)'.

3.2.2   Upon shaking hands

שלום עליכם! [sholəmaléykhəm] 'How do you do?' (lit. 'Peace unto you').

Response:

עליכם שלום! [aleykhəmshóləm] 'How do you do?' (lit. 'Unto you peace').

The handshake is usually clenched simultaneous with the stressed syllable of עליכם שלום! or שלום עליכם!.

3.2.3   Upon greeting a stranger

פֿון וואַנעט קומסטו? [funvánət kúmstə?] 'Where do you come from? (familiar)'.

פֿון וואַנעט קומט איר? [funvánət kúmtir?] 'Where do you come from? (formal)'.

פֿון וואַנעט ביסטו אַ לאַנדסמאַן? [funvánət bista lántsman?] 'Where do you come from?' (especially current in America and other immigration centres).

פֿון וואַנעט זײַט איר אַ לאַנדסמאַן? [funvánət zaytir a lántsman?] 'Where do you come from? (formal)' (especially current in America and other immigration centres).

פֿון וואַנעט קומט מען? [funvánət kúmtmən?] 'Where do you come from?' (lit. 'Where does one come from?').

פֿון וואַנעט קומט אַ ייִד? [funvánət kumt a yíd?] 'Where do you come from, my friend?' (lit. 'Where does a Jew come from?').

Response:

— פֿון 'from (+ name of place)', e.g. פֿון ניו־יאָרק [fun nuyórk] 'from New

York', פֿון פּאַריז [fun paríz] 'from Paris'. If the place name is the name of a city or town, -ער (f. ־ערין) may be suffixed to the name of the city to form an agentive noun, e.g. איך בין אַ ניו־יאָרקערין 'I'm a New Yorker (f.)', איך בין אַ פּאַריזער 'I'm a Parisian (m.)' (→ §5.12.1).

3.2.4   Asking a stranger his or her name

?ווי הייסטו [vi héystə?] 'What's your name? (familiar)'.

?ווי הייסט איר [vi héystir?] 'What's your name? (formal)' (lit. 'How are you called?').

Response:

—איך הייס [(i)khhéys —] 'My name is ...'

3.2.5   Upon answering the telephone

האַלאָ 'Hello'.

Response (when caller is known):
—האַלאָ with name of caller, e.g. האַלאָ חיים [halò | Kháyim], האַלאָ מאַשע [halò | Máshə].

3.2.6   Welcoming in person

!ברוך הבא [bor(ə)khabó] 'Welcome! (sg.)' (lit. 'Blessed is the comer').

!ברוכים הבאים [brukhimabóim] 'Welcome! (pl.)' (lit. 'Blessed are the comers').

Responses:

!ברוך הנמצא [bor(ə)khanímtsə] 'Thank you for the welcome (sg.)' (lit. 'Blessed is the one to be found here, i.e. the resident').

46

ברוכים היושבים! [brukhimayóyshvim] 'Thank you for the welcome (pl.)'
(lit. 'Blessed are the people who stay here, i.e. the residents').

יישר כוח! [(yi)sh(ər)kóyakh] 'Good of you to ask; well said' (lit.
'congratulations' but also traditionally used for 'thank you').

3.2.7 Upon parting

זײַ געזונט! [záy gəzúnt] 'Be Well!; Goodbye' (familiar).

זײַט געזונט! [záyt gəzúnt] 'Be Well!; Goodbye' (formal).

כל טוב! [kól túv] 'All the best'.

אַ גוטן! [a gútn] 'All the best' (lit. 'A good (...)').

4 Nouns

4.0   OVERVIEW

Nouns occur in three genders — masculine, feminine and neutral. They usually inflect for pluralization and diminutivization. Diminutives may have the sense of physical smallness. They frequently add subjective emotional nuances, affectionate or pejorative, to the noun. They combine to form compound nouns.

4.1   GENDER

The gender of nouns is historically fixed and must be learned with each noun. It would not, for example, be possible to determine logically that 'table' is masculine (דער טיש), 'notebook' feminine (די העפֿט) and 'country' neutral (דאָס לאַנד). Nevertheless, there are rules and tendencies covering gender assignment for many nouns. The first principle assigns natural masculines to masculine and natural feminines to feminine. The dynamic tendency evident for nouns that exhibit no inherent sex is evident in gender assignment for new words and occasional realignments of old ones. It assigns masculinity to nouns ending in a consonant (e.g. דער אויטאָמאָביל [o(y)tomobíl] 'automobile') and femininity to nouns ending in a vowel (e.g. די טעכנאָלאָגיע [tekhnológyə] 'technology'). There is some acceptable variation in gender within literary Yiddish. A noun's gender should be checked with a dictionary.

4.1.1 Masculinity

Masculinity may be determined semantically, morphologically or derivationally. The masculine definite article is דער (which inflects to דעם in both object cases → §§5.3.2 – 5.3.3).

4.1.1.1 Semantic masculinity

Nouns referring to biological males, and agentives without a feminizing suffix, are masculine. Semantic masculinity overrides morphological and derivational factors.

SAMPLES OF SEMANTIC MASCULINITY

דער אָקס ox

דער גנב [gánəv] thief

דער זון son

דער זיידע grandfather

דער מאַן man

דער מלך [méyləkh] \ דער קעניג [kéynig] king

4.1.1.2 Morphological masculinity

Nouns with the following suffixes are generally masculine. An example follows each suffix.

יזם-:   דער ייִדישיזם [yidishízm] 'Yiddishism'

syllabic ל: דער אַרבל 'sleeve'

syllabic ן-:   דער בראָנפֿן [brómfn] 'whiskey'

עם-:   דער פֿאָדעם 'thread'

ער-:   דער זומער 'summer'

4.1.1.3 Masculine agentives

Semantic and morphological masculinity overlap in the case of the masculine agentivizing suffixes ‏אָר‎-, ‏יסט‎- (stressed), ‏ניק‎-, ‏ענט‎- (stressed), ‏עץ‎-, ‏ער‎- and pejorative ‏וק‎- and ‏(י)אַק‎- (both stressed). An example follows each.

‏אָר‎-:   ‏דיקטאַטאָר‎ [diktátor] 'dictator'

‏יסט‎-:   ‏ייִדישיסט‎ [yidishíst] 'Yiddishist'

‏ניק‎-:   ‏נודניק‎ 'bore; pest; poor conversationalist'

‏ענט‎-:   ‏פּרעזידענט‎ [prezidént] 'president'

‏עץ‎-   ‏מאַלאָדיעץ‎ [malodyéts] 'man who can get things done'

‏ער‎-:   ‏לערער‎ 'teacher'

‏וק‎-:   ‏שנײַדערוק‎ [shnaydərúk] 'tailor who is not a nice person'

‏יאַק‎-:   ‏פּאַסקודניאַק‎ [paskudnyák] 'malicious person'

4.1.1.4   Derivational masculinity

Nominalizations of verb stems are masculine, e.g. ‏דער שטופּ‎ 'push (n.)' from ‏שטופּן‎ [shtúpm] 'push (v.)'. Note that where past participles undergo vowel change (→ §§7.6.2.2–7.6.2.5), the nominalization frequently derives from the stem of the past participle, e.g. ‏דער שפּרונג‎ 'jump (n.)' (cf. ‏שפּרינגען‎ 'jump (v.)', past participle ‏געשפּרונגען‎).

4.1.2   Femininity

Femininity may be determined semantically, morphologically or derivationally. The feminine definite article is ‏די‎ (which inflects to ‏דער‎ in dative → §5.3.3).

4.1.2.1   Semantic femininity

Nouns referring to biological females, and agentives with a feminizing suffix, are feminine. Semantic femininity overrides morphological and derivational factors.

SAMPLES OF SEMANTIC FEMININITY

די טאָכטער daughter

די באָבע grandmother

די פֿרוי woman

די מלכה [málkə] queen

די מומע aunt

די קו cow

4.1.2.2 Morphological femininity

Nouns that end in one of the following tend to be feminine. The inclusion of
ע-, אָ- and ה- in the list dictates that all nouns ending in an unstressed vowel
are feminine, except where in conflict with semantic masculinity, e.g. דער
טאַטע 'father'. Note that nouns ending in two of the listed endings, ות- and
עניש-, may alternatively be neutral (→ §4.1.3). An example follows each.

אָ-:	די דוגמא [dúgmə] 'example'
ה-:	די כלה [kálə] 'bride'
הײַט-:	די פֿרײַהײַט 'freedom'
ונג-:	די שטימונג 'mood'
ור-:	די ליטעראַטור [litəratúr] 'literature'
ות-:	די\דאָס עקשנות [akshónəs] 'stubbornness'
יק-:	די גראַמאַטיק [gramátik] 'grammar'
ע-:	די קאַװע 'coffee'
עניש-:	די\דאָס צעמישעניש [tsəmíshənish] 'confused situation'
ענץ-:	די קאָנפֿערענץ [konfərénts] 'conference'
עק-:	די ביבליאָטעק [bibl(y)oték] 'library'
ערײַ-:	די בעקערײַ [bekəráy] 'bakery'
קײַט-:	די שיינקײַט 'beauty'
שאַפֿט-:	די פֿרײַנדשאַפֿט [fráyntshaft] 'friendship'

51

4.1.2.3 Feminine agentives

Semantic and morphological femininity overlap in feminine agentive suffixes
‑טע (most frequent feminizer of Semitic component agentives), ‑יצע and ‑קע.
Some agentives may be feminized with either ‑ין or ‑קע, e.g. (דער) לערער
'teacher (m.)' → לערערין (די) = (די) לערערקע 'teacher (f.)'. An example
follows each feminine agentive suffix.

‑טע: די גנבטע [gánəftə] 'thief (f.)'

‑יצע: די קראָסאַוויצע [krasávitsə] 'beautiful girl / woman'

‑ין: די בעקערין 'baker (f.)'

‑קע: די פּרעזידענטקע [prezidéntkə] 'president (f.)'

4.1.2.4 Derivational femininity

Nominalizations of adjective stems are feminine. Note that where comparative
adjectives undergo vowel change (→ §5.10), the nominalization derives from
the stem of the comparative, e.g. די לענג 'length' (cf. לאַנג 'long', לענגער
[léyngər] 'longer'), די קעלט 'cold(ness)' (cf. קאַלט 'cold', קעלטער 'colder').

4.1.3 Neutrality

Neutrality may be determined semantically, morphologically or
derivationally. The neutral definite article is דאָס (which inflects to דעם in
dative → §5.3.3). Neutrality varies in a number of words with the other two
genders, most frequently femininity. Where variation does exist in the
literary language, the modern trend is away from neutral.

4.1.3.1 Semantic neutrality

Diminutives in ‑ל and ‑עלע (→ §§4.3.1 – 4.3.2) are neutral irrespective of
the gender of the base form of the noun, hence דאָס טישל 'the little table'

and דאָס טישעלע 'the very little table' from דער טיש 'the table'; analogously, דאָס געסל 'the little street' and דאָס געסעלע 'the very little street', from די גאַס 'the street'. There are two words in which semantic masculinity and femininity conflict rather sharply with the neutrality of diminutives – ייִנגל 'boy' and מיידל 'girl'. Both sets of variants – דער ייִנגל and דאָס ייִנגל, די מיידל and דאָס מיידל are equally acceptable. Historically, ייִנגל is the diminutive of יונג and מיידל of מויד. Native speakers do not, however, perceive ייִנגל and מיידל as diminutives in the modern language. The base nouns have become emotionally charged epithets that combine with adjectives in stock phrases, usually to mark indelicacy. They may explicitly be negatively charged, e.g. (דער) גראָבער יונג 'fellow with no manners or concern for other people', (די) אַלטע מויד 'old maid'. They often serve to denote physical strength, and are accompanied by 'spaced out' pronunciation, e.g. אַ געזונטער יונג! [à | gə | zún | tər | yúng] '(He's) a healthy (= powerful) fellow!', אַן אײַזערנע מויד! [àn | áy | zər | nə | móyd] '(She's) an iron lady!'.

4.1.3.2   Morphological neutrality

Nouns that begin or end in one of following affixes are generally neutral. Note that nouns suffixed by -ות and -עניש (and occasionally, -ערײַ), enumerated as feminine (→ §4.1.2.2), may also be neutral. Virtually none of the neutral affixes serves to produce new nouns in the modern language, but all are encountered in stock items.

-גע:	דאָס געשלעג [gəshlég] 'fight'
-וואַרג:	דאָס רויוואַרג 'raw material'
-טום:	דאָס ייִדנטום 'Jewry'
-ס:	דאָס שלעכטס 'evil'
-עכץ:	שרײַבעכץ [shráybəkhts / shráybakhts] 'bad writing'

4.1.3.3   Derivational neutrality

Nominalizations of infinitives are neutral, hence דאָס לויפֿן 'running (n.)' from לויפֿן 'run (v.)', דאָס זינגען 'singing (n.)' from זינגען 'sing (v.)'. Nominalizations of adjectives ending in -ע are neutral, hence דאָס אויסערגעוויינטלעכע 'the extraordinary', from אויסערגעוויינטלעך 'extraordinary'.

4.1.4   Two genders in dialectal usage

Northeastern Yiddish has only two genders — masculine and feminine. Nouns appearing as neutral in the other dialects and the standard language are assigned either masculinity or femininity. Inanimate objects tend toward feminine (e.g. די לאַנד for standard דאָס לאַנד 'country'). Diminutives have the gender of their base nouns (e.g. דער טישל for standard דאָס טישל 'table', cf. base form דער טיש).

4.2   PLURALS

Plurals, like gender, must be learned with each noun. There are few inviolable rules, but overall patterns can account for the vast majority of nouns in the language. Most capricious are the nouns undergoing vowel change with or without the -ער pluralizing ending. A dictionary should be consulted for a noun's plural.

4.2.1   Plural ending -(ע)ן

Nouns ending in a consonant or stressed vowel usually pluralize by suffixation of ‍‍ן- (or ען- after מ, נ, a stressed vowel or diphthong, נג, נק, or consonant + ל → §2.2.9).

SAMPLES OF NOUNS PLURALIZING WITH ‍-(ע)ן

אַרמיי [arméy] 'army' → אַרמייען

אַבאַן)(בּאַן 'train' → (אײזן)באַנען(אײזן

בעט 'bed' → בעטן

גאַס 'street' → גאַסן

האָטעל 'hotel' → האָטעלן

מענטש 'person; good human being' → מענטשן

פּראָפֿעסאָר [profésor] 'professor' → פּראָפֿעסאָרן [profəsórn]

שול 'traditional synagogue; school' → שולן

שותּפֿות [shútfəs] 'partnership' → שותּפֿותן

שעה [sho] 'hour' → שעהן [shóən] (also spelled שעהען)

4.2.2 Plural ending ס-

The plural ending ס- is frequently pronounced somewhere between [s] and [z]. A number of categories of nouns take ס-.

4.2.2.1 Nouns ending in unstressed ע-

Nouns ending in unstressed ע- usually pluralize by suffixation of ס-. A number of nineteenth-century borrowings from German have plurals in ‍ן-, especially in political terminology, e.g. (די) מאַסע 'mass' → מאַסן '(the) masses'. Some have alternate plurals in ס- and ‍(ע)ן-. The (ע)ן- endings predominate in journalistic and parliamentary styles and usually denote a more abstract sense, e.g. פֿראַגע 'question' pluralizes to פֿראַגעס 'questions (in the everyday sense)' and פֿראַגן 'questions (of major importance, e.g. to society)'. Cf. §15.8.

SAMPLES OF NOUNS ENDING IN UNSTRESSED ־ע PLURALIZING WITH ־ס

הע
נ
טשקע 'glove' ← העַנטשקעס

קאַװע 'coffee' ← קאַװעס

קעשענע 'pocket' ← קעשענעס

שמאַטע 'rag' ← שמאַטעס

4.2.2.2 Internationalisms ending in an unstressed nonreduced vowel

Internationalisms ending in a vowel that is not stressed but that retains its full vowel colour usually pluralize by suffixation of ־ס.

SAMPLES OF INTERNATIONALISMS ENDING IN AN UNSTRESSED

NONREDUCED VOWEL PLURALIZING WITH ־ס

אויטאָ 'car' ← אויטאָס

עגאָ 'ego' ← עגאָס

ראַדיאָ 'radio' ← ראַדיאָס

4.2.2.3 Family names

Family names pluralize by suffixation of ־ס (or ־עס after sibilants ז, זש, טש, ס, צ, or ש).

SAMPLES OF FAMILY NAMES PLURALIZING WITH ־(ע)ס

גאָלדבערג 'Goldberg' ← די גאָלדבערגס 'the Goldbergs'

האָדסאָן 'Hudson' ← די האָדסאָנס 'the Hudsons'

פלודערמאַכער 'Pludermacher' ← די פלודערמאַכערס 'the Pludermachers'

ראַבינאָװיטש 'Rabinowitz' ← די ראַבינאָװיטשעס 'the Rabinowitzes'

ראַפּאָפּאָרט 'Rappaport' ← די ראַפּאָפּאָרטס 'the Rappaports'

4.2.2.4 Nouns ending in ־ס in an unstressed syllable

Nouns ending in ־ס in an unstressed final syllable usually pluralize by suffixation of -ס.

SAMPLES OF NOUNS ENDING IN ם- IN AN UNSTRESSED

FINAL SYLLABLE PLURALIZING WITH ס-

אַקוואַריום 'aquarium' → אַקוואַריומס

לחיים [ləkháyim] '(alcoholic) drink' → לחיימס

שטורעם 'storm' → שטורעמס

4.2.2.5 Nouns ending in (ע)ן- in an unstressed final syllable

Nouns ending in ן- (or ען-) in an unstressed final syllable usually pluralize by suffixation of -ס.

SAMPLES OF NOUNS ENDING IN UNSTRESSED (ע)ן-

PLURALIZING WITH ס-

וואָלקן 'cloud' → וואָלקנס

קוימען 'chimney' → קוימענס

קישן 'pillow' → קישנס

4.2.2.6 Nonhuman nouns ending in ער-

Nonhuman nouns ending in ער- usually pluralize by suffixation of ס-.

SAMPLES OF NONHUMAN NOUNS ENDING IN

UNSTRESSED ער- PLURALIZING WITH ס-

זומער 'summer' → זומערס

טיגער 'tiger' → טיגערס

קלויסטער 'church' → קלויסטערס

4.2.3 Plural ending עס-

The plural ending עס- is frequently pronounced between [əs] and [əz].

4.2.3.1 Slavonic component nouns ending in a consonant

Some nouns, mostly of Slavonic derivation, pluralize by suffixation of -עס. There are occasional concomitant vowel changes.

SAMPLES OF SLAVONIC COMPONENT NOUNS PLURALIZING WITH -עס

כוליגאַן [khuligán] 'ruffian; hooligan' → כוליגאַנעס [khuligánəs]

טשוואָק [tshvok] 'nail' → טשוועקעס [tshvékəs]

נודניק [núdnik] 'bore; pest; poor conversationalist' → נודניקעס [núdnikəs]

4.2.4 Semitic component plurals

Most Semitic component nouns are pluralized by -ים ([im] or [əm]) or -ות [əs]. Where suffixation of -ים or -ות results in a syllable being added, stress shifts to the new penultimate syllable (→ §2.3.2.1). There are frequent vowel changes in pluralization.

4.2.4.1 Semitic component plural in -ים

Semitic component nouns ending in a consonant are usually pluralized by suffixation of -ים (pronounced [im] or [əm]). A sizable minority of nouns ending in unstressed -ה or -א, including virtually all semantically masculine agentives, also pluralize with -ים, dropping final -ה. A few non-Semitic component nouns regularly pluralize with -ים, e.g. דאָקטער '(medical) doctor' → דאָקטוירים [doktóyrim], נאַר 'fool' → נאַראָנים [narónim], and פּויער 'peasant' → פּויערים [póyərim]. Pluralizing -ים used with nouns ending in -ער or -אָר (→ §4.1.1.3) has a sarcastic or pejorative effect, e.g. וואונדער 'miracle' → וואונדיירים [vundéyrim] 'not-so-impressive miracles', פּראָפֿעסאָר 'professor' → פּראָפֿעסוירים [profəsóyrim] 'not-so-impressive professors'. The normal plurals are וואונדער (also וואונדערס), and פּראָפֿעסאָרן [profəsórn].

58

SAMPLES OF SEMITIC COMPONENT NOUNS PLURALIZING WITH ‑ים

גנב [gánəv] 'thief' → גנבים [ganóvim / ganóvəm]

חבר [khávər] 'friend' → חברים [khavéyrim / khavéyrəm]

שיכור [shíkər] 'drunkard' → שיכורים [shikúrim / shikúrəm]

שכן [shókhn] 'neighbour' → שכנים [shkhéynim / shkhéynəm]

רב [rov] 'rabbi' → רבנים [rabónim / rabónəm]

שבת [shábəs] 'Saturday; Sabbath' → שבתים [shabósim / shabósəm]

שוטה [shóytə] 'fool' → שוטים [shóytim / shóytəm]

שונא [sóynə] 'enemy' → שונאים [sónim / sónəm]

תלמיד [tálməd] 'student' → תלמידים [talmídim / talmídəm]

4.2.4.2 Semitic component plural in ‑ות

Semitic component nouns ending in unstressed ‑ה or ‑א usually pluralize by
suffixation of ‑ות, dropping final ‑ה, and falling together phonetically with
phonetic system ‑עס. A minority of nouns ending in a consonant also pluralize
by suffixation of ‑ות.

SAMPLES OF SEMITIC COMPONENT NOUNS PLURALIZING WITH ‑ות

דאגה [dáygə] 'worry' → דאגות [dáygəs]

דוגמא [dúgmə] 'example' → דוגמאות [dugmóəs] (var. דוגמות [dúgməs])

חלום [khóləm] 'dream' → חלומות [khalóyməs]

חתונה [khásənə] 'wedding' → חתונות [khásənəs]

חתימה [khsímə] 'signature' → חתימות [khsíməs]

טענה [táynə] 'complaint; point (in discussion)' → טענות [táynəs]

טובה [tóyvə] 'favour' → טובות [tóyvəs]

לשון [lóshn] 'language' → לשונות [ləshóynəs]

מקור [mókər] 'source' → מקורות [məkóyrəs] (var. מקורים [məkóyrim])

משפחה [mishpókhə] 'family' → משפחות [mishpókhəs]

סברא [svórə] 'supposition; possibility' → סברות [svórəs]

4.2.5 Plural ending in ען-

The plural ending in ען- ([əkh / akh]) is restricted to nouns ending in syllabic ל-. Where the noun is a diminutive, the composite pluralizing לעך- is obligatory (→ §§4.3.2, 4.3.3) but there are a number of non-diminutive nouns for which both ען- and ען- are acceptable, e.g. שליסל 'key' → שליסלען or שליסלעך.

SAMPLES OF NOUNS ENDING IN ל- PLURALIZING WITH ען-

אייניקל 'grandchild' → אייניקלען

ברידערל '(little) brother (lovingly)' → ברידערלען

יינגל 'boy' → יינגלען

מיידל 'girl' → מיידלען

צעטל 'note' → צעטלען

צענטל 'tenth' → צענטלען

שװעסטערל '(little) sister (lovingly)' → שװעסטערלען

שפיצל 'prank; dirty trick' → שפיצלען

4.2.6 Plural ending in ער-

Nouns that pluralize by suffixation of ער- do not fit into any morphological categories. They are frequently words that have been in the language since its inception. ער- may pluralize on its own, but it is frequently accompanied by vowel shifts.

4.2.6.1 ער- with no vowel change

SAMPLES OF NOUNS PLURALIZING WITH ער-

איי 'egg' → אייער

בילד 'picture' → בילדער

האַנטעך 'towel' → האַנטעכער

הונדערט 'hundred' → הונדערטער

4.2.6.2   ע → אַ   with   -ער

SAMPLES OF NOUNS PLURALIZING WITH -ער AND ע → אַ

לענדער ← 'country; land' לאַנד

מענער ← 'man; husband' מאַן

פלענער ← 'plan' פלאַן

פלעצער ← 'place' פלאַץ

פלעשער ← 'bottle' פלאַש

4.2.6.3   ע → אָ   with   -ער

Although not reflected in the orthography of the traditional system, Semitic component פנים [pónəm] 'face', is part of the series. It pluralizes to פנימער [pénəmər].

SAMPLES OF NOUNS PLURALIZING WITH -ער AND ע → אָ

גערטנער ← 'garden' גאָרטן

לעכער ← 'hole' לאָך

רעדער ← 'wheel' ראָד

4.2.6.4   י → ו   with   -ער

SAMPLES OF NOUNS PLURALIZING WITH -ער AND י → ו

ביכער ← 'book' בוך

הינער ← 'hen; chicken' הון

צינגער ← 'tongue' צונג

4.2.6.5   יי → וי   with   -ער

SAMPLES OF NOUNS PLURALIZING WITH -ער AND יי → וי

בײכער ← 'stomach' בויך

הײזער ← 'house' הויז

מײלער ← 'mouth' מויל

4.2.6.6 עֶר- **with various vowels** → ײ

SAMPLES OF NOUNS PLURALIZING WITH עֶר- AND VARIOUS SHIFTS TO ײ

ביימער 'tree' → בוים

(var. ציין) ציינער 'tooth' → צאָן

4.2.7 Plural by vowel change only

Like nouns pluralizing by suffixation of עֶר-, those pluralizing by vowel change alone tend to be ancient items in the language.

4.2.7.1 אַ → ע

SAMPLES OF NOUNS PLURALIZING WITH אַ → ע

הענט 'hand' → האַנט

ווענט 'wall' → וואַנט

קעץ 'cat' → קאַץ

קלעם 'blow (to body / ego / mood)' → קלאַם

4.2.7.2 אָ → ע

SAMPLES OF NOUNS PLURALIZING WITH אָ → ע

טעג 'day' → טאָג

נעמען 'name' → נאָמען

קעפ 'head' → קאָפ

שטעט 'city' → שטאָט

4.2.7.3 ו → י

SAMPLES OF NOUNS PLURALIZING WITH ו → י

ברידער 'brother' → ברודער

זין 'son' → זון

פֿוס 'foot' → פֿיס

שוך 'shoe' → שיך

4.2.7.4 יַ → וי

SAMPLES OF NOUNS PLURALIZING BY וי → יַ

לויז 'louse' → לײַז

מויז 'mouse' → מײַז

4.2.8 Same form for singular and plural

A number of nouns have plurals identical with the singular form of the noun.

4.2.8.1 Human nouns ending in -ער

Human nouns in -ער usually have no separate plural form. Minority usage does pluralize by -ס for agentives denoting professions, e.g. שנײַדערס 'tailors' for שנײַדער, שרײַבערס 'writers' for שרײַבער. פֿעטער 'uncle' exceptionally pluralizes by suffixation of -ס, hence פֿעטערס.

SAMPLES OF HUMAN NOUNS ENDING IN -ער WITH IDENTICAL PLURALS

אַמעריקאַנער 'American' → אַמעריקאַנער

אַרבעטער 'worker' → אַרבעטער

וועגעטאַריער 'vegetarian' → וועגעטאַריער

טענצער 'dancer' → טענצער

לערער 'teacher' → לערער

ענגלענדער 'Englishman' [éynglǝndǝr] → ענגלענדער

קאַנאַדער 'Canadian' → קאַנאַדער

שוועסטער 'sister' → שוועסטער

שנײַדער 'tailor' → שנײַדער

שרײַבער 'writer' → שרײַבער

4.2.8.2 Various nouns with identical plurals

בײנגל 'bagel' → בײגל

בריוו 'letter' → בריוו

פֿינגער 'finger' → פֿינגער

פֿיש 'fish' → פֿיש

פֿערד 'horse' → פֿערד

פֿרײַנד [fraynt] 'friend' → פֿרײַנד

שטערן 'star' → שטערן

4.3   DIMINUTIVES

There is a two-tier system comprising a first diminutive and a second diminutive. In its simplest form, the first diminutive denotes 'smallness' and the second diminutive 'more smallness' or 'tinyness'. Many nouns, however, usually for morphological reasons, have no more than one of the two. The diminutives may evoke emotions and attitudes instead of, or in addition to, size. Some diminutives have lost their diminutive sense and are used as base nouns which 'happen to be' morphologically diminutive. The major diminutives are of neutral gender. Many diminutives undergo the internal vowel shifts אַ/אָ → ע; ו → י; וי → ײ, various → ײ. They are the same shifts applicable in pluralization (→ §§4.2.6.2 – 4.2.6.6).

4.3.1   Morphology of the first diminutive

The first diminutive is formed by suffixation of syllabic ל- (→ §2.2.8). Its plural is formed by further suffixation of עך- [əkh / akh], giving plural first diminutive suffix לעך- where ל, at the beginning of a syllable, is not syllabic.

SAMPLES OF DERIVATION OF THE FIRST DIMINITUVE

(די) טישלעך .pl ,'little table' (דאָס) טישל ← 'table' (דער) טיש

(די) קעצלעך .pl ,'little cat; kitten' (דאָס) קעצל ← 'cat' (די) קאַץ

(די) ביכלעך .pl 'little book' (דאָס) ביכל ← 'book' (דאָס) בוך

4.3.1.1 Nouns ending in ‑ן

Nouns ending in ‑ן attract ‑דל rather than ל, and pluralize by further suffixation of ‑עך, e.g. שטיין (דער) 'stone' → שטיינדל (דאָס) 'little stone; pebble', pl. שטיינדלעך (די).

4.3.1.2 Nouns ending in ‑ל

Nouns ending in ‑ל attract ‑(ע)ל rather than ל‑, and pluralize by further suffixation of ‑עך, e.g. מויל (דאָס) 'mouth' → מיילעל (דאָס) (or מיילל) 'little mouth', pl. מיילעלעך (די) or מיילללעך (די).

4.3.1.3 Semitic component plurals

Semitic component plurals in ‑ים are diminutivized by suffixation of ‑לעך, occasionally with accompanying semantic nuances, e.g. חברים [khavéyrim] 'friends' → חברימלעך [khavéyrimlakh] 'shady friends; cronies' (cf. sg. חבר (דער) [khávər] 'friend'); ענינים [inyónim] 'matters' → ענינימלעך [inyónimlakh] 'little matters' (cf. sg. ענין (דער) [ínyən] 'matter').

4.3.1.4 Nouns with no first diminutive

Nouns ending in syllabic ‑ל (e.g. לעפל (דער) 'spoon'), and nouns stressed two or more syllables from the last (e.g. אָנשיקעניש (די\דאָס) [ónshikənish] 'nuisance; pain in the neck') cannot attract the first diminutive. Nouns ending in a vowel (e.g. כמאַרע (די) 'threatening cloud') are incapable of attracting the first diminutive, but personal names occasionally accept it (→ §4.3.7).

4.3.2 Morphology of the second diminutive

The second diminutive is formed by suffixation of עלע- [ələ, alə]. Its plural is formed by further suffixation of ך-. The resulting sequence עלעך- is pronounced [alakh], [aləkh] or [ələkh] (→ §2.1.2.3).

SAMPLES OF THE SECOND DIMINUTIVE

(די) טישעלעך .table' → טישעלע (דאָס) 'tiny table', pl' (דער) טיש

קאַץ (די) 'cat' → קעצעלע (דאָס) 'little kitten', pl. קעצעלעך (די)

(די) ביכעלעך .book'→ ביכעלע (דאָס) 'pamphlet', pl' (דאָס) בוך

4.3.2.1 Nouns ending in ל-

Nouns ending in ל- attract the second diminutive by means of the ל assuming the added role of the ל of second diminutive suffix עלע-, with the two required עs added on either side, e.g. לעפֿל (דער) 'spoon' → לעפֿעלע (דאָס), pl. לעפֿעלעך (די).

4.3.2.2 Nouns ending in an unstressed vowel

Nouns ending in an unstressed vowel (i.e. ע-, ה, or א), attract the second diminutive by means of the unstressed vowel assuming the added role of the first ע of second diminutive suffix עלע-, with the remaining sequence לע- suffixed thereafter, e.g. פֿראַגע (די) 'question' → פֿראַגעלע (דאָס) 'little question', pl. פֿראַגעלעך (די); גמרא (די) [gəmórə] 'Gemora / Gemara (major part of the Talmud; select reading therefrom; cf. §§7.3.2.1, 15.17.15)' → גמראלע (דאָס) [gəmórələ] 'brief reading / lesson of the Talmud', pl. גמראלעך (די) [gəmórələkh].

4.3.2.3 Nouns with no second diminutive

Nouns ending in a consonant with stress on a syllable other than the last (e.g. פּלימעניק (דער) [pliménik] 'nephew') cannot attract the second diminutive.

Those ending in syllabic ל- are exempted from the restriction, hence (דער)
פֿידל 'fiddle' → פֿידעלע (דאָס) 'little fiddle (endearing)'. Nouns ending in
syllabic ן- rarely accept the second diminutive. When they do, the ן- is
dropped, e.g. שטעקן (דער) 'stick' → שטעקעלע (דאָס) [shtékalə] 'little
stick'.

4.3.3   Suffix קע- with inanimate nouns

Suffix קע- used with inanimate nouns does not usually form a diminutive
noun from a base noun. It is rather used to coin nouns denoting objects that
happen to be small, e.g. אַגראַפֿקע [agráfkə] 'safety pin', קאַסעטקע [kasétkə]
'cassette tape'. Where base and derived forms do exist, the derived קע- form
usually signifies an object distinct from its base noun, e.g. מאַשינקע (די)
(also שרײַבמאַשינקע) 'typewriter' from מאַשין 'machine'. It occasionally
invokes a humorous mood, e.g. מאַכאַרײַקע (די) [makharáykə] 'contraption;
gizmo'. Unlike other diminutives, those in קע- are feminine. Cf. §4.3.7.1 on
קע- with proper names.

4.3.4   Diminutives as new base nouns

While many diminutives represent inflections of their base nouns denoting
smallness (first diminutive) or tinyness (second diminutive), many
diminutives of both categories have acquired lives of their own by assuming
special connotations, e.g. הײַזל (דאָס) 'brothel' from הויז (דאָס) 'house',
פֿינגערל (דאָס) 'ring' from פֿינגער (דער) 'finger', חנדל (דאָס) [kheyndl]
'flirtatious / coquettish gesture' from חן [kheyn] 'grace; beauty'. In a
number of instances, the notion of size is retained as a secondary factor in
tandem with the diminutive itself becoming the everyday name for a thing,

e.g. קעמל (דער) קאַם from ,'pocket comb' (דאָס) קעמעלע ,'comb' (דאָס) קעמל
which is now so rare that its use would imply a rather huge comb. In a
number of instances, the base form of a noun and a diminutive thereof
denote related but distinct objects, e.g. זײגער (דער) 'clock (in general); wall
clock; pocket watch' vs. זײגערל (דאָס) 'wristwatch'.

4.3.5   The second diminutive as sentimentality marker
The second diminutive may mark warmth, affection and sentimentality with
nonhuman nouns. In many instances, the first diminutive marks physical
reduction in size while the second diminutive invokes affection. For some
speakers, the pronunciation of the first ע in singular עלע- and both עs in
plural ending עלעך- increasingly approach [a] in direct proportion to
increasing sentimentality, hence the frequent sentimental realizations [-alə]
and [alakh] (→ §§ 2.1.2.2 – 2.1.2.3).

SAMPLES OF THE SECOND DIMINUTIVE AS SENTIMENTALITY MARKER

הונט (דער) 'dog' → הינטל (דאָס) → הינטעלע (דאָס)

לאָמפּ (דער) 'lamp' → לעמפּל (דאָס) → לעמפּעלע (דאָס)

קאָפּ (דער) 'head' → קעפּל (דאָס) → קעפּעלע (דאָס)

4.3.6   The first diminutive as pejorative
The first diminutive applied to masculine agentives, especially those denoting
professions, is decidedly pejorative. It generally means that the person is
either incompetent at his work, not a nice person, or both.

SAMPLES OF THE FIRST DIMINUTIVE AS PEJORATIVE

אַדוואָקאַט (דער) 'lawyer' → אַדוואָקאַטל (דאָס) 'small time lawyer'

לערער (דער) 'teacher' → לערערל (דאָס) 'bad teacher'

(דער) מאָלערל ← 'artist' (דאָס) מאַלעערל 'very minor artist'

(דער) שריַיבער 'writer' ← (דאָס) שריַיבערל 'bad writer; graphomaniac'

4.3.7 Diminutives as love markers

The first, and, especially, the second diminutive can be applied to traditional Jewish proper forenames to denote warmth, affection and love. While most prolific for children's names, diminutive forenames are often retained through life. On the whole, they follow the morphological patterns of diminutives generally (→ §§4.3.2 – 4.3.3.4). Note, however, that (ע)בֿל-(→ §4.3.1.2) does not occur with proper names, and that names ending in a vowel may occasionally accept the first diminutive (unlike common nouns which cannot → §4.3.1.4).

SAMPLES OF DIMINUTIVES AS LOVE MARKERS

אבֿרהם [avróm] (m.) → אבֿרהמל [avréml] → אבֿרהמעלע [avrémalə]

חיה [kháyə] (f.) → חיהלע [kháyalə]

לאה [léyə] (f.) → לאהלע [léyalə]

משה [móyshə] (m.) → משהל [móyshl] → משהלע [móyshalə]

סענדער [séndər] (m.) → סענדערל [séndərl]

שמואל [shmúəl] (m.) → שמועלע [shmúalə]

שרה [sórə] (f.) → שרהל [sórl] → שרהלע [sóralə]

4.3.7.1 Suffix -קע as love marker

As an alternative to the usual -ל and -עלע diminutivizing suffixes, love may be shown by -קע suffixed to proper forenames. The -קע forms occur most extensively in Northeastern Yiddish. For increased endearment, -עלע may follow upon -קע, subject to the usual morphological constraints (→ §§4.3.1.4,

4.3.2.4, 4.3.7). The compounded suffix קעלע- is usually restricted to children's names and use as a term of endearment in intimate relationships.

SAMPLES OF SUFFIXES קע- AND קעלע- AS LOVE MARKERS

אברהם [avróm] (m.) → אברהמקע [avrémkə] → אברהמקעלע [avrémkalə]

חיה [kháyə] (f.) → חיהקע [kháykə] → חיהקעלע [kháykalə]

לאה [léyə] (f.) → לאהקע [léykə] → לאהקעלע [léykalə]

משה [móyshə] (m.) → משהקע [móyshkə] → משהלע [móyshkalə]

סענדער [séndər] (m.) → סענדערקע [séndərkə]

שמואל [shmúəl] (m.) → שמואלקע [shmúlkə] → שמואלקעלע [shmúlkalə]

שרה [sórə] (f.) → שרהקע [sórkə] → שרהקעלע [sórkalə]

4.3.7.2   Suffixes יק- and טשיק- as love markers

יק- is most frequent with masculine forenames ending in ל-. The masculine forename איציק has developed as a popular alternate to the more formal יצחק [yítskhok], which corresponds with the Biblical 'Isaac'. Its diminutive is איציקל. Occasionally, צע- (or טשע-) may be encountered as a feminine counterpart to יק-, e.g. חנצע [khántsə] or חנטשע [khántshə] from חנה [khánə]. A variant love marker is טשיק-, which may replace the last syllable of the stem of the name, e.g. אליהו [eylióhu] → עלטשיק [éltshik] (m.), with spelling according to the phonetic system for ease of reading. For increased endearment, ל- may follow upon יק- or טשיק-. The compounded suffixes יקל- and טשיקל- are usually restricted to children's names and to use as terms of endearment in intimate relationships. יק- or טשיק- do not generally trigger internal vowel shifts.

SAMPLES OF SUFFIX יק- AND טשיק- AS LOVE MARKERS

ישראל [yisró(ə)l] (m.) → ישראליק [(yi)srólik] → ישראליקל [(yi)srólikl]

שמואל [shmúəl] (m.) → שמואליק [shmúlik] → שמואליקל [shmúlikl]

אברהם [avróm] (m.) → אברהמטשיק [avrómtshik]

4.4   COMPOUND NOUNS

A compound noun comprises a noun joined together with another word (an adjective, verb stem, or another noun) to function as a single new noun. The first member of the compound (which needn't be a noun) has primary stress. Stress in the second (which must be a noun) is lowered in deference to the compound (→§§2.3.1.1, 2.3.1.4). Gender and plural are determined by the second. There is considerable variation in the written language as to whether compound nouns are written as one word, as two, or hyphenated. Well established and familiar compounds are written as one word (except where one of the two is spelled according to the traditional system). The dynamic tendency that is developing is implicitly linked with pronunciation. Where a well established compound is pronounced as one word, with no internal phonetic pause, it is written as one word. Less well known compounds, and those created at will, are generally written as two words or hyphenated. The longer the compound, the stronger the inclination to write it as two words. There is a clear (if slow-moving) trend away from hyphenation.   In the samples that follow, internal phonetic pause is marked by |.

SAMPLES OF COMPOUND NOUNS

auto mechanic [o(y)tomobíl | məkhànikər] מעכאַניקער אויטאָמאָביל (דער)

university student [universitét | studènt] סטודענט אוניװערסיטעטס (דער)

homework [héymarbət] היימאַרבעט (די)

traditional yeshiva student [yəshívəbòkhər] ישיבֿה־בחור (דער)

teacher training course [lérər | kùrs] לערער־קורס (דער)

great-grandfather [éltərzeydə] עלטערזיידע (דער)

kindergarten [kíndərgortn] קינדערגאָרטן (דער)

pickpocket [késhənəgànəv] קעשענע־גנבֿ (דער)

registration form [registrátsyə | blànk] בלאַנק רעגיסטראַציע (דער)

title page [shárblat] שער־בלאַט (דער)

4.4.1 Compounding ס

Many compounds comprising two nouns have a ס (often pronounced between [s] and [z]) suffixed to the first to mark compounding and ease pronunciation. The ס is not a productive compound-forming suffix anymore. It is usually retained where it exists in stock compounds, but some traditional ס compounds have developed alternate forms without it. Compounding ס is frequent in instances where the first member is אַרבעט 'work', לעבן [lébm] 'life', פֿאָלק 'people; folk; nation' or a noun ending in suffix ־ונג. The hyphen is usually used in writing, except where the compound is pronounced as a single word, e.g. לאַנדסמאַן [lántsman] 'compatriot' (lit. 'land man'). Compounding ס is encountered extensively in journalistic prose, and is especially prominent in political and scientific terminology of the twentieth century.

SAMPLES OF COMPOUNDING ס

(די) אַנטװיקלונגס‎≠‎מעגלעבקײטן development opportunities

(דער) אַרבעטס‎≠‎פּלאַן plan of action (lit. 'work plan')

(דער) דערציאונגס‎≠‎מיניסטעריום ministry of education

(די) לעבנס‎≠‎פֿראַגע question of life or death (lit. 'life question')

(דאָס) פֿאָלקסליד folksong

(די) פֿאָלקס‎≠‎מעשה [fólks | màysə] folktale

4.4.2 Compounding נ

Many compounds comprising two nouns have a נ suffixed to the first as a compounding marker. It is, generally speaking, no longer productive but is retained where it exists. It is most consistently used in names of trees.

SAMPLES OF COMPOUNDING נ

באַרנבױם pear tree

weekly newspaper וואָכנבלאַט

orange juice מאַראַנצן-זאַפֿט

fig tree פֿײגנבוים

magician (lit. 'maker of tricks') קונצנמאַכער (דער)

4.4.3   The construct state in the Semitic component

Compound nouns in European languages comprise describer (attribute) plus described (head) as evident in the Yiddish compounds cited. Semitic languages, on the other hand, have the construct state with reverse order: described (head) followed by describer (attribute), corresponding with the use of 'of' in European languages. Yiddish preserves a large number of Hebrew and Aramaic constructs as stock phrases. Stress is usually on the second element. Most constructs occur within the Semitic component but there are a few exceptions, e.g. סוף-וואָך(ן) (דער) [sòvvókh] 'weekend'. Constructs are hyphenated or written separately.

SAMPLES OF CONSTRUCTS

waste of (valuable) time [biṭl zmán] ביטול-זמן (דער)

traditional rabbinical court [bézdn] בית-דין (דער)

rabbinical court proceeding / trial [din tóyrə] דין-תורה (דער\די)

spinal cord [khut ashédrə] חוט-השדרה (דער)

a taste of paradise (said esp. of good food) [tam ganéydn] טעם גן-עדן

eclipse of the sun [likə khámə] ליקוי-חמה (די)

place of rest; refuge [mòkəm mənúkhə] מקום-מנוחה (דער)

devotion, selflessness, self-sacrifice [məsirəs néfəsh] מסירת-נפֿש (דער\דאָס)

head of a traditional Talmudic academy [rosh yəshívə] ראש-ישיבֿה (דער)

wild idea; temporary insanity [ruəkh shtús] רוח-שטות (דער)

tuition fee [skhar líməd] שֹכֹר-לימוד (דער)

4.4.3.1 Productive construct former בעל

בעל [bal] forms a large number of Semitic component constructs within Yiddish. Its plural form is בעלי [bálə]. A number of בעל nouns are however pluralized solely by pluralization of the second element (by Semitic component pluralizing suffixes ים- [əm/im] and וֹת- [əs], and occasionally by phonetic system ס-. בעל is in effect a masculine agentive former, but a few בעל constructions have evolved feminine equivalents. Its force derives from the older sense of 'master of'. It joins naturally only with Semitic component nouns. Constructs formed with בעל may be hyphenated or written separately. Note that the phonetic system is used for באַלעבאַס [baləbós] 'boss; married man; master of the household', and its plural באַלעבאַטים [baləbátim]. The plural using the traditional system (בעלי־בתים), may also be encountered. Where the singular בעל־הבית is encountered the reference is usually to the learned [baal habáyis], as in Ashkenazic Hebrew, referring strictly to 'master of the household' in traditional contexts. בעל־מצווה [balmítsvə] is a traditional alternate to בר־מצווה [barmítsvə] 'Bar Mitsvah'.

SAMPLES OF CONSTRUCT AGENTIVES WITH בעל

debtor [balkhóyv] בעל חוב (pl. בעלי חובֿות [baləkhóyvəs])
dreamer [balkhalóyməs] בעל חלומות (pl. בעלי חלומות [baləkhalóyməs])
master; artisan [balməlókhə] בעל מלאָכה (pl. בעל מלאכֿות [balməlókhəs])
coachman; simple man [balagólə] בעל עגלה (pl. בעל עגלוֹת)
man who earns a good living [balparnósə] בעל פרנסה (pl. בעלי פרנסה)
reader of the Torah in synagogue [balkóyrə] בעל קורא (pl. בעל קוראס)
kindhearted, merciful person [balrákhmim] בעל רחמים (pl. בעלי רחמים)
passionate man [baltáyvə(nik)] בעל תאווה(ניק) (pl. בעל תאווה(ניק)ס)
passionate woman [baltáyvənitsə] בעל תאווהניצע (pl. בעל תאווהניצעס)
practical person [baltákhləs] בעל תכליֿת (pl. בעלי תכליֿת [balətákhləs])
penitent; returnee to Judaism [baltshúvə] בעל תשובה (pl. בעלי תשובֿה)

4.4.4   Compound names

Most traditional forenames are double-barrelled. It is important to bear in mind that the second of these is not a 'middle name' or 'middle initial'. The two names are used together as one. Some traditional compound forenames, especially male names deriving from names of animals, comprise the Hebrew and Yiddish for the 'same' name, e.g. דוֹבּ≈בּער [dovbér]. דוֹבּ is the Hebrew for Yiddish בּער 'bear'. Analogously, אריה≈לײב [aryəléyb], lit. 'lion lion', צבֿי≈הירש [tsvihírsh], lit. 'deer deer' and זאבּ≈װאָלף [ze(y)vvólf], lit. 'wolf wolf'. The second of the two compounded names is stressed. The individuals so known formally would be known to their friends and relatives by the diminutives of the second (Yiddish) name alone – בּערל (or בּערקע), לײבל (or לײבקע), הערשל (or הירשקע) and װעלװל (or װעלפֿקע). Cf. §§5.8.1, 5.14.2, 5.15.1.2 on traditional names.

SAMPLES OF MALE COMPOUND NAMES

Arn-Vélvl אהרן≈װעלװל

Hirshə-Dóvid הירשע≈דוד

Yoshə-Bér יאָשע≈בּער

Moyshə-Kálmən משה≈קלמן

Shloymə-Zálmən שלמה≈זלמן

SAMPLES OF FEMALE COMPOUND NAMES

Blumə-Díshə בלומע≈דישע

Khayə-Sórə חיה≈שרה

Mashə-Dvóyrə מאַשע≈דבֿורה

Simə-Léyə סימע≈לאה

5 NOUN PHRASES

5.0 OVERVIEW

A noun phrase is a noun alone or with its articles and/or adjectives. Noun phrases occur in three cases (nominative, accusative and dative) determined by the noun phrase's relation to the verb phrase. It is the articles and adjectives within the noun phrase that regularly inflect for case and for gender. With a few easily defined exceptions, Yiddish nouns themselves do not inflect.

5.1 CASE

Case is the situation of the noun phrase relative to the verb phrase. Because the singular noun itself does not usually inflect, its case is evident from its articles and adjectives, which do. While case exists abstractly across the board, its morphological effects are evident only in the singular. In the plural, the definite article is always די, and the adjective ending always -ע, irrespective of case or gender.

5.1.1 Nominative (subject)

Nominative is the situation of the noun phrase as subject of a sentence. The noun phrase in nominative is not dominated by any verb phrase. It simply exists, or itself dominates a verb phrase.

SAMPLES OF NOUN PHRASES IN NOMINATIVE

The fellow is here   דער בחור [bókhər] איז דאָ

The woman is reading   די פֿרוי לייענט

The house is pretty   דאָס הויז איז שײן

5.1.2 Accusative (verbal object)

Accusative is the situation of the noun phrase as the direct object of a verb.

SAMPLES OF NOUN PHRASES IN ACCUSATIVE

I see the fellow   איך זע דעם בחור

I'm photographing the woman   איך פֿאָטאָגראַפֿיר די פֿרוי

I'm repairing the house   איך פֿאַרריכט דאָס הויז

5.1.3 Dative (prepositional object)

Dative is the situation of the noun phrase as the direct object of any preposition (and hence, frequently, the indirect object of a verb).

SAMPLES OF NOUN PHRASES IN DATIVE

I'm speaking to the fellow   איך רעד מיט דעם בחור

I'm running from the girl   איך לויף פֿון דער מײדל

I'm looking at the house   איך קוק אויף [af] דעם הויז

5.1.3.1 Dative with understood preposition

A number of verbs, most frequently with a human object, impose dative upon their noun phrase, although no preposition appears. These are instances of the understood preposition. There is no preposition to mediate between verb phrase and noun phrase, but the action of the verb nevertheless does not 'strike' its object directly or physically. The most frequent prepositions left out and understood are צו 'to' and פֿאַר 'for'. Depending on its use in a sentence, one and the same verb may impose accusative or dative (with understood preposition). Cf. e.g. accusative איך שיק זי אין קאַליפֿאָרניע 'I'm sending her to California' vs. dative איך שיק איר אַ בריװ 'I'm sending her a letter' (understood preposition צו); accusative געפֿין מיך 'Find me!' vs. dative געפֿין מיר אַ צימער 'Find me a room' (understood preposition פֿאַר). On accusative and dative pronouns → §§ 6.1.2 – 6.1.3.

SAMPLES OF THE USE OF DATIVE WITH UNDERSTOOD PREPOSITION

| I'm writing (to) the fellow | איך שרײַב דעם בחור |
| I'll tell the woman what I know | איך װעל זאָגן דער פֿרױ װאָס איך װײס |

VERBS THAT MAY IMPOSE DATIVE WITHOUT A PREPOSITION

believe (somebody) [gléybm]	גלײבן
give (something to somebody) [gébm]	געבן
tell; recount (to somebody)	דערצײילן
show (to somebody)	װײַזן
say; tell	זאָגן
telephone	טעלעפֿאָנירן
hint; allude [mərámez]	מרמז זײַן
answer; reply (to somebody)	ענטפֿערן
send (to somebody)	שיקן
write (to somebody) [shráybm]	שרײַבן

5.1.3.2   לערנען and פֿרעגן

פֿרעגן 'ask (a question)' and לערנען 'teach' (→ §7.3.2.1) may take accusative, e.g. פֿרעג זי 'Ask her (familiar)!' and לערנט זי 'Teach her (formal)!'. Both may be replaced by alternate forms with prepositions (that

naturally impose dative) – בײַ פֿרעגן [ba] 'ask (of)' and מיט לערנען 'teach',
e.g. פֿרעג בײַ אים! [ba] 'Ask (familiar) her!' and לערנט מיט איר! 'Teach
(formal) her!'.

5.2 INDEFINITE ARTICLES

The indefinite article, 'a(n)', which precedes the noun, is always singular. It
is אַ with nouns beginning with a consonant, אַן with nouns beginning with a
vowel, hence אַ פֿראַגע 'a question' vs. אַן ענטפֿער 'an answer'. The
indefinite article does not inflect for case or gender.

5.3 SINGULAR DEFINITE ARTICLES

The singular definite article inflects for the gender ($\rightarrow$ §4.1) and case
($\rightarrow$§5.1) of its noun.

5.3.1 Singular definite articles in nominative

The singular definite article 'the' has the following forms in nominative.

masculine:	דער
feminine:	די
neutral:	דאָס

SAMPLES OF SINGULAR DEFINITE ARTICLES IN NOMINATIVE
The student (m.) is here   דער סטודענט איז דאָ

The student (f.) is here   די סטודענטקע [studéntkə] איז דאָ

The house is pretty   דאָס הויז איז שיין

5.3.2 Singular definite articles in accusative: only masculine inflects

The masculine singular definite article inflects in accusative. Feminine and neutral are identical with their nominative forms.

masculine:	דעם → דער
feminine:	די
neutral:	דאָס

SAMPLES OF SINGULAR DEFINITE ARTICLES IN ACCUSATIVE

I see the student (m.)   איך זע דעם סטודענט

I see the student (f.)   איך זע די סטודענטקע

I see the house   איך זע דאָס הויז

5.3.3 Singular definite articles in dative: all three inflect

masculine:	דעם → דער
feminine:	דער → די
neutral:	דעם → דאָס

SAMPLES OF SINGULAR DEFINITE ARTICLES IN DATIVE

I'm looking at the student (m.)   איך קוק אויף [af] דעם סטודענט

80

I'm looking at the student (f.) איך קוק אויף <u>דער</u> סטודענטקע

I'm looking at the house איך קוק אויף <u>דעם</u> הויז

5.3.3.1 Contractions of prepositions with דעם

דעם, the masculine and neutral definite article in dative, contracts with a number of prepositions to form a single word. These contracted forms are acceptable in all styles, including the most formal.

אויף דעם [avdem] → אויפֿן [afn] 'on / to the'

אונטער דעם → אונטערן 'under the'

איבער דעם → איבערן 'over the'

אין דעם → אינעם 'in the'

אָן דעם → אָנעם 'without the'

בײַ דעם [badem] → בײַם [bam] 'at the' (→ §15.1)

ביז דעם → ביזן (N.E. var. ביזל) 'until the'

דורך דעם [du(r)kh] → דורכן [du(r)khn] 'through the'

לויט דעם → לויטן 'according to the'

מיט דעם → מיטן 'with the'

נאָך דעם [noghdem] → נאָכן 'after the'

פֿאַר דעם → פֿאַרן 'before / for the'

פֿון דעם → פֿונעם 'from / of the'

צוליב דעם → צוליבן [tsulíbm] 'because of the'

צו דעם → צום 'to the'

5.3.3.2 Prepositions without definite articles

The masculine and neutral definite articles may be omitted with the prepositions אין 'in; to', פֿון 'from' and לעבן [lébm] 'near', if no adjective intervenes between the preposition and the noun that is its object. The feminine definite article is usually retained, e.g. לעבן [lébm] דער סטאַנציע

'near the station' but it too may be omitted with נאָס (די) 'street' and (די) שטאָט 'city'.

SAMPLES OF פֿון AND לעבן, אין WITHOUT DEFINITE ARTICLES

Let's meet in the building (= [bínyən] דער בנין) לאָמיר זיך טרעפֿן אין בנין

It's not far from the house (= דאָס הויז) ס'איז ניט ווײַט פֿון הויז

It's wet in the street (= די נאָס) אין נאָס איז נאָס

5.4   PLURAL DEFINITE ARTICLES

The plural definite article is always די.

SAMPLES OF PLURAL DEFINITE ARTICLES

I see the students (m.)   איך זע די סטודענטן

The students (f.) are here   די סטודענטקעס זײַנען דאָ

I'm looking at the houses   איך קוק אויף די הײַזער

5.5   SINGULAR ADJECTIVES

Singular adjectives inflect for the case and gender of the noun they modify. They are unaffected by articles, except for the neutral indefinite which loses its inflection when used with an indefinite article in nominative and accusative. It optionally loses its inflection in dative.

5.5.1   Singular adjectives in nominative

Endings are ער- in masculine and ע- in feminine and neutral definite. There is no ending in neutral indefinite. Model adjective is גוט 'good'. Definite and

82

indefinite articles are supplied to illustrate agreement.

masculine definite:	דער גוטער
masculine indefinite:	אַ גוטער
feminine definite:	די גוטע
feminine indefinite:	אַ גוטע
neutral definite:	דאָס גוטע
neutral indefinite:	אַ גוט

SAMPLES OF SINGULAR ADJECTIVES IN NOMINATIVE

masculine

The good student (m.) is here   דער גוטער סטודענט איז דאָ

A good student (m.) is here   אַ גוטער סטודענט איז דאָ

feminine

The good student (f.) is here   די גוטע סטודענטקע איז דאָ

A good student (f.) is here   אַ גוטע סטודענטקע איז דאָ

neutral

The good house is pretty   דאָס גוטע הויז איז שיין

A good house is pretty   אַ גוט הויז איז שיין

5.5.2   Singular adjectives in accusative:
only masculine inflects

The masculine ending, -ער, inflects to -ן. Feminine and neutral remain uninflected. Model adjective is גוט 'good'. Definite and indefinite articles are supplied to illustrate agreement.

masculine definite: <u>דער</u> גוטער   →   <u>דעם</u> גוטן

masculine indefinite: אַ גוטער   →   אַ גוטן

feminine definite: <u>די</u> גוטע

feminine indefinite: אַ גוטע

neutral definite: <u>דאָס</u> גוטע

neutral indefinite: אַ גוט

SAMPLES OF SINGULAR ADJECTIVES IN ACCUSATIVE
masculine

I see the good student (m.)   איך זע <u>דעם</u> גוטן סטודענט

I see a good student (m.)   איך זע אַ גוטן סטודענט

feminine

I see the good student (f.)   איך זע <u>די</u> גוטע סטודענטקע

I see a good student (f.)   איך זע אַ גוטע סטודענטקע

neutral

I see the good house   איך זע <u>דאָס</u> גוטע הויז

I see a good house   איך זע אַ גוט הויז

5.5.3   Singular adjectives in dative:
all three inflect

All three genders inflect, but inflection is optional for the neutral indefinite. Model adjective is גוט 'good'. Definite and indefinite articles are supplied to illustrate agreement.

masculine definite: <u>דער</u> גוטער   →   <u>דעם</u> גוטן

masculine indefinite: אַ גוטער   →   אַ גוטן

feminine definite:	דער גוטער → די גוטע	
feminine indefinite:	א גוטער → א גוטע	
neutral definite:	דעם גוטן → דאָס גוטע	
neutral indefinite:	(אַ גוטן) → אַ גוט	

SAMPLES OF SINGULAR ADJECTIVES IN DATIVE
masculine

I'm looking at the good student (m.) איך קוק אויף [af] דעם גוטן סטודענט

I'm looking at a good student (m.) איך קוק אויף אַ גוטן סטודענט

feminine

I'm looking at the good student (f.) איך קוק אויף דער גוטער סטודענטקע

I'm looking at a good student (f.) איך קוק אויף אַ גוטער סטודענטקע

neutral

I'm looking at the good house איך קוק אויף דעם גוטן הויז

I'm looking at a good house איך קוק אויף אַ גוט(ן) הויז

5.5.4   Variants of inflected adjective ending ן-

The masculine and neutral adjective ending ן- has several variants, depending on how the adjective stem ends. Following ם or a stressed vowel or diphthong, it is ען- (e.g. װאַרעם 'warm' → װאַרעמען, בלוי 'blue' → בלויען). Following נ it is עם- (e.g. שײן 'beautiful' → שײנעם). The adjective נײ 'new' anomalously takes עם-, hence נײעם. Note that ן- is retained in inflected adjective endings following נג- and נק-. Cf. §2.2.9.

5.5.5   Inflected adjectives in letter formulas

The three alternative salutations are inflecting adjectives. They are טײערער

(lit. 'dear') and ליבער (lit. 'beloved') for friendly letters, and חשובער [khóshəvər] (lit. 'esteemed; respected') for more formal letters. The most common is טײערער. The ער- ending is used for masculine, the ע- ending for feminine and plural. Preposition מיט 'with' usually launches the closing greeting, e.g. מיט פֿרײנדשאַפֿט 'with friendship'. Any adjectives in the closing greeting inflect as usual, e.g. מיט פֿרײנדלעכע גרוסן 'with kind (lit. 'friendly') regards', and its singular counterpart מיט פֿרײנדלעכן גרוס. Possessive pronouns (→ §6.2.1.1) are used for signing off – דײַן 'Your (familiar)' and אײַער 'your (formal)'. On dating letters → §13.3.4.

SAMPLES OF ADJECTIVAL SALUTATIONS

טײערע דעבי   Dear Debbie

טײערער אַלעקס   Dear Alex

טײערע קאָלעגן   Dear Colleagues

חשובער רעדאַקטאָר   Dear Editor

5.6   PLURAL ADJECTIVES

The plural adjective ending is ע- in all cases and genders.

SAMPLES OF PLURAL ADJECTIVES

I'm looking at the good students (m.)   איך קוק אויף די גוטע סטודענטן

The good students (f.) are here   די גוטע סטודענטקעס זײַנען דאָ

I see the good houses   איך זע די גוטע הײַזער

5.7   PREDICATE ADJECTIVES

Predicate adjectives describe their noun from a greater distance than the more frequently used attributive adjectives. They follow איז 'is' and זײַנען 'are' or other verbs of being (e.g. בלײַבן 'remain', שטײן 'stand'). They occur only in nominative.

5.7.1 Singular predicate adjectives without an article

Singular predicate adjectives without an article are uninflected. The adjective stem appears on its own. Whether the noun has a definite or indefinite article does not affect the predicate adjective. The construction may be used to make a general statement.

SAMPLES OF THE PREDICATE ADJECTIVE WITHOUT AN ARTICLE

The table is white   דער טיש איז װײַס

The story is long   די מעשה [máysə] איז לאַנג

The house is new   דאָס הױז איז נײַ

A forest is beautiful (= Forests are beautiful)   אַ װאַלד איז שײן

5.7.2 Singular predicate adjectives with indefinite article

Predicate adjectives with the indefinite article agree with their nouns as adjectives generally do (→ §5.5) except for the neutral indefinite which attracts suffix ס-. They usually modify nouns that themselves have a definite article. Repetition of that definite article with the predicate adjective would endow the construction with comparative force (→ §5.10.2). Model adjective is גוט 'good'. Indefinite articles are supplied.

masculine:	אַ גוטער
feminine:	אַ גוטע
neutral:	אַ גוטס

SAMPLES OF PREDICATE ADJECTIVES WITH INDEFINITE ARTICLE

The table is white (/ a white one)   דער טיש איז אַ וויסער

The story is long (/ a long one)   די מעשה איז אַ לאַנגע

The house is good (/ a good one)   דאָס הויז איז אַ גוטס

5.7.3   Plural predicate adjectives

Plural predicate adjectives may be uninflected. Alternatively, they may have the plural ע- ending which has the force of English 'ones' used to avoid repeating a noun. Plural predicate adjectives tend to have demonstrative force and the definite article preceding their nouns is often best translated 'these' (→ §6.3).

SAMPLES OF PLURAL PREDICATE ADJECTIVES

masculine

The tables are white   די טישן זײַנען װײַס

The tables are white ones   די טישן זײַנען װײַסע

feminine

The stories are long   די מעשיות [máysəs] זײַנען לאַנג

The stories are long ones   די מעשיות [máysəs] זײַנען לאַנגע

neutral

The houses are new   די הײַזער זײַנען נײַ

The houses are new ones   די הײַזער זײַנען נײַע

5.8   ADJECTIVES FOLLOWING THE NOUN

Adjectives may follow the noun with an article intervening (resulting in repetition of the article). They inflect as do normal attributive adjectives (→ §5.5). The construction is particularly prominent in poetry, folktales and certain narrative styles.

SAMPLES OF USE OF ADJECTIVES FOLLOWING THE NOUN

An old tree stood over here אַ בוים אָן אַלטער איז דאָ געשטאַנען

I saw the old tree איך האָב געזען דעם בוים דעם אַלטן

5.8.1 Adjectives following the noun as proper names

In East European villages, an adjective with definite article describing a
person, with definite article, following the name, was on occasion used as a
name by which an individual was known, e.g. יאָסל דער רויטער 'Yosl the
redhead', שמואל-יאַנקל דער מלמד [shmulyánkl der məlámməd] 'Shmúəl-
Yankl the school teacher' (from מלמד 'teacher in a traditional חדר [khéydər]
or primary school'). A number of figures from ancient Jewish history, mostly
biblical, are known in Yiddish by their traditional Hebrew names following
the same pattern, i.e. name plus descriptive title. Cf. §§4.4.4, 5.14.2, 5.15.1.2
on traditional names.

SAMPLES OF TRADITIONAL NAMES FROM ANCIENT JEWISH HISTORY

Adam (lit. 'Adam the First') [òdəm horíshn] אדם הראשון

Abraham (lit. 'Abraham our Father') [avròm ovínu] אברהם אבינו

Moses (lit. 'Moses our Teacher') [mòyshə rabéynu] משה רבינו

Deborah (lit. 'Deborah the Prophetess') [dvòyrə hanəvíə] דבורה הנביאה

Samson (lit. 'Samson the Strong Man') [shìmshn hagíbər] שמשון הגיבור

David (lit. 'David the King') [dòvid haméyləkh] דוד המלך

Solomon (lit. 'Solomon the King') [shlòymaméyləkh] שלמה המלך

Elijah (lit. 'Elijah the Prophet') [eyliòhu hanóvi] אליהו הנביא

Isaiah (lit. 'Isaiah the Prophet') [yəshàyə hanóvi] ישעיהו הנביא

Jeremiah (lit. 'Jeremiah the Prophet') [yirmiyòhu hanóvi] ירמיהו הנביא

Esther (lit. 'Esther the Queen') [èstər hamálkə] אסתר המלכה

Haman (lit. 'Haman the Evil Man')   [hòmən horóshə]   המן הרשע

Judah the Maccabee   [yəhùdə hamakábi]   יהודה המכבי

5.9   ADJECTIVE QUANTIFIERS

The major adjective quantifiers are אַ ביסל 'a little; slightly', גאַנץ 'quite; rather; pretty' and זייער 'very'.

5.9.1   אַ ביסל

אַ ביסל 'a little; slightly' immediately precedes uninflected predicate adjectives. Before predicate adjectives with the indefinite article, it precedes the indefinite article. Cf §6.4.6 on partitive pronoun אַ ביסל.

SAMPLES OF ADJECTIVE QUANTIFIER אַ ביסל

The film is slightly boring   דער פֿילם איז אַ ביסל נודנע

The film is a slightly boring one   דער פֿילם איז אַ ביסל אַ נודנער

His films are slightly boring   זײַנע פֿילמען זײַנען אַ ביסל נודנע

5.9.2   גאַנץ

גאַנץ 'quite; rather; pretty' immediately precedes attributive and predicate adjectives. It follows the indefinite article.

SAMPLES OF ADJECTIVE QUANTIFIER גאַנץ

They're showing quite a boring film   מ'ווײַזט אַ גאַנץ נודנעם פֿילם

The film is quite boring   דער פֿילם איז גאַנץ נודנע

The film is quite a boring one   דער פֿילם איז אַ גאַנץ נודנער

His films are quite boring   זײַנע פֿילמען זײַנען גאַנץ נודנע

5.9.3 זייער

זייער [zéyər / zeyr / zer] 'very' immediately precedes attributive and predicate adjectives. When זייער quantifies an attributive adjective with the indefinite article, it may precede or follow the indefinite article (אַ זייער = זייער אַ). When it quantifies a predicate adjective with the indefinite article, זייער אַ is generally used.

SAMPLES OF ADJECTIVE QUANTIFIER זייער

I saw the very boring film   איך האָב געזען דעם זייער נודנעם פֿילם

The film is very boring   דער פֿילם איז זייער נודנע

His films are very boring   זײנע פֿילמען זײנען זייער נודנע

מ'ווײזט זייער אַ נודנעם פֿילם = מ'ווײזט אַ זייער נודנעם פֿילם

They're showing a very boring film

The film is a very boring one   דער פֿילם איז זייער אַ נודנער

5.10   COMPARATIVE ADJECTIVES

The comparative is formed by suffixing -ער to the adjective stem. Normal adjective endings are then suffixed to the -ער. Many comparatives have concomitant vowel changes, frequently אַ/אָ/וי $\rightarrow$ ע and ו $\rightarrow$ י, which must be learned with the relevant adjective. Note the special comparatives גוט 'good' $\rightarrow$ בעסער 'better', שלעכט 'bad' $\rightarrow$ ערגער 'worse'. There are four comparative link words corresponding with 'than' — conjunctions ווי and איידער which leave the compared noun phrase that follows them in nominative, and prepositions פֿאַר and פֿון which place it in dative ($\rightarrow$ §5.5.3).

SAMPLES OF COMPARATIVE ADJECTIVES

ניו־יאָרק איז גרעסער ווי אַ סך [asákh] אַנדערע שטעט

New York is larger than many other cities

(cf. גרויס 'large')

די יינגערע שװעסטער איז קליגער פֿאַר דער עלטערער

The younger sister is cleverer than the older one

(cf. יונג 'young', קלוג 'clever', אַלט 'old')

די טײַערע פֿאָטאָגראַפֿיעס זײַנען שענער איידער די ביליקע

The expensive photographs are prettier than the cheap ones

(cf. שײן 'pretty')

מ'קען האָבן מער צוטרוי צו אַ נײַערן אויטאָמאָביל

You can have more faith in a newer car

(cf. נײַ 'new')

5.10.1 Comparative predicate adjectives

Comparative predicate adjectives are formed by using the definite article after איז 'is' or זײַנען 'are' (or another verb of being). They inflect as subject adjectives generally (→§5.5.1). Comparative affix -ער- appears between the comparative stem and the appropriate inflectional ending.

SAMPLES OF COMPARATIVE PREDICATE ADJECTIVES

The old table is the nicer one — דער אַלטער טיש איז דער שענערער

The big city is the more beautiful one — די גרויסע שטאָט איז די שענערע

The new house is the smaller one — דאָס נײַע הויז איז דאָס קלענערע

5.10.2 Predicate base adjectives with comparative force

Repetition of the definite article with any predicate adjective tends to give

the adjective comparative force (in contrast to the indefinite article →
§5.7.2). The pattern of inflection follows attributive adjectives (→ §5.5.1).

SAMPLES OF PREDICATE BASE ADJECTIVES WITH COMPARATIVE FORCE

The old table is the nice one   דער אַלטער טיש איז דער שיינער

The big city is the beautiful one   די גרויסע שטאָט איז די שיינע

The new house is the small one   דאָס נײַע הויז איז דאָס קליינע

5.11   SUPERLATIVE ADJECTIVES

The superlative is formed by suffixing -סט to the adjective stem. The usual
adjective endings are then suffixed to the סט sequence. Superlatives are
generally processed by the same אַ / אָ / וי → ע and ו → י vowel
changes as their corresponding comparatives. These vowel changes must be
learned along with each of the adjectives affected. Note the special
superlatives גוט 'good' → בעסט- 'best', שלעכט 'bad' → ערגסט- [erkst]
'worst'.

SAMPLES OF SUPERLATIVE ADJECTIVES

ניו־יאָרקער זאָגן נאָך אַז דער „עמפּײַער סטייט בילדינג"

איז דער העכסטער בנין אין דער וועלט

New Yorkers still say that the Empire State Building is the tallest building in

the world

(cf. הויך 'tall; high')

דאָס איז די לענגסטע מעשה [léynkstə máysə] אין בוך

This is the longest story in the book

(cf. לאַנג 'long')

ער איז דער נאַרישסטער פֿון זיי אַלעמען

He is the most foolish of them all

(cf. נאַריש 'foolish')

זי איז אַוועק צו דער באַליבטסטער מומע

She went to her most beloved aunt

(cf. באַליבט 'beloved')

5.11.1 Superlative predicate adjectives

Superlative predicate adjectives are formed by using the definite article after איז 'is' or זײַנען 'are'. They inflect as nominative adjectives generally (→ §5.5.1). The superlative affix -סט- appears between the comparative (/superlative) stem and the appropriate inflectional ending. They offer an alternative to attributive superlatives.

SAMPLES OF SUPERLATIVE PREDICATE ADJECTIVES

The old table is the nicest one   דער אַלטער טיש איז דער שענסטער

The big city is the most beautiful one   די גרויסע שטאָט איז די שענסטע

The new house is the smallest one   דאָס נײַע הויז איז דאָס קלענסטע

5.11.2 Superlative intensifier סאַמע

The superlative intensifier סאַמע [sámə] 'very (–st)', immediately precedes the superlative. סאַמע does not inflect.

SAMPLES OF SUPERLATIVE INTENSIFIER סאַמע

This is your (familiar) very best idea   דאָס איז דײַן סאַמע בעסטער אײַנפֿאַל

You have the most beautiful pictures   דו האָסט די סאַמע שענסטע בילדער

They are the very greatest fools   זיי זײַנען די סאַמע גרעסטע נאַראָנים

5.12 SPECIAL TYPES OF ADJECTIVES

5.12.1 Invariant adjectives

Adjectives formed by suffixation of -ער to the names of cities and towns (and occasionally countries) do not inflect. They retain the -ער ending in all cases, numbers and genders. Internal modifications of the stem are encountered in the names of some culturally central cities. In addition to their adjectival use, they all double as agentives denoting a person from the named place. As agentives they attract the feminizing suffix -ין (→ §§ 3.2.3, 4.1.2.3).

SAMPLES OF INVARIANT ADJECTIVES

American אַמעריקאַנער

of / from Oxford אָקספּאָרדער

of / from Warsaw װאַרשעװער (cf. Warsaw װאַרשע)

of / from Vilna װילנער

of / from Jerusalem [yərusholáymər] ירושלימער

(cf. Jerusalem [yərusholáyim] ירושלים)

of / from Montreal מאָנטרעאַלער

of / from Melbourne מעלבורנער

of / from New York ניו⸗יאָרקער

Parisian פּאַריזער

of / from Cracow קראָקעװער (cf. Cracow קראָקע)

of / from Tel Aviv [telavívər] תל⸗אביבער

5.12.2 Adjectives from names of substances

Adjectives derived from names of traditionally known substances frequently attract suffix -ערנ, to which the appropriate adjective endings are further suffixed. Note that גאָלד 'gold' attracts נ- alone, hence גאָלדן- (→ §5.12.3).

SAMPLES OF ADJECTIVES FROM NAMES OF SUBSTANCES WITH SUFFIX -ערן

(of) iron אײַזערן- (cf. אײַזן 'iron')

(of) glass גלעזערן- (cf. גלאָז 'glass')

wooden הילצערן- (cf. האָלץ 'wood')

(of) copper קופּערן- (cf. קופּער 'copper')

SAMPLES OF THE USE OF ADJECTIVES DERIVED FROM NAMES OF SUBSTANCES

I have two wooden boxes איך האָב צוויי הילצערנע קעסטלעך

Don't break the glass table צעברעך ניט דעם גלעזערנעם טיש

5.12.3   ADJECTIVES WITH FINAL SYLLABIC נ-

Adjectives with a base form ending in syllabic נ- (→ §2.2.9) replace the
syllabic נ- with ענ- in inflected forms (other than predicate indefinite with
ending ס- → §5.7.2), e.g. base form אָפֿן [ofn] 'open' vs. masculine singular
accusative/dative אָפֿענעם [ófənəm], plural אָפֿענע [ófənə]; base form גאָלדן
[goldn] 'golden' vs. masculine singular accusative/dative גאָלדענעם
[góldənəm], plural גאָלדענע [góldənə].

5.13   DIMINUTIVES OF ADJECTIVES

There are two suffixes by which adjectives are diminutivized. One of these,
לעך-, reduces the force of the adjective, and has a number of nuances. The
second, ינק-, applies affection and sentimentality. Unlike diminutives of
nouns (→ §4.3), diminutives of adjectives do not undergo internal vowel
shifts.

5.13.1 Adjective diminutive in ‎-לעך

The adjective diminutive in ‎-לעך mitigates the force of the base adjective, and is often used to soften a stark statement or mitigate an insult. It derives from the adverb diminutive in ‎-לעך (→ §10.5). ‎-לעך usually occurs with monosyllabic adjective stems. The diminutivized adjective is pronounced slowly in falsetto. It is often accompanied by a gentle forward and downward thrust of the head and the opened palm of one hand, with optional horizontal vibration of the same hand and its fingers, and a slight smile. Cf. §10.5 on diminutives of adverbs.

SAMPLES OF ADJECTIVE DIMINUTIVE ‎-לעך

rather difficult; delicate   שווערלעך (from שווער 'difficult')

somewhat chilly; not very cold   קאַלטלעך (from קאַלט 'cold')

somewhat hot   הייסלעך (from הייס 'hot')

somewhat ugly [mísləkh]   מיאוסלעך (from מיאוס [mís] 'ugly')

SAMPLES OF THE USE OF ADJECTIVE DIMINUTIVE ‎-לעך

It's a rather delicate matter   ס'איז אַ שווערלעכער ענין

It's a somewhat chilly day   ס'איז אַ קאַלטלעכער טאָג

It's a somewhat hot day   ס'איז אַ הייסלעכער טאָג

Her boyfriend is not exactly handsome   איר חבֿר [khávər] איז מיאוסלעך

5.13.2 Adjective diminutive in ‎-ינק

The adjective diminutive ‎-ינק, to which normal adjective endings are suffixed, marks warmth, affection and sentimentality. Its usage parallels the second diminutive of nouns in ‎-עלע (→ §4.3.5). The adjective אַלט 'old', which is often personified to refer informally and affectionately to an elderly person, takes ‎-יטש, e.g. דער אַלטיטשקער קומט 'The old chap is coming'.

SAMPLES OF ADJECTIVE DIMINUTIVES IN ־ינק

white װײַסינק (from װײַס 'white')

little קלײנינק (from קלײן 'little')

beautiful שײנינק (from שײן 'beautiful')

5.14   NOUNS THAT INFLECT FOR CASE

A minority of nouns, nearly all of them referring to people, may inflect for one or both of the objective cases. They attract inflectional ending ־ן (ען- following ה, ו, a stressed vowel or diphthong, or the sequences נג, נק or consonant plus ל). They fall into two categories: intimate nouns and proper names. Personal pronouns inflect internally rather than by suffixation (→ §§6.1.2 − 6.1.3).

5.14.1   Intimate nouns

The intimate nouns are from family and traditional life.

5.14.1.1   Masculine intimate nouns

Masculine intimate nouns are inflected in both accusative and dative. Note that inflection for ייד and מענטש is optional.

טאַטע 'father' → טאַטן

זײדע 'grandfather' → זײדן

ייד 'Jew; fellow; guy' (→ יידן)

מענטש 'person; fellow; human' (→ מענטשן)

רבי [rébə] '(traditional) school teacher; Chassidic rebbe' → רבין [rébm]

SAMPLES OF INFLECTED MASCULINE INTIMATE NOUNS

Lloyd George knows my father   לויד דזשאָרדזש קען דעם טאַטן

I'm speaking with grandfather   איך רעד מיטן זיידן

Did you see that fellow?   האָסט געזען דעם מענטשן?

Have you been to see the rebbe?   [bam rébm] ?ביסט געווען ביים רבין

5.14.1.2   Feminine intimate nouns

Feminine intimate nouns are inflected in dative. They optionally inflect in accusative. Inflection of מומע is optional even in dative.

מאַמען ← 'mother' מאַמע

[bobm] באָבען ← 'grandmother' באָבע

(← מומען) 'aunt' מומע

SAMPLES OF INFLECTED FEMININE INTIMATE NOUNS

Are you going to (see) mother?   גייסט צו דער מאַמען?

Have you heard from grandmother?   האָסט געהערט פֿון דער באָבען?

I'm writing to my aunt   איך שרײַב דער מומען

5.14.1.3   Neutral intimate האַרץ

The one surviving neutral inflecting noun is האַרץ 'heart' which inflects to האַרצן in dative. Inflection signals that האַרץ is being used in its metaphoric sense, e.g. אין האַרצן 'at heart', זיך נעמען צום האַרצן 'take to heart' אַ שטאָך [afn] שווער אויפֿן 'depressed' (lit. 'heavy on the heart'), אין האַרצן 'devastating shock; blow to the ego' (lit. 'stab in the heart'). The absence of inflection in dative signals that 'heart' is being used in a more strictly physical sense, e.g. דער פּאַציענט לײַדט פֿון ווייטיק אין האַרץ 'The patient is suffering heart pain'.

5.14.2 Proper names

A single proper name, whether forename or surname, may inflect for either objective case. Where both names are used, only the surname inflects. משיח [məshíəkh] 'Messiah' is a proper name in Yiddish and therefore inflects to משיחן [məshíəkhn]. Analogously, biblical names comprising name plus descriptive title (→ §5.8.1) are treated as single names and it is therefore the descriptive title that inflects, e.g. אליהו הנביא [eylióhu hanóvi] 'Elijah the Prophet' → אליהו הנביאן [eylióhu hanóvin]. Cf. §§4.4.4, 5.15.1.2 on traditional Yiddish names.

SAMPLES OF INFLECTIONS OF PROPER NAMES

בערל Béri (m.) → בערלען [bérlən]

טײבעלע Táybalə (f.) → טײבעלען [táybalən]

לאה Léyə (f.) → לאהן [léyən]

קלמן Káimən (m.) → קלמנען [káimənən]

מאָסקאָוויטש Móskovitsh → מאָסקאָוויטשן [móskovitshn]

שלמה רובין Shlóymə Rúbin → שלמה רובינען [shlóymə rúbinən]

5.14.2.1 Optionality scale

The degree of optionality in the inflection of proper names depends in large measure upon the familiarity of the name in the language. Traditional names are most frequently inflected, well known modern names often inflected, and strange sounding foreign names (in the subjective view of the speaker or writer) only rarely inflected. Inflection is consciously avoided where confusion could result as to whether the name itself does or does not end in [n]. Thus the Japanese name Tokiko might at first not be inflected (to ensure that the hearer or reader does not mistakenly infer that the name is 'Tokikon'), but upon increasing acquaintance with the name, the rate of inflection could increase proportionately. Use of inflection with names not rooted in the language is encountered in formal styles as a 'supergrammatical' feature, and in the opinion of some, a pedantic one. In informal styles, inflection of non-traditional names may be used for humorous effect.

SAMPLES OF INFLECTIONS OF NON-TRADITIONAL PROPER NAMES

טשאָק בערין 'Chuck Berry' → טשאָק בערי

לויד דזשאָרדזשן 'Lloyd George' → לויד דזשאָרדזש

נאַדינען 'Nadine' → נאַדין

ניקסאָנען 'Nixon' → ניקסאָן

5.15 POSSESSIVES

Possession by humans is marked by suffixation of the possessive ending -ס. Possession by nonhumans (institutions, abstract notions, etc.) is generally expressed by the preposition פֿון.

5.15.1 Human possessors

Possession by humans is marked by suffixation of ס- (usually pronounced between [s] and [z]), to the possessor's name (or an agentive noun) e.g. מענדעלעס סטיל 'Mendele's style'. If the possessor has a definite article, the article is inflected for dative (→ §5.1.3), e.g. דעם פֿײַערלעשערס טאָכטער 'the fireman's daughter', דער לערערינס צימער 'the teacher's (f.) room', דעם קינדס צאַצקע 'the child's toy'. The understood preposition is פֿון, denoting relation to the possesor. If the name or agentive ends in one of the sibilants ז, ס, צ, ש, the suffix is עס-, e.g. האָראָװיצעס היטל 'Horowitz's hat', דעם באַלעבאָסעס אַדרעס 'the boss's address'. The older usage of an apostrophe before possessive ס is still encountered.

5.15.1.1 Intimate nouns as human possessors

Possessives of the masculine intimate nouns מענטש and ייד, זיידע, טאַטע
רבי (→§5.14.1.1) are formed by adding possessive ס to the inflected ‏־ן form
of each (‏רבין‎ and ‏טאַטן, זיידן, יידן, מענטשן‎). The resulting possessives are
דעם רבינס and דעם מענטשנס, דעם יידנס, דעם זיידנס, דעם טאַטנס
[rébnz].

5.15.1.2 Possessives as proper names

In traditional Yiddish-speaking communities, people are often known by their
forenames followed by the possessive of one of their parents' forenames.
Alternatively, the possessive of the agentive of a parent's profession may be
used. The construction, which has the force of 'son of' and 'daughter of', is
well represented in Yiddish literature, both as pen names of authors and in
names of major works. Cf. §§4.4.4, 5.8.1, 5.14.2 on traditional names.

SAMPLES OF POSSESSIVES FORMING PROPER NAMES

יצחק באַשעװיס (בת‑שבֿע‎ from)

Yítskhok Bashévis 'Isaac son of Bath-Sheba'

(Isaac Bashevis Singer)

מאָטל פּײסי דעם חזנס

Motl Péysə-dem-kházns ('Motl son of the Cantor Peysə')

(name of book by Sholem Aleichem)

שלמה ר' חיימס

Shloymə Reb Kháyims ('Solomon son of Chaim')

(name of book by Méndələ Móykhər Sfórim)

5.15.2 Nonhuman possessors

Possession by nonhumans is generally marked by explicit use of the preposition פֿון 'of', e.g. דער גרינדער פֿון דער אָרגאַניזאַציע 'the founder of the organization', דער כאַראַקטער פֿון שטאָט 'the city's character'.

6 PRONOUNS

6.0 OVERVIEW

There are four types of pronouns — personal, possessive, demonstrative and partitive.

6.1 PERSONAL PRONOUNS

Personal pronouns replace a specifically named or understood person or thing. There are seven singular and three plural personal pronouns. Most pronouns inflect for accusative and for dative. For samples of the use of personal pronouns → §§ 7.5.1–7.5.2, 7.6.1.1–7.6.1.2, 7.7.1–7.7.2, 7.9.1–7.9.2.

6.1.1 Pronouns in nominative

6.1.1.1 Singular

איך	I
דו	you (familiar)
איר	you (formal)
ער	he
זי	she
מ׳ \ מען \ מע	people; one; we
ס׳ \ עס \ סע	it

6.1.1.2 Plural

מיר we

איר you

זיי they

6.1.2 Pronouns in accusative

6.1.2.1 Singular

מיך me

דיך you (familiar)

אײַך you (formal)

אים [em] him

זי her

עס it

6.1.2.2 Plural

אונדז us

אײַך you

זיי them

6.1.3 Pronouns in dative

ס' \ עס \ סע 'it' do not occur in dative.

6.1.3.1 Singular

מיר me

דיר you (familiar)

you (formal) אײַך

him [em] אים

her איר

6.1.3.2 Plural

us אונדז

you אײַך

them זײ

6.1.4 Single objective case in dialectal usage

Minority usage, based upon Northeastern Yiddish, uses the dative forms for both accusative and dative of the singular personal pronouns. Bearing in mind that the plural paradigms are universally identical for both accusative and dative, this usage results in a single objective case for all personal pronouns. Use of the unified objective case, as follows, may be encountered in the literary language.

me מיר

you (familiar) דיר

you (formal) אײַך

him [em] אים

her איר

6.1.5 Morphology of the third person indefinite pronoun

The third person human indefinite may occur in any of three forms before the verb — מ' (most frequent in Yiddish literature and in contemporary written Yiddish) מען [mən] (most frequent in journalistic style) or מע [mə] (the favourite of speakers and writers hailing from Southeastern Yiddish speech territory). After the verb, only מען occurs. The same pattern is also followed by the third person nonhuman indefinite. It may occur in any of three forms before the verb — 'ס, עס [əs] or סע [sə], with usage distribution paralleling that of 'ה, מען and מע, respectively. After the verb, only עס occurs.

6.1.6   Semantic features of personal pronouns

6.1.6.1   (אײַך) איר (דיר / דיך) דו and

The second person singular דו forms are traditionally used with intimate friends and small children. The technically 'plural' איר (cf. French *vous*, German *Sie*) is used as a singular with persons with whom one has a more formal relationship. In Eastern Europe, a child would often address his or her own grandparent with איר; a girl and boy in love would be taking a daring step by switching to דו before marriage. The division between דו and איר continues to depend on a number of social variables. Nevertheless, it is clear that except in the most traditional communities, דו has steadily encroached upon the semantic territory of איר in the course of the last century. This is most marked in the English-speaking world and in Israel, where the coterritorial English and Hebrew lack the distinction, but the trend is evident among younger speakers even in Paris and Montreal, where the distinction is supported by the coterritorial French. The major factor in the degree to which דו and איר are distinguished by younger people today seems to be the level of 'traditionalness' of a speech community or circle. Among younger Yiddish speakers born and raised in the West, it has become customary in recent years to ask permission upon first acquaintance to dispense with איר

and to proceed straight onward to דו. It, is, however, important to use איר with adult members of traditional communities as well as with older generation East-European-born speakers of all cultural persuasions.

6.1.6.2   Use of 'מ

מ' (/ מען / מע) is widely used in Yiddish where English uses 'we', 'people (in general)', 'one', 'you'. It frequently occurs where English uses a passive.

SAMPLES OF THE USE OF 'מ

We've already been there   מ'איז שוין געװען דאָרטן

People say so   מ'זאָגט אַזוי

What do people say about it?   װאָס זאָגט [vozzókt] מען װעגן דעם?

One can't say for certain   [avzíkhər] מ'קען ניט זאָגן אויף זיכער

The truth is not known   דעם אמת [éməs] װײס מען ניט

You're not allowed in there   מ'טאָר ניט אַרײַנגײן דאָרטן

6.1.6.3   Use of 'ס

ס' (/ עס / סע) may serve to provide a grammatically necessary subject in a sentence with no 'real' subject. It may also occur where Yiddish requires a subject at the beginning of a phrase to meet the inflected-verb-second rule (→ §14.1). It prefixes the predicatives איז דאָ 'there is' and זײַנען דאָ 'there are' (→ §14.6).

SAMPLES OF THE USE OF 'ס

It could be / Maybe   ס'קען זײַן

Maybe not   ס'קען זײַן אַז ניט

It's raining in London   ס'גײט [zgeyt] אַ רעגן אין לאָנדאָן

Father is coming   ס'קומט דער טאַטע

An apple tree is growing in the garden   ס'װאַקסט אַן עפּלבוים אין גאָרטן

It's fine / Things are good   ס'איז [sigút] גוט

6.2 POSSESSIVE PRONOUNS

Possessive pronouns occur both before and after the noun. Where possession is clear from context, the definite article is generally used instead of a possessive pronoun (→ §15.13).

6.2.1 Preceding the possessed noun

Possessive pronouns preceding the possessed noun inflect for the number of the possessor and the number of the possession. The gender of the possessor is evident only in the third person singular where there are separate pronouns – זייַן 'his' vs. איר 'her'. Possessive pronouns preceding the possessed noun also inflect for gender when the indefinite article is used in a special construction (→ §6.2.1.5).

6.2.1.1 Singular possessor with singular possession

my	מייַן
your (familiar)	דייַן
your (formal)	אײַער
his	זייַן
her	איר

6.2.1.2 Singular possessor with plural possessions

my	מייַנע
your (familiar)	דייַנע
your (formal)	אײַערע
his	זייַנע
her	אירע

6.2.1.3   Plural possessors with singular possession

אונדזער   our

אײער   your

זײער   their

6.2.1.4   Plural possessors with plural possessions

אונדזער<u>ע</u>   our

אײער<u>ע</u>   your

זײער<u>ע</u>   their

6.2.1.5   The possessive-indefinite construction

Possessive pronouns preceding the possessed noun inflect for gender and case when the indefinite article occurs with the noun. The construction has the force of 'a — of mine/yours etc.'.   It is most frequent with nouns designating humans.

SAMPLES OF USE OF THE POSSESSIVE-INDEFINITE CONSTRUCTION

מײנער אַ פֿעטער קומט הײַנט

An uncle of mine is coming today

מײנע אַ מומע קומט הײַנט אױף דער נאַכט

An aunt of mine is coming this evening

איך זע אונדזערן אַ באַקאַנטן

I see an acquaintance (m.) of ours

6.2.2   Following the possessed noun

Possessive pronouns following the possessed noun may be synonymous with

110

the simpler forms preceding the noun. Used with the definite article, the construction may have demonstrative force (→ §6.3). Possessive pronouns following the noun inflect for everything – number of the possessor and the possession, gender of the possessor and the possession, and case. The arrow (→) marks the regular changes for both accusative and dative (AD) or, where applicable, for dative (D) only. Sample nouns are שירעם (דער) 'umbrella', זאַך (די) 'thing' and הויז (דאָס) 'house'.

6.2.2.1   First person possessor with single possession

דעם שירעם מײַנעם (AD) → דער שירעם מײַנער

דער זאַך מײַנער (D) → די זאַך מײַנע

דעם הויז מײַנעם (D) → דאָס הויז מײַנס

6.2.2.2   Familiar second person possessor with single possession

דעם שירעם דײַנעם (AD) → דער שירעם דײַנער

דער זאַך דײַנער (D) → די זאַך דײַנע

דעם הויז דײַנעם (D) → דאָס הויז דײַנס

6.2.2.3   Formal second person possessor with single possession

דעם שירעם אײַערן (AD) → דער שירעם אײַערער

דער זאַך אײַערער (D) → די זאַך אײַערע

דעם הויז אײַערן (D) → דאָס הויז אײַערס

6.2.2.4   Third person masculine possessor with single possession

דעם שירעם זײַנעם (AD) → דער שירעם זײַנער

דער זאך זײַנער (D) → די זאך זײַנע

דעם הויז זײַנעם (D) → דאָס הויז זײַנס

6.2.2.5 Third person feminine possessor with single possession

דעם שירעם אירן (AD) → דער שירעם אידער

דער זאך אירער (D) → די זאך אידע

דעם הויז אירן (D) → דאָס הויז אירס

6.2.2.6 Singular possessor with plural possessions

די שירעמס \ זאַבן \ הײַזער מײַנע

די שירעמס \ זאַבן \ הײַזער דײַנע

די שירעמס \ זאַבן \ הײַזער אײַערע

די שירעמס \ זאַבן \ הײַזער זײַנע

די שירעמס \ זאַבן \ הײַזער אידע

6.2.2.7 First person possessors with single possession

דעם שירעם אונדזערן (AD) → דער שירעם אונדזערער

דער זאך אונדזערער (D) → די זאך אונדזערע

דעם הויז אונדזערן (D) → דאָס הויז אונדזערס

6.2.2.8 Second person possessors with single possession

דעם שירעם אײַערן (AD) → דער שירעם אײַערער

דער זאך אײַערער (D) → די זאך אײַערע

דעם הויז אײַערן (D) → דאָס הויז אײַערס

6.2.2.9 Third person possessors with singular possession

דעם שירעם זייערן (AD) → דער שירעם זייערער

דער זאָך זייערער (D) ‏→ די זאָך זייערע

דעם הויז זייערן (D) ‏→ דאָס הויז זייערס

6.2.2.10   Possessors with plural possessions

די שירעמס \ זאָקן \ הײזער אונדזערע

די שירעמס \ זאָקן \ הײזער אײערע

די שירעמס \ זאָקן \ הײזער זייערע

6.3   DEMONSTRATIVE PRONOUNS

6.3.1   'this'

Demonstrative 'this' may be expressed by phonetic stress alone, in which case it is implicit in written texts, or explicitly by a demonstrative pronoun.

6.3.1.1   Implicit 'this': stressed definite article

The definite articles (in any of the cases) can double as demonstratives by being stressed. In written texts, demonstrative use of an article is inferred from the context or evident from bold typeface (or spacing out of letters to denote emphasis). Noun phrases used as demonstratives are frequently jumped to the front of a sentence, further strengthening the sense of 'this'/'these' rather than 'the' (→ §§14.4.7, 14.10).

SAMPLES OF IMPLICIT 'THIS'

דעם בחור קען איך

[dém bókhər kénəkh] I know this fellow

cf. [dəm bókhər kénəkh] I know the fellow

די מיידל איז דאָ פֿריער געװען

[dí méydl i(z) do fríər gəvén] This girl was here before

cf. [dəméydl i(z) do fríər gəvén] The girl was here before

דאָס בוך איז לאַנג

[dóz búkh iz láng] This book is long

cf. [dəz búkh iz láng] The book is long

די גאַסן זײַנען שמאָל

[dí gásn zaynən shmól] These streets are narrow

cf. [də gásn zaynən shmól] The streets are narrow

6.3.1.2 Explicit 'this'

There are several demonstrative formulas: אָט and אָ אָט preceding the definite article; אָ alone following it; adjectively inflected דאָזיק- following it. Two or more may be used redundantly in combination for proportionately increasing emphasis. A series of demonstratives for a single noun serves to emphasize identity and is occasionally used for humorous or hostile effect. In the samples provided, demonstrative force may be said to increase with each line.

SAMPLES OF EXPLICIT 'THIS'

(→ §6.3.1.1 FOR TRANSLATIONS)

אָט דעם בחור קען איך

אָט אָ דעם בחור קען איך

דעם אָ בחור קען איך

דעם דאָזיקן בחור קען איך

אָט דעם דאָזיקן בחור קען איך

אָט אָ דעם דאָזיקן בחור קען איך

אָט די מיידל איז דאָ פֿריער געוזמען

אָט אָ די מיידל איז דאָ פֿריער געוזמען

די אָ מיידל איז דאָ פֿריער געוזמען

די דאָזיקע מיידל איז דאָ פֿריער געוזמען

אָט די דאָזיקע מיידל איז דאָ פֿריער געוזמען

אָט אָ די דאָזיקע מיידל איז דאָ פֿריער געוזמען

אָט דאָס בוך איז לאַנג

אָט אָ דאָס בוך איז לאַנג

דאָס דאָזיקע בוך איז לאַנג

אָט דאָס דאָזיקע בוך איז לאַנג

אָט אָ דאָס דאָזיקע בוך איז לאַנג

אָט די גאַסן זײַנען שמאָל

אָט אָ די גאַסן זײַנען שמאָל

די אָ גאַסן זײַנען שמאָל

די דאָזיקע גאַסן זײַנען שמאָל

אָט די דאָזיקע גאַסן זײַנען שמאָל

אָט אָ די דאָזיקע גאַסן זײַנען שמאָל

6.3.2   'that'

Stressed definite articles are used in many instances where English has 'that', e.g. ‏וואָס איז דאָס?‏ [vósə dós?] 'What's that?'. Where 'thatness' is however explicitly required, ‏דער צווייטער‏, ‏דער אַנדערער‏ or ‏יענער‏ are used.

6.3.2.1   ‏דער צווייטער / דער אַנדערער‏

As an attributive adjective before a noun, ‏דער אַנדערער‏ 'the other / next one' may signify 'thatness' for any noun, but on its own, it substitutes for a person — 'that one; the other person; the second one; the next one'. As an adjective, אַנדער is anomalous insofar as it declines only with the definite article (e.g. דער אַנדערער מאַן 'the other man', די אַנדערע פֿרױ 'the other woman'); with the indefinite article it is usually left as invariant אַנדער, e.g. אַן אַנדער מאַן 'an other man', אַן אַנדער פֿרױ 'an other woman'. Plural is always אַנדערע. In singular only, דער צװײטער (lit. 'the second one') may be used interchangeably with דער אַנדערער.

SAMPLES OF THE USE OF דער אַנדערער AND דער צװײטער

דעם אַדנערן (\ דעם צװײטן) דאַרף מען פֿרעגן
We should ask the other man (/ that man)

דער אַנדערער (\ דער צװײטער) איז דער עקספּערט
It's the other one who's the expert

די אַנדערע (\ די צװײטע) קומט מאָרגן
The other lady is coming tomorrow

די אַנדערע קען איך נאָך ניט
I don't know the others yet

6.3.2.2   יענער

As an attributive adjective before a noun, יענער may signify 'thatness' for any noun, but on its own it substitutes for a person — 'that one; the other person'. The old neutral nominative form in ס- (יענס, also spelled יענץ) is very rare nowadays. When used with a neutral it is increasingly lining up with feminine in nominative and with masculine in accusative and dative (cf. interrogative װעלכער → §11.3.1.1 and relative װעלכער → §14.7). יענער is frequently (but not necessarily) aggressive or derogatory. When used with the definite article, ‏דער יעניקער‎, usually aggressive and occasionally humorous, may be substituted for ‏יענער‎. ‏יענער‎ demonstrates the speaker or writer's wish to project distance between him or herself and the person spoken of by labelling him or her with 'otherness'.

SAMPLES OF THE USE OF ‏יענער‎

‏יענער ווייס ניט וואָס ער רעדט‎

That man (lit. 'that one') doesn't know what he's talking about

‏יענע ווייס ניט וואָס זי רעדט‎

That woman (lit. 'that one') doesn't know what she's talking about

‏יענעם קען מען ניט געטרויען‎

That man can't be trusted

‏דער יעניקער איז שוין ווידער דאָ‎

There he is again!

6.3.2.3 ‏דער זעלבער / דער זעלביקער‎

As an attributive adjective before a noun, ‏זעלב(יק)-‎ may signify 'sameness' for any noun, but on its own it substitutes for a person — 'the same one; the same person'.

SAMPLE OF THE USE OF ‏דער זעלביקער‎

‏דער זעלביקער האָט אַמאָל געהאַלטן אַנדערש‎

The same man once held a rather different view

6.4   PARTITIVE PRONOUNS

Partitive pronouns provide for a limitation to a single person or a conceptual proportional relation to a perceived group of people, or people in general.

6.4.1   אײנער and אײנע

אײנער 'a/one (person); a man' and אײנע 'a woman' inflect for case and gender as adjectives. Cf. §§12.1.1–12.1.1.1 on numerals אײן and אײנס.

SAMPLES OF THE USE OF אײנער AND אײנע

אײנער איז דאָ הײַנט געװען   One (m.) of them was here today

אײנע איז דאָ הײַנט געװען   One (f.) of them was here today

אײנעם װאָלטסט געדאַרפֿט פֿאַרבעטן   You should invite one of them

אײנער זאָגט אַזױ, אײנער זאָגט אַזױ   One says one thing, one says another

6.4.2   עמעצער

עמעצער 'somebody; anybody (positive)' is usually pronounced [éymətsər]. It inflects for case as an adjective. עמעצער is exclusively a pronoun.

SAMPLES OF THE USE OF עמעצער

עמעצער [éymətsər] איז דאָ?   Is anybody here?

איך האָב עמעצן [éymətsn] געזען   I saw somebody

6.4.3   קײנער

קײנער 'nobody; anybody (negative)' inflects for case as an adjective. Where the negative phrase does not already contain the negative particle ניט, קײנער ניט is used, e.g. װער איז דאָ? 'Who's there?' is answered negatively by קײנער ניט 'Nobody'. קײנער is exclusively a pronoun.

SAMPLES OF THE USE OF קיינער

זאָלסט קיינעם ניט דערציילן   Don't tell anybody

איך האָב קיינעם ניט געזען   I didn't see anybody

Nobody's here?   קיינער איז דאָ ניטאָ?

6.4.4   טייל

טייל 'some (people); part', which takes a plural verb, does not inflect. טייל is also a common noun and an invariant adjective that may refer to inanimate objects.

SAMPLES OF THE USE OF טייל

טייל זאָגן יאָ טייל זאָגן ניין   Some say 'yes', some say 'no'

טייל וועלן מסכים [máskim] זײַן   Some will agree

6.4.5   אַ פּאָר / עטלעכע

עטלעכע, or אַ פּאָר 'a few', which take a plural verb, do not inflect. עטלעכע and אַ פּאָר are also common nouns and invariant adjectives that may refer to inanimate objects.

SAMPLES OF THE USE OF עטלעכע AND אַ פּאָר

איך קען נאָר אַ פּאָר פֿון זיי   I know only a few of them

עטלעכע וועלן קומען   A few people will come

6.4.6   אַ ביסל

אַ ביסל 'a small number; a few', which takes a plural verb, does not inflect. When used as a common noun or invariant adjective, אַ ביסל has the sense of 'a little'. Cf. §5.9.1 on adjective quantifier אַ ביסל.

SAMPLES OF THE USE OF ביסל אַ

A few people remained   אַ ביסל זײַנען געבליבן

A few people will be unhappy   אַ ביסל װעלן זײַן אומצופֿרידן

6.4.7   אַ סך

אַ סך [asákh] 'many', which takes a plural verb, does not inflect. It is also a common noun and invariant adjective that may occur with inanimate objects.

SAMPLES OF THE USE OF סך אַ

Many people are still here   אַ סך זײַנען נאָך דאָ

Many have already left   אַ סך זײַנען שוין אַװעק

6.4.8   (די) מערסטע

(די) מערסטע 'most', which takes a plural verb, does not inflect. (די) מערסטע is also a common noun and invariant adjective that may refer to inanimate objects.

SAMPLES OF THE USE OF מערסטע (די)

Most people are still here   (די) מערסטע זײַנען נאָך דאָ

Most have already left   (די) מערסטע זײַנען שוין אַװעק

6.4.9   איטלעכער / יעדערער / יעדער איינער

איטלעכער / יעדערער / יעדער איינער 'everyone; everybody', which take a singular verb, inflect for case and gender as adjectives. איטלעכער now occurs mostly in literary styles. They are exclusively pronouns.

SAMPLES OF THE USE OF איטלעכער / יעדערער / יעדער איינער

Everyone knows he's crazy   יעדער איינער װייסט אַז ער איז משוגע

איך האָב געזען יעדן איינעם פֿון זײ   I saw every one of them

דאָס װײס יעדערער   Everyone knows that

איטלעכער איז צופֿרידן   Everyone is happy

יעדערער האָט זײנע משוגעתן [məshugásn]   Everyone has his foibles

6.4.10   יעדער איינציקער

יעדער איינציקער 'each and every one; every single one', which takes a singular verb, inflects for case and gender as an adjective. It is exclusively a pronoun.

SAMPLES OF THE USE OF יעדער איינציקער

איך קען יעדן איינציקן   I know every single one

יעדער איינציקער װעט הײַנט קומען   Every single person will come today

מ'װעט פֿאַרבעטן יעדן איינציקן   We will invite every single one of them

6.4.11   אַלע

אַלע 'everyone' which takes a plural verb, optionally inflects to אַלעמען in either objective case when serving as a pronoun referring to humans. When substituting for inanimate objects, אַלע is retained uninflected in all cases. Hence האָסט אַלע ביכער? 'Do you have all the books?' may be answered by איך האָב זײ אַלע ' I have them all'.

SAMPLES OF THE USE OF אַלע AND אַלעמען

אַלע קענען די מעשה? [máysə]   Does everyone know the story?

האָסט אַלעמען דערצײילט די מעשה?   You told everyone the story?

7 VERBS

7.0   OVERVIEW

The Yiddish verb system combines synthetic and analytic constructions. Synthetic verbs synthesize grammatical information into a single word by inflecting the verb as required. Only the present tense is fully synthetic in Yiddish. Person and number are marked by appropriate endings. The past and future are formed by combining a synthetic helping verb with an uninflected (unchanging) main verb. In the past, the unchanging main verb is the past participle.   In the future it is the infinitive.   The essential morphology therefore comprises the suffixes of the stem in the present tense and the conjugations of the helping verbs used to form the past and future. Analytic verbs are discussed in §9.

7.1   THE INFINITIVE

The infinitive is the traditional point of reference for any verbal paradigm. The synthetic infinitive is formed by suffixing ן (or ען after ח; נ;   נג;   נק;   a stressed vowel or diphthong;   ל following a consonant) to the stem. Preposition צו 'to', unlike its English counterpart, appears only rarely with the infinitive.

SAMPLES OF INFINITIVES

אַנטװיקלען develop

זאָגן say

טאַנצן dance

לאַכן laugh

קוקן look

שרײַען yell

7.2 THE PRESENT PARTICIPLE

The present participle is formed by suffixation of דיק- (or ענדיק- after ם, נ,
נג, נק, ל following a consonant, or a stressed vowel) to the stem of the
verb. It denotes the ongoingness of the verbal action — 'while doing / being
something; in the course of; during'. Its use frequently corresponds with
English -ing when so used. Syntactically, דיק- functions as an adverb (→
§14.4.1).

SAMPLES OF THE USE OF PRESENT PARTICIPLES

איך בין אַרײַן אין צימער האַלטנדיק די ביכער אין האַנט

I entered the room, holding the books in my hand

זיצנדיק אין שענק האָבן מיר געבלאָפט אַ שיינע פאָר לחיימס [ləkháyimz]

Sitting in the pub, we had quite a few drinks

זי איז אַוועק טראַכטנדיק וועגן דעם

She left thinking about it

שמועסנדיק אַ גאַנצע נאַכט האָט מען געפֿונען דעם ענטפֿער

Talking a whole night, the answer was found

שרײַענדיק וועסטו קיין זאַך ניט אויפֿטאָן [úfton]

You won't accomplish anything by yelling

7.3   THE VERBAL ADDITIVE: זיך

The verbal additive is זיך. It is only pronounced [zikh] when stressed for contrast.   It is normally reduced to [zəkh] or [zakh] and although written separately, it is nearly always pronounced as a suffix of the preceding verb. When the part of the verb preceding זיך ends in one of the voiceless consonants [f], [k], [kh], [p], [s], [sh], [t], [s] – most frequently [t] of the third person singular ending – that voiceless consonant may undergo the usual regressive voiceless assimilation and become voiced in deference to the [z] of זיך (→§2.2.3), e.g. וואָס הערט זיך העראָס [vos hérdzakh?] 'What's new?; How are you?'. זיך following a verb ending in a voiceless consonant is, however, one of the instances where assimilation may be progressive, leading to the devoicing of the second consonant – the ז of זיך – hence the equally widespread [vos hértsakh?]. זיך follows the present tense verb but usually precedes the past participle in the past tense and the infinitive in the future tense (→ §§7.5, 7.6, 7.9, 14.3.1, 14.3.3.1, 14.5.1, 14.5.3.1).

7.3.1   זיך as an inherent part of the verb

Some verbs are historically accompanied by זיך (literally 'oneself; itself'). In these instances, זיך always occurs with the verb, and is listed with it in dictionaries. Many inherent זיך verbs have different meanings when used on their own, e.g. בעטן 'ask' vs. זיך בעטן 'beg'.

SAMPLES OF VERBS WITH INHERENT זיך

זיך אַרויסדרייען [aróyzdreyən]   extricate oneself; get out of

זיך אַריַינמישן   interfere; mix in

זיך באַמיַען   try

זיך באַקלאָגן   complain

זיך חבֿרן [khávərn] (מיט)   be friends (with)

זיך טומלען make noise

זיך סטאַרען try

זיך פֿאַרפּלאָנטערן become tied up / entangled

זיך קװענקלען hesitate; be indecisive

7.3.2 זיך as intransitivity and reflexivity marker

זיך may designate intransitivity or a reflexive mood in a verb that is transitive when it appears alone (not to be confused with the grammatical reflexive → §14.8). זיך adds the notion that it is the subject him or herself that is undergoing the action.

SAMPLES OF זיך AS AN INTRANSITIVITY AND REFLEXIVITY MARKER

dress up elegantly פּוצן זיך אויספּוצן (cf. פּוצן 'polish' trans. v.)

hide (oneself) באַהאַלטן זיך (cf. באַהאַלטן 'hide' trans. v.)

get washed װאַשן זיך (cf. װאַשן 'wash' trans. v.)

wish for oneself װינטשן זיך (cf. װינטשן 'wish' trans. v.)

comfort / console oneself טרייסטן זיך (cf. טרייסטן 'console' trans. v.)

forgive oneself פֿאַרגעבן זיך (cf. פֿאַרגעבן 'forgive' trans. v.)

7.3.2.1 לערנען זיך and לערנען

לערנען (→ §5.1.3.2) may mean both 'teach' and 'study'. Where the meaning is unclear from context, זיך לערנען may be used for 'study' to avoid ambiguity. זיך לערנען occurs much more frequently in discussions of modern education. In discussion of traditional studies, לערנען appears on its own, e.g. לערנען חומש [khúməsh] 'study Khúməsh [the Five Books of Moses]', לערנען אַ בלאַט גמרא [gəmórə] 'master a section of the Talmud (lit. learn a leaf (= two sided page) of Talmud)'. Cf. §§ 4.3.2.2, 5.1.3.2, 15.17.15.

7.3.3 זיך as a solitude marker

זיך may be attached at will to a number of verbs to denote solitude, the state of being on one's own, or wishing to be alone, e.g. איך גיי 'I am going; walking' vs. ...איך גיי מיר זיך 'I am walking along by myself...'. It may have the force of 'minding one's own business' and is commonly used to anticipate an interruption or harassment from another party.

7.3.4 Prepositional constructions with זיך

זיך combines with a number of prepositions to form widely used prepositional phrases. Occasionally, the construction is used creatively. The best known example comes from the literary movement associated with the introspectivist Yiddish literary journal אין זיך, launched in New York in 1920. Its name derives from אין זיך 'in oneself', hence – introspectivist. The group's adherents are known as the אינזיכיסטן ' *inzikhists / introspectivists*'.

SAMPLES OF PREPOSITIONAL CONSTRUCTIONS WITH זיך

around oneself; in one's circle / environment אַרום [arúm] זיך

at home; in one's own possession; בײַ [ba] זיך

with oneself מיט זיך

independently; alone פֿאַר [fárzəkh] זיך

recover; get well קומען צו זיך

7.3.5 Inflection of זיך for person in dialectal usage

In Southern Eastern Yiddish (comprising Mideastern and Southeastern Yiddish), verbal additive זיך is generally reserved for the third person only and for the general sense of 'oneself'. The first person singular is מיך and the second person singular דיך. Less consistently encountered are אונדז for first person plural and אײַך for second person plural. Cf. e.g. איך װאַש מיך 'I'm washing myself' for standard איך װאַש דיך. Use of inflected forms of דיך may be encountered in the literary language.

7.4.   NEGATION

The negator is ניט (N.E.) or נישט (S.). It is ניט קײן ט(ש)ני [nit kin / nit ka] with an indefinite noun as object. ני(ש)ט is only stressed when emphasis is required. On its position in the sentence → §§14.3.3, 14.5.3.

7.5   PRESENT TENSE

The present tense is formed by suffixation of the appropriate ending to the stem. There is no ending in the first person singular. Note that the formal second person singular איר form is taken from the plural. דיך follows the present tense verb. The first person singular is identical with the stem of the verb. The first person plural is usually identical with the infinitive (but cf. §§7.5.3, 14.9).

7.5.1   Present singular endings

first person:	no ending
second person familiar:	‑סט
second person formal:	‑ט
third person:	‑ט

imperative familiar: no ending

imperative formal: ‑ט

SAMPLE OF PRESENT SINGULAR: זאָגן 'say'

I say   איך זאָג

you (familiar) say   דו זאָגסט

you (formal) say   איר זאָגט

he says   ער זאָגט

she says   זי זאָגט

it is said / people say / one says   מ'זאָגט

say! tell me! (familiar)   זאָג!

say! tell me! (formal)   זאָגט!

7.5.2   Present plural endings

first person: ‑(ע)ן

second person: ‑ט

third person: ‑(ע)ן

imperative: ‑ט

SAMPLE OF PRESENT PLURAL: זאָגן 'say'

we say   מיר זאָגן

you say   איר זאָגט

they say   זײ זאָגן

say! tell me!   זאָגט !

SAMPLE VERBS WITH REGULAR PRESENT

visit   באַזוכן

bless (esp. 'say the traditional grace after meals') בענטשן

yearn for; miss בענקען

remember געדענקען

live (= dwell) וואוינען

dream [khóləmən] חלומען

dance טאַנצן

think טראַכטן

run לױפֿן

read [léyənən] לייענען

think (= be of the opinion) מיינען

eat עסן

go (by vehicle) פֿאָרן

come קומען

sleep שלאָפֿן

converse שמועסן

7.5.3 Reduced ע in verb endings

There are a few verbs with first and third person plural ending ־ען that have infinitives in ־ן. The ־ען forms are expected with stems ending in a stressed vowel or diphthong (→ §2.2.9). Cf. מיר \ זיי גייען [géyən] 'we / they are going', מיר \ זיי זעען [zéən] 'we / they see', מיר \ זיי שטייען [shtéyən] 'we / they are standing' vs. infinitives גיין 'go', זען 'see', שטיין 'stand'. Note that the ע that appears in verb endings in the expected phonetic contexts should not be confused with the organic ע of stems that happen to end in ע. Where a stem ends in ע, the ע is retained throughout the conjugation, e.g. stem כראָפּע 'snore', infinitive כראָפּען, third person ער \ זי כראָפּעט 'he/she is snoring'.

7.5.4 Variants in the regular present tense

7.5.4.1 Stem ending in ט in third person singular

Stems ending in ט, conjugated for third person singular (where the present tense ending is also ט), would result in two consecutive t's. Double consonants do not generally occur (although they appear in writing in compounded words to preserve the integrity of both stems, e.g. פֿאַרדרופֿן 'call together' from prefix -פֿאַר and infinitive רופֿן → §6.1.5). The potential טט sequence that would result in the third person singular of stems ending in ט is averted by obligatory collapse in both speech and writing to a single ט, e.g. זי אַרבעט 'she works' (infinitive אַרבעטן), ער האַלט 'he holds / is holding' (infinitive האַלטן), מ'וואַרט 'people are waiting; everybody is waiting' (infinitive וואַרטן).

7.5.4.2 Stem ending in ד in third person singular

Stems ending in ד in third person singular (where the present tense ending is ט), would result in ד followed by ט. The דט sequence is retained in writing, but never pronounced, hence זי רעדט [zi ret] 'she talks / is talking'.

7.5.5 Anomalies

7.5.5.1 No ending in third person singular

The third person singular forms of a number of helping verbs that serve to form analytic verbs (→ §9.1) do not have the usual ט- ending.

דאַרף 'has to; must' (→ §9.1.2)

חיל 'wants' (→ §9.1.6)

זאָל 'should' (→ §9.1.8)

מוז 'must' (→ §9.1.12)

מעג 'may' (→ §9.1.13)

טאָר (ניט) 'may not' (→ §9.1.13)

קען 'can; is able' (→ §9.1.16)

7.5.5.2   Optional ט ending in third person singular

The irregular װײסן 'know (something that is not generally studied)' (→ §15.4) may or may not have the usual -ט ending in third person singular, hence זי װײסט = זי װײס 'she knows'.

7.5.6   Imperative additives טאָ and זשע

טאָ [tə; to] immediately precedes the imperative and זשע [zhə] immediately follows it. They can be used independently of each other or they may surround the imperative for increased effect. Both טאָ and זשע invoke affection, love or familiarity to support a suggestion, request or command, often having the force of 'please', 'do please' or 'come on'. טאָ occasionally translates 'then; in that case' in support of the imperative, and usually occurs after the other party has made some remark about the request. Both טאָ and זשע frequently serve to impose guilt upon the listener or reader in support of the request made (→ §11.4 on interrogative additives טאָ and זשע). In less intimate contexts, the non-emotional זײַ אַזוי גוט or זײַט אַזוי גוט (familiar) or גוט (lit. 'Be so good'), may be used for 'please'.

SAMPLES OF IMPERATIVE ADDITIVES טאָ and זשע

טאָ זאָג מיר   Then tell me

זאָג זשע מיר   Come on, please tell me

טאָ זאָג זשע מיר (You owe it to me!)   Then come on, please tell me

7.6   PAST TENSE

7.6.1   Regular past

The regular past is formed by combining the appropriate **present** tense form of helping verb הָאָבן [hóbm] 'have' with the **past participle** of the main verb. The regular past participle is formed by prefixing גע- and suffixing -ט to the stem, giving the template גע+STEM+ט. The גע- prefix disappears in the past participles of verbs with unstressed prefixes ($\rightarrow$ §8.1), e.g. פֿאַרשטײן 'understand' $\rightarrow$ past participle פֿאַרשטאַנען 'understood'. It also disappears in verbs with stressed suffix -ירן, e.g. אָרגאַניזירן [organizírn] 'organize' $\rightarrow$ past participle אָרגאַנאַזירט 'organized'.

7.6.1.1   Singular present of הָאָבן

איך הָאָב I have

דו הָאָסט you (familiar) have

איר הָאָט you (formal) have

ער הָאָט he has

זי הָאָט she has

מ'הָאָט people have /we have / one has

SAMPLE SINGULAR PAST USING הָאָבן: זאָגן 'say'

איך הָאָב געזאָגט I (have) said

דו הָאָסט געזאָגט you (familiar) (have) said

איר הָאָט געזאָגט you (formal) (have) said

ער הָאָט געזאָגט he says

זי הָאָט געזאָגט she says

מ'הָאָט געזאָגט it was said / people said / one said

7.6.1.2 Plural present of הָאָבן

מיר הָאָבן [hobm] we have

איר הָאָט you have

זיי הָאָבן [hobm] they have

SAMPLE PLURAL PAST USING הָאָבן: זאָגן 'say'

מיר הָאָבן <u>געזאָגט</u> we (have) said

איר <u>הָאָט געזאָגט</u> you (have) said

זיי <u>הָאָבן געזאָגט</u> they (have) said

SAMPLE VERBS WITH REGULAR PAST AND THEIR PAST PARTICIPLES

געברענט burn → ברענען

געגלייבט believe → גלייבן

געוויינט cry → וויינען

געזוכט look for; search → זוכן

געטומלט make noise → טומלען

געלאַכט laugh → לאַכן

גערייניקט clean (up) → רייניקן

געשטערט bother → שטערן

7.6.2 Past participle in -(ע)ן

Some participles are historically of the shape גע+STEM+ן (or גע+STEM+ען if the stem ends in מ, נ, נג, נק, ל, following a consonant, or a stressed vowel). Participles in -(ע)ן are frequently accompanied by internal vowel shift.

7.6.2.1 Participle in (ע)ן with no vowel shifts

געבעטן ← בעטן 'ask for; request'

גראָבן 'dig' ← געגראָבן

האַלטן 'hold; be of the opinion' ← געהאַלטן

טראָגן 'wear; carry; be pregnant' ← געטראָגן

וואַשן 'wash (trans.)' ← געוואַשן

שאַפֿן 'create' ← געשאַפֿן

שלאָגן 'hit; strike; beat' ← געשלאָגן

7.6.2.2 Participle in (ע)ן with שׂ ← י

(ט ← ד) אויסמײַדן 'avoid' ← אויסגעמיטן

בײַטן 'change' ← געביטן

בײַסן 'bite' ← געביסן

ווײַזן 'show' ← געוויזן

טרײַבן [tráybm] 'drive; propel; chase' ← געטריבן [gətríbm]

(ט ← ד) לײַדן 'suffer' ← געליטן

לײַען 'lend' ← געליגן (var. געלינן)

קלײַבן [kláybm] 'collect' ← געקליבן [gəklíbm]

זיך קלײַבן [kláybm] 'prepare to; ready oneself' ← געקליבן [gəklíbm] זיך

זיך רײַבן [ráybm] 'rub' ← געריבן [gəríbm] זיך

רײַסן 'tear' ← געריסן

שווײַגן 'remain silent' ← געשוויגן

שמײַסן 'whip' ← געשמיסן

(ט ← ד) שנײַדן 'cut' ← געשניטן

שרײַבן [shráybm] 'write' ← געשריבן [gəshríbm]

שרײַען 'yell; scream' ← געשריען (S. var. געשרינן)

7.6.2.3 Participle in (ע)ן with ע ← אָ

מעסטן 'measure' ← געמאָסטן

שעלטן 'slaughter' ← געשאָלטן

נעשאָנקען 'give (as a gift)' → שענקען

7.6.2.4 Participle in (ע)ן with י → ו

נעבונדן 'tie (up)' → בינדן

נעדרונגען 'infer' → דרינגען

נעהונקען 'limp' → הינקען

נעוואונטשן 'wish (somebody something)' → ווינטשן

נעזונגען 'sing' → זינגען

נעזונקען 'sink' → זינקען

נעטרונקען 'drink' → טרינקען

נעצוואונגען 'force' → צווינגען

נעשלונגען 'swallow' → שלינגען

נעוואונען 'win' → נעווינען

7.6.2.5 Various vowel and consonant changes

זיך נעבוינין 'bend down' → זיך בייגן

נעברענגט 'bring' → נעבראָכט (S. var. [gəbréynkt]) ברענגען

אויפֿנעהויבן 'lift' → אויפֿהייבן [úfheybm] [úfgəhoybm]

נענומען 'take' → נעמען

פֿאַרלאָרן 'lose' → פֿאַרלוירן (N.E. var. פֿאַרלירן)

פֿאַרשטאַנען 'understand' → פֿאַרשטיין

נעשוואָרן 'swear' → נעשוואוירן (N.E. var. שווערן)

7.7 MINORITY PAST TENSE: THE זײַן VERBS

A minority of verbs form their past by combining the appropriate present of זײַן 'be', rather than האָבן 'have' with the past participle (cf. French être,

German *sein*). All זײַן verbs have past participles in (ע)ן, usually with vowel shift. All are intransitive.

7.7.1   Singular present of זײַן

איך בין   I am

דו ביסט   you (familiar) are

(זענט .S. var)   איר זײַט   you (formal) are

ער איז   he is

זי איז   she is

מ'איז   we are / people are / one is

SAMPLE SINGULAR PAST USING זײַן: שלאָפֿן 'sleep'

איך בין געשלאָפֿן   I (have) slept

דו ביסט געשלאָפֿן   you (familiar) (have) slept

איר זײַט געשלאָפֿן   you (formal) (have) slept

ער איז געשלאָפֿן   he (has) slept

זי איז געשלאָפֿן   she (has) slept

מ'איז געשלאָפֿן   we/people (have) slept; one slept

7.7.2   Plural present of זײַן

(זענען .S. var)   מיר זײַנען   we are

איר זײַט   you are

(זענען .S. var)   זיי זײַנען   they are

SAMPLE PLURAL PAST USING זײַן: שלאָפֿן 'sleep'

מיר זײַנען געשלאָפֿן   we (have) slept

איר <u>זײַט</u> געשלאָפֿן   you (have) slept

די <u>זײַנען</u> געשלאָפֿן   they (have) slept

7.7.3   Basic זײַן verbs

The basic זײַן verbs generally have to do with motion, motionlessness, states of existence, and the life cycle. Where a זײַן verb acquires a transitive meaning, it automatically joins the more usual האָבן verbs (→ §7.6), e.g. transitive העַנגען 'hang (something / somebody)' with האָבן vs. intransitive העַנגען 'hang; be hanging' with זײַן.

BASIC VERBS WITH PAST WITH זײַן AND THEIR PAST PARTICIPLES

געבליבן [gəblíbm] ← 'remain' [bláybm] בלײַבן

נעגאַנגען ← 'go; walk' גיין

געלונגען ← 'be successful (in doing something)' געלינגען

געראָטן ← 'turn out as planned' געראָטן

געשען ← 'happen; occur' [gəshén] געשען

(העַנגען 'hang' (S. var. געהאַנגען) געהאַנגען)

געוואַקסן ← 'grow' וואַקסן

געוואָרן ← 'become' ווערן

געווען ← 'be' זײַן

געזעסן ← 'sit' זיצן

געלאָפֿן ← 'run' לויפֿן

געלעגן ← 'lie' ליגן

געפֿאַלן ← 'fall' פֿאַלן

געפֿאָרן ← 'go (by vehicle)' פֿאָרן

געפֿלויגן ← 'fly' פֿליען

געקומען ← 'come' קומען

נעקראָבן ← קריכן 'climb; crawl'

נעשטאָרבן ← שטאַרבן 'die'

נעשטאַנען ← שטיין 'stand'

נעשלאָפֿן ← שלאָפֿן 'sleep'

נעשפרונגען ← שפרינגען 'jump'

7.7.4 Derivative זײַן verbs

Derivative זײַן verbs are prefixed forms of basic זײַן verbs. As is often the case with prefixed verbs (→ §8), they may in the course of centuries wander far from the meanings of the base verbs from which they derive. Derivative זײַן verbs preserve the major grammatical features of the base verbs from which they derive – past with זײַן, past participle in ‎(ע)ן, and intransitivity. One of the זײַן verbs, ווערן 'become' can itself be used to form analytic verbs, all of which automatically form their past tense with זײַן (→ §9.1.7).

SAMPLES OF DERIVATIVE זײַן VERBS

אויסגעגאַנגען [óyzgəgangən] ← אויסגײן [óyzgeyn] 'die; run out'

אויסגעשטאַנען ← אויסשטײן 'put up with'

אַרײַנגעפֿאַלן ← אַרײַנפֿאַלן 'commit a blunder; fall in; be deceived'

בײַגעוען ← בײַזײַן [báyzayn] 'be present'

פֿאָרגעקומען ← פֿאָרקומען 'happen; occur'

7.8 PLUPERFECT PAST TENSE

The pluperfect past is formed by inserting געהאַט (past participle of האָבן) before the past participle of the main verb. The pluperfect is rarely encountered with זײַן verbs.

SAMPLES OF THE PLUPERFECT PAST

איך האָב אײַך געהאַט געוואָרנט איר זאָלט ניט גײן

I had warned you (formal) not to go

דאָס האָבן זײ אונדז געהאַט געזאָגט פֿריִער

That is what they had told us beforehand

דעם דאָזיקן פֿילם האָבן מיר געהאַט געזען

We had seen that film

7.9 FUTURE TENSE

The future tense is formed by combining the appropriate part of וועלן 'will / shall' with the infinitive. The conjugation of וועלן is irregular. In normal speech, the appropriate part of וועלן used to form the future tense is phonetically reduced as transcribed (→ §§7.9.1 – 7.9.2). Future helping verb וועלן should not be confused with וועלן 'want' (→ §9.1.6). The infinitives are identical but the present tense conjugations differ markedly.

7.9.1 Singular future with וועלן

I will [ikh vel / khvel / ikhl] איך וועל

you (familiar) will [du vest / duəst / dust] דו וועסט

you (formal) will [ir vet / irət / irt] איר וועט

he will [er vet / erət / ert] ער וועט

she will [zi vet / ziət / zit] זי וועט

we will / people will / one will [məvét / mət] מ'וועט

SAMPLE SINGULAR FUTURE: זאָגן 'say'

I will say   איך וועל זאָגן

you (familiar) will say   דו וועסט זאָגן

you (formal) will say   איר וועט זאָגן

he will say   ער וועט זאָגן

she will say   זי וועט זאָגן

people will say / we will say / one will say   מ'וועט זאָגן

7.9.2   Plural future with וועלן

we will   [mir veln / miln (N.E.) / mirn (S.)]   מיר וועלן

you will   [ir vet / irət / irt]   איר וועט

they will   [zey veln / zeyln / zeln / zəln]   זײ וועלן

SAMPLE PLURAL FUTURE: זאָגן 'say'

we will say   מיר וועלן זאָגן

you (plural/formal singular) will say   איר וועט זאָגן

they will say   זײ וועלן זאָגן

7.10   IMMEDIATE FUTURE TENSE

The immediate future is formed by the appropriately conjugated present
tense of גיין 'go'. It denotes the intention to carry out the action in the
nearer rather than in the more distant future.

SAMPLES OF THE IMMEDIATE FUTURE

I'm going to buy a book   איך גײ קױפֿן אַ בוך

I'm going to tell him off   איך גײ אים [em] אַרײנזאָגן

They're going to think about it   זײ גײען טראַכטן וועגן דעם

7.11   PLUPERFECT FUTURE TENSE

The pluperfect future is formed by the appropriate part of וועלן ($\rightarrow$ §§7.9.1 – 7.9.2) plus infinitive האָבן plus the past participle of the main verb.

SAMPLES OF THE PLUPERFECT FUTURE

איך וועל איך האָבן געוואָרנט איר זאָלט ניט גיין

I will have warned you (formal) not to go

דאָס וועלן זיי אונדז האָבן געזאָגט פריער

That is what they will have told us beforehand

דעם דאָזיקן פילם וועלן מיר האָבן געזען

We will have seen that film

8 PREFIXED VERBS

8.0 OVERVIEW

A prefix can provide a verb with a special nuance or a completely new meaning. The modern meanings of many prefixed verbs may be distantly related, or not obviously related at all, to those of their unprefixed base forms. Many prefixes have become so attached to certain verbs that the verb on its own provides an imperfective mood suggesting that the action is somehow incomplete. There are two types of verbal prefixes: unstressed prefixes and stressed prefixes. Stressed prefixes emerge as separate words in the present tense.

8.1 UNSTRESSED PREFIXES

Unstressed prefixes are retained in all tenses. In the past tense, the past participle prefix גע- disappears; its function is assumed by the unstressed prefix itself. Some of the six unstressed prefixes do have some general primitive meaning. Use over the centuries has, however, obscured it in many instances. For many, a historical connection may be inferred (e.g. אַנטדעקן 'discover' from אַנט + דעקן 'cover'; cf. English 'dis' + 'cover').

8.1.1 אַנט-

General meaning: negation; distancing from; undoing of.

142

אַנטדעקן   [andékn] 'discover' (→ past participle אַנטדעקט)

זיך אַנטזאַגן   [andzágn] 'refuse'   (→ past participle זיך אַנטזאַגט)

אַנטלאָפֿן װערן   'run away from' (→ past participle אַנטלאָפֿן געװאָרן)

אַנטמוטיקן   'discourage' (→ past participle אַנטמוטיקט)

אַנטשלאָפֿן װערן   'fall asleep' (→ past participle אַנטשלאָפֿן געװאָרן)

8.1.2. -בא

General meaning: transitivization of intransitive verbs; application of one thing to another; thoroughness of action; bringing a state of existence into being.

באַהאַלטן   'hide' (→ past participle באַהאַלטן)

באַזוכן   'visit' (→ past participle באַזוכט)

באַלײדיקן   'insult' (→ past participle באַלײדיקט)

באַמערקן   'notice' (→ past participle באַמערקט)

באַרואיקן   'calm (someone) down'   (→ past participle באַרואיקט)

זיך באַרואיקן   'calm (oneself) down' (→ past participle זיך באַרואיקט)

8.1.3. -גע

-גע is a relic prefix. Most of the stems of the גע- verbs do not survive as unprefixed verbs.

געבוירן װערן   (N.E. var. געבאָרן װערן) 'be born' (→ past participle

(נעבאָרן געוואָרן געוואָרן; N.E. var. נעבוירן געוואָרן)

נעדענקען	[gədéynkən] 'remember' (→ past participle נעדענקט)
געוואויר ווערן	(N.E. var. געוואָר ווערן) 'find out' (→ past participle געוואָר געוואָרן; N.E. var. געוואויר געוואָרן)
נעוויינען	'win' (→ past participle נעוואונען)
נעטרויען	'trust' (→ past participle נעטרויט)
זיך נעזעגענען	'say goodbye (to one another)' (→ past participle זיך נעזעגנט)
נעפֿינען	'find' (→ past participle נעפֿונען)
נעשען	[gəshén] 'happen; occur' (→ past participle נעשען)

8.1.4   דער- (frequently [da])

General meaning: completeness of action; carrying through of the action to its conclusion.

SAMPLES OF דער-

דערהרגענען	[dahárgənən] 'kill' (→ past participle דערהרגעט [dahárgət])
זיך דערפֿרייען	'rejoice (esp. with the company or presence of another person)' (→ past participle זיך דערפֿרייט)
דערציילן	'tell (a story); recount' (→ past participle דערציילט)
דערקענען	'recognize' (→ past participle דערקענט)
דערשיסן	'shoot (dead)' (→ past participle דערשאָסן)

8.1.5   פֿאַר-

General meaning: completeness of action; initiation of a change in circumstances; debasement of the value or success of the action.

SAMPLES OF -פֿאַר

פֿאַרבעסערן	'improve' (→ past participle פֿאַרבעסערט)
פֿאַרגעסן	'forget' (→ past participle פֿאַרגעסן)
פֿאַרדעלבטיקן	'suspect' (→ past participle פֿאַרדעלבטיקט)
פֿאַרדרייען	'entangle; mess up' (→ past participle פֿאַרדרייט)
זיך פֿאַרדרייען	'get tied up in' (→ past participle זיך פֿאַרדרייט)
פֿאַרלירן	'lose' (→ past participle פֿאַרלוירן; N.E. var. פֿאַרלאָרן)
פֿאַרפֿירן	'lead astray; seduce' (→ past participle פֿאַרפֿירט)
פֿאַרשטאַרקן	'strengthen' (→ past participle: פֿאַרשטאַרקט)
פֿאַרשענערן	'make (more) beautiful' (→ past participle: פֿאַרשענערט)

8.1.6   -צע

General meaning: coming apart; spreading out; in all directions; spacing out of the verbal action; total undoing of something.

SAMPLES OF -צע

צעברעכן	'break' (→ past participle צעבראָכן)
צעגיסן	'spill all over the place' (→ past participle צעגאָסן)
צעטומלען	'confound' (→ past participle צעטומלט)
צעטרענצלען	'squander completely' (→ past participle צעטרענצלט)
צעכאַפן	'grab up; buy out' (→ past participle צעכאַפט)
צעקאַליעטשען	'ruin; cripple' (→ past participle צעקאַליעטשעט)

8.2   STRESSED PREFIXES

Like their unstressed counterparts, stressed prefixes are deeply rooted in the history of the language, and the primitive senses of the prefixes have often been lost. The heavy stress of stressed prefixes relegates the stem to secondary stress status (→ §§2.3.1.3 — 2.3.1.4). In the present tense, the stressed prefix separates off and appears *after* the verb. In the past tense, -גע is infixed *between* the stressed prefix and the stem to form a one-word past participle. The status of the stressed prefix as a distinct entity is so strong that it often blocks consonant assimilation of voice or voicelessness (→ §2.2.1 — 2.2.4), especially when sentence rhythm provides for heavy wordstress; cf. e.g. heavily stressed [óys gə mátərt] 'completely exhausted' vs. less heavily stressed [óyzgəmatərt] 'exhausted' for אויסגעמאַטערט (past participle of אויסמאַטערן). Model verb is צוזאָגן [tsúzogn] 'promise'.

SAMPLE OF CONJUGATION OF STRESSED PREFIX: צוזאָגן

present singular

I promise   [zog tsú] איך זאָג צו

you (familiar) promise   [zokst tsú] דו זאָגסט צו

you (formal) promise   [zokt tsú] איר זאָגט צו

he promises   [zokt tsú] ער זאָגט צו

she promises [zokt tsú] זי זאָגט צו

it is promised / people promise / one promises   [məzòkt tsú] מ'זאָגט צו

Promise! (familiar)   [zog tsú] זאָג צו!

Promise! (formal)   [zokt tsú] זאָגט צו!

present plural

we promise   [zogn tsú] מיר זאָגן צו

you promise   [zokt tsú] איר זאָגט צו

they promise   [zogn tsú] זיי זאָגן צו

Promise!   [zokt tsú] זאָגט צו!

present participle

(while) promising   [tsúzogndik] צוזאָגנדיק

past singular

I (have) promised [tsúgəzokt] איך האָב צוגעזאָגט

you (have) promised (familiar) דו האָסט צוגעזאָגט

you (have) promised (formal) איר האָט צוגעזאָגט

he (has) promised ער האָט צוגעזאָגט

she (has) promised זי האָט צוגעזאָגט

it was promised / people promised / one promised מ'האָט צוגעזאָגט

past plural

we (have) promised מיר האָבן צוגעזאָגט

you (have) promised איר האָט צוגעזאָגט

they (have) promised זיי האָבן צוגעזאָגט

future singular

I will promise איך װעל צוזאָגן

you (familiar) will promise דו װעסט צוזאָגן

you (formal) will promise איר װעט צוזאָגן

he will promise ער װעט צוזאָגן

she will promise זי װעט צוזאָגן

they will promise / we will promise / one will promise מ'װעט צוזאָגן

future plural

we will promise מיר װעלן צוזאָגן

you will promise איר װעט צוזאָגן

they will promise זיי װעלן צוזאָגן

8.2.1   אויס-

General meaning: completeness of action; lengthiness of the action; undoing of a prior situation; suddenness; outward action.

SAMPLES OF אויס-

אויסהרגענען [óys hargənən] 'annihilate; wipe out completely' (→ past participle אויסגעהרגעט [óys gə hargət] / [óyzgəhargət])

אויסוואַשן 'wash (thoroughly)' (→ past participle אויסגעוואַשן)

זיך אויסוויינען 'cry one's eyes out' (→ past participle זיך אויסגעוויינט)

אויסזאָגן 'reveal' (→ past participle אויסגעזאָגט [óyzgəzokt])

אויסלעשן 'extinguish' (→ past participle אויסגעלאָשן)

אויסמײַדן 'avoid' (→ past participle אויסגעמיטן)

אויסשרײַען 'yell suddenly' (→ past participle אויסגעשריִען; S. var. אויסגעשריגן)

8.2.2   אויפֿ- [úf]

General meaning: completeness of action;   Cf. English *up*. Note that the pronunciation [úf] does not reflect the spelling.

SAMPLES OF אויפֿ-

אויפֿהייבן [úfheybm] 'pick up;   lift' (→ past participle אויפֿגעהויבן [úfgəhoybm])

אויפֿווײַזן [úfvayzn] 'demonstrate; document' (→ past participle אויפֿגעוויזן [úfgəvizn])

אויפֿעפֿענען [úfefənən] 'open up' (→ past participle אויפֿגעעפֿנט [úfgəefnt])

אויפֿשטיין [úfshteyn] 'get up' (→ past participle אויפֿגעשטאַנען [úfgəshtanən])

148

8.2.3 אומ-

General meaning: return to former state.

SAMPLES OF -אומ

אומברעגנגען '(systematically / officially) kill' (→ past participle
אומגעברעאָלט; S. var. אומגעברעגגט [úmgəbreynkt])

אומקומען '(systematically/officially) be killed' (→ past participle
(אומגעקומען

אומקערן 'give back; return' (→ past participle אומגעקערט)

זיך אומקערן 'come back; return' (→ past participle זיך אומגעקערט)

8.2.4 אונטער-

General meaning: under; at the bottom of; secretly; moderately; not quite fully.

SAMPLES OF -אונטער

אונטערהינקען 'limp; be less than proficient' (→ past participle
(אונטערגעהונקען

זיך אונטערפוילן 'be lazy temporarily / for a specific task' (→ past
participle זיך אונטערגעפוילט)

אונטערדרוקן 'secretly hand over (to)' (→ past participle
(אונטערגערוקט

אונטערשרײַבן [úntərshraybm] 'sign (one's name)' (→ past participle
אונטערגעשריבן [úntərgəshribm])

8.2.5 איבער-

General meaning: completeness of the action; repetition of the action; action through time or space; excessiveness.

SAMPLES OF -איבער

149

SAMPLES OF -איבער

| איבערזעצן | 'translate' (→ past participle איבערגעזעצט) |

איבערזעצן — 'translate' (→ past participle איבערגעזעצט)

איבערטרײַבן — [íbərtraybm] 'exaggerate' (→ past participle איבערגעטריבן [íbərgətribm])

איבערלאָפֿן — 'have a snack' (→ past participle איבערגעלאָפֿט)

איבערמאַכן — 'make over; renew' (→ past participle איבערגעמאַכט)

איבערקוקן — 'look over' (→ past participle איבערגעקוקט)

8.2.6 -אײַנ

General meaning: enter a new state; change of situation.

SAMPLES OF -אײַנ

זיך אײַנגעװײנען — 'get used to' (→ past participle זיך אײַנגעװײנט)

אײַנװיקלען — 'wrap up' (→ past participle אײַנגעװיקלט)

זיך אײַנלעבן — 'get used to living (in a place)' (→ past participle זיך אײַנגעלעבט [áyngəlept])

אײַנרעדן — 'talk into' (→ past participle אײַנגערעדט [áyngəret])

אײַנשטימען — 'agree' (→past participle אײַנגעשטימט)

זיך אײַנעקשנען — [áynakshənən] 'be stubborn about something' (→ past participle זיך אײַנגעעקשנט [áyngəakshnt])

8.2.7 -אָנ

General meaning: specification of the action.

SAMPLES OF -אָנ

אָנדרודלען — 'incite (someone's anger against a third party)' (→ past participle אָנגעדרודלט)

150

אָנהייבן   [ónheybm] 'start' (→ past participle אָנגעהויבן
                      [óngəhoybm])

אָנווײַזן   'point out' (→ past participle אָנגעוויזן)

אָנטאַפן   [óntapm] 'touch' (→ past participle אָנגעטאַפט)

אָנשרײַבן   [ónshraybm] 'write' (→past participle אָנגעשריבן
                      [óngəshribm])

8.2.8   -אָפּ

General meaning: completion of the action. Note that in the past tense, the prefix may be pronounced [óp] or [ó].

SAMPLES OF -אָפּ

אָפּאַרבעטן   'complete a period of work' (→ past participle
            אָפּגעאַרבעט [ó(p)gəarbət])

אָפּטאָן   'play a trick' (→ past participle אָפּגעטאָן
            [ó(p)gəton])

אָפּלײגן   'postpone; procrastinate' (→ past participle אָפּגעלײגט
            [ó(p)gəleykt])

אָפּענדיקן   'finish completely' (→ past participle אָפּגעענדיקט
            [ó(p)gəendikt])

אָפּעסן   'finish eating' (→ past participle אָפּגעגעסן
            [ó(p)gəgesn])

8.2.9   -בײַ

General meaning: by; at.

SAMPLES OF -בײַ

בײַוווינן   'attend' (→ past participle בײַגעוווינען [báygəven])

בײַלײגן   'enclose' (→ past participle בײַגעלײגט [báygəleykt])

בײַקומען	'overcome' (→ past participle בײַקומען)
בײַשטײַערן	'make a contribution' (→ past participle בײַגעשטײַערט)

8.2.10 -פֿאָר

General meaning: anticipate; come before.

SAMPLES OF -פֿאָר

פֿאָרלײגן	'propose' (→ past participle פֿאָרגעלײגט [fórgəleykt])
פֿאָרשלאָגן	'propose (in more formal/parliamentary style)' (→ past participle פֿאָרגעשלאָגן [fórgəshlogn])
פֿאָרשטעלן	'introduce' (→ past participle פֿאָרגעשטעלט)
זיך פֿאָרשטעלן	'imagine; suppose' (→ past participle פֿאָרגעשטעלט זיך)
פֿאָרקומען	'occur' (→ past participle פֿאָרגעקומען)

8.2.11 -צו

SAMPLES OF -צו

זיך צוהערן	'listen to; pay (careful) attention to; obey' (→ past participle צוגעהערט זיך)
צוזאָגן	'promise' (→ past participle צוגעזאָגט [tsúgəzokt])
צוטשעפּ(ען)ען	[tsútshepənən] 'add on; affix; attach' (→ past participle צוגעטשעפּעט [tsúgətshépət])
זיך צוטשעפּ(ען)ען	'become attached; become a nuisance/pest (to)' (→ past participle צוגעטשעפּעט זיך)
צולויפֿן	'run over (to)' (→ past participle צוגעלאָפֿן)
צונעמען	'take away' (→ past participle צוגענומען)
זיך צופּאַסן	'fit in; conform' (→ past participle צוגעפּאַסט זיך)
(זיך) צוקוקן	'watch; observe' (→ past participle צוגעקוקט זיך)

8.2.12 Free stressed prefixes

The free stressed prefixes retain much of the historic force of their meanings, and can usually be prefixed at will to verbs. They often mark the direction of movement or action, or some prepositional aspect (e.g. with what or whom). Most can double as adverbs or prepositions on their own. A number of them, however, have entered into fixed combinations with specific verbs, yielding new meanings that cannot always be inferred from the base verb, e.g. דורכֿקומען [dú(r)khkumən] 'work it out; compromise' (from דורך 'through' plus קומען 'come'), נאָכֿקרימען 'mimic' (from נאָך 'after' plus זיך קרימען 'make faces'), פֿאָרויסזאָגן [foróyszogn] 'predict' (from פֿאָרויס 'before' plus זאָגן 'say').

FREE STRESSED PREFIXES

through [(a)dú(r)kh] -(אַ)דורכֿ-

(over) there; to there; thither אַהינ-

(over) here; to here; hither אַהער-

away אַוועק-

with מיט-

opposite; vis-à-vis; in reply to אַ(נט)קעגנ-

down אַנידער-

down אַראָפֿ-

out אַרויס-

upward [arúf] -אַרויפֿ-

around אַרומ-

in אַרײנ-

down אַרונטער-

over אַריבער-

after נאָכֿ-

past; by פֿאַרבײַ-

פֿאָרויס- before

פֿונאַנדער- apart; in all directions

צוזאַמען- together

צונויפֿ- bring together

SAMPLES OF FREE STRESSED PREFIXES

(אַ)דורכ-	(אַ)דורכפֿאָרן 'pass through (by vehicle)'
אַהינ-:	אַהינגיין 'go there'; אַהינשװימען 'swim there'
אַהער-:	אַהערקומען 'come here'
אַװעק-:	אַװעקגיין [avéggeyn] 'go away; leave'; אַװעקװאַרפֿן 'throw away'
אַ(נט)קעגנ-:	זיך אַ(נט)קעגנשטעלן 'oppose'
אַנידער-:	זיך אַנידערזעצן 'sit down'
אַראָפֿ-:	אַראָפֿברענגען 'bring down'; אַראָפֿשפרינגען 'jump down'
אַרויס-:	אַרויסװאַרפֿן 'throw out'; אַרויסלאָזן 'let out; release'
אַרויפֿ-:	אַרויפֿקריכן [arúfkrikhn] 'climb up'; אַרויפֿטראָגן [arúftrogn] 'carry up'
אַרום-:	אַרומזוכן 'look around for; search'; אַרומפֿאָרן 'travel around'
אַרונטער-	אַרונטערלאָזן 'let down; lower'
אַרײַנ-:	אַרײַנזאָגן 'tell off; scold' (lit. 'tell in'); אַרײַנלאָזן 'let in'
אַריבער-	אַריבערשפרינגען 'jump over'
מיט-	מיטלײַדן 'suffer together with'; מיטנעמען 'take with';
נאָכ-	נאָכלויפֿן 'run after'
פֿאַרבײַ-	פֿאַרבײַפֿאָרן [farbáyforn] 'travel past; pass through'
פֿונאַנדער-	זיך פֿונאַנדערלויפֿן 'run in all directions; scatter'

154

פֿאָרויס-   פֿאָרויסלויפֿן 'run in front of'

צוזאַמען-   צוזאַמענאַרבעטן 'work (well) together'

צונויפֿ-   צונויפֿזאַמלען [tsənóyfzamlən] 'gather together'

8.2.12.1   Free stressed prefixes without main verbs

The free stressed prefixes אַדורך- (but not its parallel form דורך-), אַוועק-, אַרײַן-, אַרויפֿ-, אַרויס-, אַרײַן-, אַרונטער and אַריבער can be used on their own without a main verb. Their past tense is formed with helping verb זײַן (→§7.7). Use of free stressed prefixes without a main verb often provides a sentence with increased dynamic force. Some have become established in idiomatic expressions, e.g. ער איז אַראָפֿ פֿון זינען 'He's off his rocker' (lit. 'gone down from sense'; cf. English 'out of his mind').

SAMPLES OF STRESSED PREFIXES WITHOUT MAIN VERBS

She left yesterday   זי איז נעכטן אַוועק

He went up the stairs [arúf]   די טרעפֿ ער איז אַרויפֿ

They entered the house   זיי זײַנען אַרײַן אין הויז

8.3   PERFECTIVE VS. NAKED VERBS

Many unstressed and stressed prefixes have become so attached to certain verbs as to render the verb on its own rare and somewhat strange sounding to native speakers. In these cases, the prefixed versions have in effect become the present day base forms of the verb, and the unprefixed 'naked' forms are reserved for situations where the action is incomplete or vague. Thus, אָנשרײַבן [ónshraybm] is the usual verb for 'write'. The use of שרײַבן on its own may be reserved for general situations e.g. וואָס שרײַבסטו? [vos shráypstə?] 'What are you writing?' Use of the unprefixed form may also signify incompleteness of the action, e.g. איך האָב געשריבן אַ בריװ 'I was writing a letter', which may imply that the letter was somehow not completed. The equivalent of 'I wrote a letter' is איך האָב אָנגעשריבן אַ בריװ. Analogously צוקומען is the basic form for 'come (somewhere)', צוגיין for 'go (somewhere)'; קומען and גיין on their own are more general concepts.

9 ANALYTIC VERBS

9.0 OVERVIEW

Unlike synthetic verbs which synthesize the main verb and its person, tense
and number into a single word by prefixing or suffixing the stem (→ §7),
analytic verbs 'analyze these out' by factoring down to the individual
grammatical components, which are maintained by a helping verb. In all
analytic verbs, by definition, the main verb is uninflected – neither prefixed
nor suffixed nor internally changed in any way, irrespective of person, tense
or number. Person, tense and number are rather indicated by the inflection
of the appropriate helping verb which accompanies it. Many everyday
synthetic verbs are used analytically when the speaker wishes to modify or
specify the meaning along the lines of one of the available helping verbs that
serve as formers of specialized analytic verbs. Some verbs, on the other hand,
are historically analytic. They are the inherently analytic verbs, which do not
exist as synthetic verbs. Analytic verbs require no detailed analysis or
conjugation because they don't change. It is the helping verbs that inflect,
and they tend to be irregular.

9.1 SPECIALIZED ANALYTIC VERBS

9.1.1 Analytic verb former נעבן א

נעבן א [gébm] 'give a' designates the action, in conceptual terms, as a single
(and usually brief) event, rather than an ongoing affair. Its present is formed

with the present tense of irregular געבן as helping verb plus indefinite article
אַ plus the stem of the main verb. In the past tense, the participle געגעבן
[gəgébm] usually follows the stem. In the future, the inflected part of
futurizing וועלן must precede the אַ plus stem sequence. The infinitive
usually follows. Many analytic געבן verbs have alternative forms with טאָן
(→ §9.1.9).

9.1.1.1   singular of helping verb געבן 'give'

I give   איך גיב

you (familiar) give   דו גיסט

you (formal) give   איר גיט

he gives   ער גיט

she gives   זי גיט

people give / we give/ one gives   מ'גיט

give! (familiar)   גיב!

give! (formal)   גיט!

9.1.1.2   plural of helping verb געבן 'give'

we give   מיר גיבן

you give   איר גיט

they give   זיי גיבן

give!   גיט!

SAMPLE ANALYTIC VERB WITH געבן: געבן אַ קוש 'give a kiss'

present singular

I am giving a kiss   איך גיב אַ קוש

You (familiar) are giving a kiss   דו גיסט אַ קוש

You (formal) are giving a kiss   איר גיט אַ קוש

He is giving a kiss   ער גיט אַ קוש

She is giving a kiss   זי גיט אַ קוש

One gives a kiss; You should give a kiss   מ'גיט אַ קוש

Give a kiss! (familiar)   גיב אַ קוש!

Give a kiss! (formal)   גיט אַ קוש!

present plural

We are giving a kiss   מיר גיבן אַ קוש

You are giving a kiss   איר גיט אַ קוש

They are giving a kiss   זיי גיבן אַ קוש

Give a kiss!   גיט אַ קוש!

past singular

I gave a kiss   איך האָב אַ קוש געגעבן

You (familiar) gave a kiss   דו האָסט אַ קוש געגעבן

You (formal) gave a kiss   איר האָט אַ קוש געגעבן

He gave a kiss   ער האָט אַ קוש געגעבן

She gave a kiss   זי האָט אַ קוש געגעבן

Everybody kissed; People gave a kiss; We gave a kiss   מ'האָט אַ קוש געגעבן

past plural

We gave a kiss   מיר האָבן אַ קוש געגעבן

You gave a kiss   איר האָט אַ קוש געגעבן

They gave a kiss   זיי האָבן אַ קוש געגעבן

future singular

I will give a kiss [khvel akúzh gebm]   איך וועל אַ קוש געבן

You (familiar) will give a kiss [dust akúzh gebm]   דו וועסט אַ קוש געבן

You (formal) will give a kiss   [irət akúzh gebm] איר וועט אַ קוש געבן

He will give a kiss   [erət akúzh gebm] ער וועט אַ קוש געבן

She will give a kiss   [zit akúzh gebm] זי וועט אַ קוש געבן

We will/People will kiss   [mət akúzh gebm] מ'וועט אַ קוש געבן

future plural

We will give a kiss   [miln / mirn a kúzh gebm] מיר וועלן אַ קוש געבן

You will give a kiss   [irət a kúzh gebm] איר וועט אַ קוש געבן

They will give a kiss   [zeln a kúzh gebm] זיי וועלן אַ קוש געבן

SAMPLE ANALYTIC VERBS WITH געבן

promise (lit. 'give a word')   אַ װאָרט געבן

advise; give (a piece of) advice   [éytsə] אַן עצה געבן

cope; manage   [éytsə] זיך אַן עצה געבן

slap / give a smack   אַ פּאַטש געבן

smile / give a smile   אַ שמייכל געבן

9.1.2   Analytic verb former דאַרפֿן

דאַרפֿן (usually pronounced [dáfn]) 'must; have to; should; ought to' is used with the infinitive of the main verb. The third person singular has no ט-, hence דאַרף 'ס\מ\זי\ער.

SAMPLES OF THE USE OF דאַרפֿן

I have to go   איך דאַרף אַװעק

Why do you have to go?   פֿאַרװאָס דאַרפֿסטו גײן?

What do you need it for? [avós dáfstəs?]   אױף װאָס דאַרפֿסטו עס

I must tell you the truth   [éməs] איך דאַרף דיר זאָגן דעם אמת

We really have to go   מ'דאַרף טאַקע גײן

9.1.3 Analytic verb former האַלטן אין

האַלטן אין 'in the process of; in the middle of; in the midst of' is formed by the appropriate part of האַלטן plus preposition אין plus infinitive. It can be applied to any verb that expresses an ongoing action, and often corresponds with English -*ing*.

SAMPLES OF USE OF האַלטן אין

זי האַלט אין שרײַבן אַ בריוו   She's in the middle of writing a letter

מיר האַלטן איצטער אין עסן   We're eating now

9.1.4 Analytic verb former האַלטן אין אײַן

האַלטן אין אײַן 'keep (on); all the time; constantly' is formed by the appropriate part of האַלטן plus אין אײַן plus infinitive. It can be applied to any verb that expresses an ongoing action.

SAMPLES OF USE OF האַלטן אין אײַן

פֿאַרוואָס האַלטסטו אין אײַן שפרינגען?   Why do you keep jumping?

זיי האַלטן אין אײַן לאַכן   They keep laughing

9.1.5 Analytic verb former וואָלטן

וואָלטן 'would' is formed with either the infinitive or the past participle of the main verb. It is used to express a conditional or contingent mood. The past participle is used most frequently. The infinitive tends to be reserved for a rather more parliamentary style.

SAMPLES OF THE USE OF וואָלטן

וואָס וואָלטסטו [voistú] געזאָגט?   What would *you* (familiar) say?

און דו וואָלטסט [voist] געגאַנגען?   And you (familiar) would go?

איך וואָלט אַנדערש געהאַנדלט   I would deal with it differently

איך װאָלט טענהן [táynən] אַנדערש   I would argue otherwise

מיר װאָלטן װעלן װיסן דעם אמת [éməs]   We would wish to know the truth

9.1.5.1   Alternative conditional with װען

A conditional mood may also be formed by conjunction װען, lit. 'when; if' that also has the sense of 'if it were the case that'. It occurs in this sense in the present tense only, but the present with װען is frequently used to cover situations in the past. װען often serves as the if-clause in a sentence in which װאָלטן occurs in the then-clause (→ §§14.4.5 – 14.4.5.1).

SAMPLES OF THE ALTERNATIVE CONDITIONAL WITH װען

װען איך בין ראָטשילד   If I were Rothschild...

װען איך װײס דעמאָלט װאָלט הײַנט געװען אַנדערש

If I had known then, things would be different today

9.1.6   Analytic verb former װעלן

װעלן 'want to' is used with the infinitive of the main verb. Although the infinitive is identical with װעלן 'will (future tense helping verb)' (→ §7.9), the rest of its conjugation differs markedly. The stem vowel of װעלן 'want to' is [י] in the present, [אַ] in the past and [ע] in the infinitive, hence in the future. While the conjugated parts of װעלן 'will' are phonetically reduced in everyday speech, those of װעלן 'want to' are not. Note the contrasting transcriptions of each in the future tense of the sample provided.

SAMPLE OF USE OF װעלן 'WANT TO': MODEL MAIN VERB גײן 'GO'

present singular

איך װיל גײן   I want to go

דו װילסט גײן   You (familiar) want to go

You (formal) want to go   איר װילט גײן

He wants to go   ער װיל גײן

She wants to go   זי װיל גײן

People want to go / Everyone wants to go   מ'װיל גײן

present plural

We want to go   מיר װילן גײן

You want to go   איר װילט גײן

They want to go   זײ װילן גײן

past singular

I wanted to go   [ikhob gəvólt géyn]   (N.E. var. גײן (נעװעלט   איך האָב געװאָלט גײן

You (familiar) wanted to go   [dust gəvólt géyn]   דו האָסט געװאָלט גײן

You (formal) wanted to go   [irət gəvólt géyn]   איר האָט געװאָלט גײן

He wanted to go   [erət gəvólt géyn]   ער האָט געװאָלט גײן

She wanted to go   [ziət gəvólt géyn]   זי האָט געװאָלט גײן

People/We wanted to go   [mət gəvólt géyn]   מ'האָט געװאָלט גײן

past plural

We wanted to go   [mir hobm gəvólt géyn]   מיר האָבן געװאָלט גײן

You wanted to go   [irət gəvólt géyn]   איר האָט געװאָלט גײן

They wanted to go   [zey hobm gəvólt géyn]   זײ האָבן געװאָלט גײן

future singular

I will want to go   [ikhl véln géyn]   איך װעל װעלן גײן

You (familiar) will want to go   [dust véln géyn]   דו װעסט װעלן גײן

You (formal) will want to go   [irət véln géyn]   איר װעט װעלן גײן

He will want to go   [erət véln géyn]   ער װעט װעלן גײן

She will want to go   [ziət véln géyn] זי חעט וועלן גיין

People will want to go [mət véln géyn] מ'חעט וועלן גיין

future plural

We will want to go   [miln / mirn véln géyn] מיר חעלן וועלן גיין

You will want to go   [irət véln géyn] איר חעט וועלן גיין

They will want to go   [zeln véln géyn] זיי חעלן וועלן גיין

9.1.7   Analytic verb former וערן

וערן 'become; be; get' is used with the past participle of the main verb to form a passive. In the present tense, the appropriately inflected part of וערן 'become' precedes the verb. In the past and future it usually follows it. וערן forms its past with זײַן (→ §7.7). Note that a few deeply rooted וערן constructions coexist in the modern language with corresponding synthetic verbs, e.g. אַנטלויפֿן = אַנטלאָפֿן וערן 'run away; escape'. Passives may also be formed using pronoun 'מ (→ §6.1.6.2). Model verb is אַרײַנגעדרייט וערן 'become entangled / tied up in something; become involved'.

SAMPLE OF USE OF וערן:

אַרײַנגעדרייט וערן 'BECOME INVOLVED'

present singular

I'm becoming involved   איך ווער אַרײַנגעדרייט

You (familiar) are becoming involved   דו ווערסט אַרײַנגעדרייט

You (formal) are becoming involved   איר ווערט אַרײַנגעדרייט

He is becoming involved   ער ווערט אַרײַנגעדרייט

She is becoming involved   זי ווערט אַרײַנגעדרייט

One becomes involved; It's easy to get entangled!   מ'חוערט אַרײַנגעדרייט

Go ahead and become involved! (familiar) *(sarcastic)* חער אַרײַנגעדרײט!

Go ahead and become involved! (formal) *(sarcastic)* חערט אַרײַנגעדרײט!

present plural

We're becoming involved   מיר חערן אַרײַנגעדרײט

You're becoming involved   איר חערט אַרײַנגעדרײט

They're becoming involved   זיי חערן אַרײַנגעדרײט

Go ahead and become involved! *(sarcastic)*   חערט אַרײַנגעדרײט!

past singular

I became involved   איך בין אַרײַנגעדרײט געוואָרן

You (familiar) became involved   דו ביסט אַרײַנגעדרײט געוואָרן

You (formal) became involved   איר זײַט אַרײַנגעדרײט געוואָרן

He became involved   ער איז אַרײַנגעדרײט געוואָרן

She became involved   זי איז אַרײַנגעדרײט געוואָרן

People became involved; We became involved   מ'איז אַרײַנגעדרײט געוואָרן

past plural

We became involved   מיר זײַנען אַרײַנגעדרײט געוואָרן

You became involved   איר זײַט אַרײַנגעדרײט געוואָרן

They became involved   זיי זײַנען אַרײַנגעדרײט געוואָרן

future singular

I will become involved   איך וועל אַרײַנגעדרײט װערן

You (familiar) will become involved   דו וועסט אַרײַנגעדרײט װערן

You (formal) will become involved   איר וועט אַרײַנגעדרײט װערן

He will become involved   ער וועט אַרײַנגעדרײט װערן

She will become involved   זי וועט אַרײַנגעדרײט װערן

(I'm warning you,) we'll become involved   מ'וועט אַרײַנגעדרייט ווערן

future plural

We will become involved	מיר וועלן אַרײַנגעדרייט ווערן
You will become involved	איר וועט אַרײַנגעדרייט ווערן
They will become involved	זיי וועלן אַרײַנגעדרייט ווערן

SAMPLE VERBS WITH ווערן

אַנטשלאָפֿן ווערן   fall asleep

געראַטעוועט ווערן   be rescued; be saved

נמאס [níməs] ווערן   be fed up with (plus reflexive → §14.6)

נתפּעל [nispóəl] ווערן   be impressed; admire

צעמישט ווערן   be / become confused

9.1.6   Analytic verb former זאָלן

זאָלן 'should; would; ought; let (...); may (...)' is used with the infinitive of the main verb. It occurs far more frequently than English 'should' (which itself frequently corresponds with דאַרפֿן → §9.1.2). In numerous contexts זאָל corresponds with English use of the infinitive alone. Frequently, זאָל provides a subjunctive mood. The third person singular has no ט-, hence ער\זי\מ'\ס' זאָל.

SAMPLES OF THE USE OF זאָלן

פֿון וואַנעט זאָל איך וויסן?   How should I know?

וואָס זאָל מען טאָן? [vózl mən tón]   What should we do?

איך האָב אים [khóbm] געזאָגט ער זאָל וואַרטן   I told him to wait

זאָל זײַן אַזוי   Let's have it your way (lit. 'Let it be like this')

זאָלן זיי שרײַען!   Let them yell!

COMMON EXPRESSIONS WITH זאָלן

זאָל זײַן אַזוי

Let's have it your way (lit. 'Let it be like this')

זאָל זײַן מיט מזל! [mazl]

Best of luck to you! (lit. 'It should be with luck!')

זאָל איך אַזוי װיסן פֿון צרות [tsórəs]

I have no idea (lit. 'So I should know of troubles')

מ'זאָל זיך נאָר טרעפֿן אויף שמחות [af símkhəs]

Let us meet only on happy occasions   (said on sad occasions)

9.1.8.1   זאָלן as an alternative imperative

Second person use of זאָלן (lit. 'you should') is frequently used as an alternative to the grammatical imperative (→ §7.5). Imperative use of זאָלן frequently has a softer tone than the grammatical imperative, implying friendly advice rather than a command. Familiar second person pronoun דו is usually omitted and זאָלסט used on its own. When דו is retained the resulting mood is one of scolding or warning (as harsh or harsher than the grammatical imperative).

SAMPLES OF זאָלן AS AN ALTERNATIVE IMPERATIVE

זאָלסט קומען פֿרי!   Come early! (familiar)

דו זאָלסט קומען פֿרי!   (I'm telling you,) come early! (familiar)

זאָלסט ניט גיין!   Don't go! (familiar)

דו זאָלסט ניט גיין!   (I warn you,) don't go!

איר זאָלט זאָגן דעם אמת [émas]   Tell the truth! (formal)

9.1.9   Analytic verb former טאָן אַ

טאָן אַ 'do a' is often interchangeable with געבן אַ (→ §9.1). It too designates the action as a single event, rather than an ongoing affair. Its present is formed with the present tense of irregular טאָן as helping verb plus indefinite article אַ plus stem. In the past, the participle געטאָן [gətón] usually follows the stem. In the future, the inflected part of futurizing וועלן must precede the אַ plus stem sequence, while the infinitive טאָן usually follows. Where both טאָן and געבן are used with the same verb, טאָן tends to have a loftier tone, געבן a more everyday tone. Thus, אַ קוש טאָן alone would be used in אַ קוש טאָן די מזוזה 'kiss the מזוזה [məzúzə] (traditional doorpost amulet) when entering or leaving a room'. אַ קוש טאָן with reference to humans may denote a higher level of love than אַ קוש געבן which denotes only the act of kissing. There is also a grammatical difference. געבן takes dative without a preposition (i.e. the understood preposition → §5.1.3.1); טאָן does not. Cf. e.g. אַ קוש טאָן די שוועסטער vs. אַ קוש געבן דער שוועסטער 'give one's sister a kiss'. There is no difference for masculine nouns, where both accusative and dative have דעם (→ §§ 5.3.2–5.3.3).

9.1.9.1   present singular of helping verb טאָן

I do / am doing	איך טו
you (familiar) do / are doing	דו טוסט
you (formal) do / are doing	איר טוט
he does / is doing	ער טוט
she does / is doing	זי טוט
people do / we do / one does	מ'טוט
Do! (familiar)	טו!
Do! (formal)	טוט!

168

9.1.9.2   present plural of helping verb טאָן

we do / are doing   מיר טוּעֶן

you do / are doing   איר טוּט

they do / are doing   זײ טוּעֶן

Do! טוּט!

SAMPLE OF אַ טאָן: MODEL VERB אַ קוק טאָן

present singular

I'm having a look   איך טו אַ קוק

You (familiar) are having a look   דו טוסט אַ קוק

You (formal) are having a look   איר טוט אַ קוק

He is having a look   עֶר טוט אַ קוק

She is having a look   זי טוט אַ קוק

One has a look; You should have a look   מ'טוט אַ קוק

Have a look (familiar)!   טו אַ קוק!

Have a look (formal)!   טוט אַ קוק!

present plural

We are having a look   מיר טוּעֶן אַ קוק

You are having a look   איר טוט אַ קוק

They are having a look   זײ טוּעֶן אַ קוק

Have a look! טוט אַ קוק!

past singular

I had a look   איך האָב אַ קוק געטאָן

You (familiar) had a look   דו האָסט אַ קוק געטאָן

You (formal) had a look   איר האָט אַ קוק געטאָן

He had a look   עֶר האָט אַ קוק געטאָן

She had a look   זי האָט אַ קוק געטאָן

People had a look; We had a look   מ'האָט אַ קוק געטאָן

past plural

We had a look   מיר האָבן אַ קוק געטאָן

You had a look   איר האָט אַ קוק געטאָן

They had a look   זיי האָבן אַ קוק געטאָן

future singular

I will have a look   [ikhl/khvel akúkton]   איך וועל אַ קוק טאָן

You (familiar) will have a look   [du(ə)st akúkton]   דו וועסט אַ קוק טאָן

You (formal) will have a look   [ir(ə)t akúkton]   איר וועט אַ קוק טאָן

He will have a look   [er(ə)t akúkton]   ער וועט אַ קוק טאָן

She will have a look   [zi(ə)t akúkton]   זי וועט אַ קוק טאָן

We will / People will have a look   [mə(və)t akúkton]   מ'וועט אַ קוק טאָן

future plural

We will have a look   [miln / mirn a kúkton]   מיר וועלן אַ קוק טאָן

You will have a look   [ir(ə)t a kúkton]   איר וועט אַ קוק טאָן

They will have a look   [ze(y)ln a kúkton]   זיי וועלן אַ קוק טאָן

SAMPLE ANALYTIC VERBS WITH טאָן

say (quickly)   אַ זאָג טאָן

think over; have a think   אַ טראַכט טאָן

give a laugh   אַ לאַך טאָן

ask   [a frékton]   אַ פֿרעג טאָן

give a scratch   אַ קראַץ טאָן

give a jump   אַ שפּרונג טאָן

9.1.10   Analytic verb former לאָזן

לאָזן 'allow; let' is used with the infinitive of the main verb. In inverted word order (→ §§11.2, 14.4), the ס of suffix -סט(ו) is frequently omitted, giving לאָזטו. Imperative לאָז followed by objective pronoun מיך obligatorily conflates to לאָמיך, e.g. לאָמיך צורו 'Leave me alone'.

SAMPLES OF USE OF לאָזן

Let me know (familiar)	לאָז וויסן
Let me know (formal)	לאָזט וויסן
Why don't you (familiar) let them come?	פֿאַרוואָס לאָזטו זיי ניט קומען?
Leave me alone / Stop harassing me (familiar)	לאָז אָפּ!
Leave me alone / Stop harassing me (formal)	לאָזט אָפּ!

9.1.11   Analytic verb former לאָמיר

לאָמיר 'let's; let us' is used with the infinitive of the main verb. It is exclusively a first person plural. Note, however, that growing usage has לאָמיר instead of לאָמיך (→ §9.1.10), e.g. לאָמיר צורו 'Leave me alone'.

SAMPLES OF USE OF לאָמיר

Come on, let's go (lit. 'Let's go already')	לאָמיר שוין גיין
Let's answer	לאָמיר ענטפֿערן
Let's not answer	לאָמיר ניט ענטפֿערן

9.1.12   Analytic verb former מוזן

מוזן 'must; be compelled to' is used with the infinitive of the main verb. It is often interchangeable with דאַרפֿן (→ §9.1.2) but can denote a stronger sense of necessity. The third person singular has no ט-, hence מוז 'ס\מ\זי\ער.

SAMPLES OF THE USE OF מוזן

I really have to go	איך מוז טאַקע גיין

מיר מוזן היַינט האָבן אַן ענטפֿער We need to have an answer today

9.1.13   Analytic verb former מעגן

מעגן 'may' is used with the infinitive of the main verb. It denotes that permission or moral authority is invoked for the action, rather than mere physical ability (cf. קענען → 9.1.16). Anomalously, the negative of מעגן is the inflected part of טאָרן, always used with ניט, giving טאָר ניט 'may not'. The third person singular of both has no ט-, hence ער\זי\מ'\ס' מעג and ער\זי\מ'\ס' טאָר ניט.

SAMPLES OF THE USE OF מעגן AND טאָר ניט

Are we allowed to use the garden?   צי מעג מען נוצן דעם גאָרטן?

It's not allowed on weekends   [sóv vókh] טאָר מען ניט סוף≠וואָך

Is touching allowed?   [óntapm] מעג מען? אָנטאַפן

9.1.14   Analytic verb former נעמען

נעמען 'take to' is used with the infinitive of the main verb. It has the sense of 'about to start; just starting; get down to doing something'. The past participle of נעמען is גענומען. Where the infinitive functions as a noun (→ §4.1.3.3), or a true noun is the thing that is about to be started, the parallel construction נעמען זיך צו is used. It is followed by the definite article (appropriately in dative following צו) plus the noun.

SAMPLES OF THE USE OF נעמען AND נעמען זיך צו

I'm about to begin studying music   איך נעם שטודירן מוזיק

We prepared to escape   מיר האָבן גענומען אַנטלױפֿן

I'm getting down to work   איך נעם זיך צו דער אַרבעט

Let's get down to the homework   לאָמיר זיך נעמען צו דער היימאַרבעט

172

9.1.15 Analytic verb former פֿלעגן

פֿלעגן 'used to' is used with the infinitive of the main verb to express the habitual past.

SAMPLES OF THE USE OF פֿלעגן

I used to live over there   איך פֿלעג דאָרטן וואוינען

We used to see each other often   מיר פֿלעגן זיך זען אָפֿט

It used to be different   [sflegd zayn ándərsh] ס'פֿלעגט זײַן אַנדערש

9.1.16 Analytic verb former קענען

קענען (var. קאָנען) 'can' is used with the infinitive of the main verb. The third person singular has no ט-, hence ער\זי\מ'\ס' קען. The conjugation of analytic verb former קענען is identical to that of קענען 'know' (→ §15.4).

SAMPLES OF THE USE OF קענען

Can you do me a favour?   [tóyvə?] קענסט מיר טאָן אַ טובֿה?

You never can tell   [məkénit vísn] מ'קען ניט וויסן

I can't make it today   הײַנט קען איך ניט קומען

9.2   INHERENTLY ANALYTIC VERBS

9.2.1   The inherently analytic verb with האָבן

In the present, the appropriate part of האָבן [hóbm] 'have' (→ §§7.6.1.1 – 7.6.1.2) must precede the main verb. In the past, the inflected part of האָבן also precedes the main verb but the past participle געהאַט may precede or follow the main verb; it usually follows. Analogously, in the future, the inflected futurizing וועלן ($\rightarrow$ §§7.91 – 7.9.2) must precede the main verb but infinitive האָבן may precede or follow the main verb; it usually follows. Note that one of the inherently analytic verbs with האָבן, פֿאַראיבל האָבן [faríbl hobm] 'be offended; take something the wrong way' is the source of נישט פֿאַראיבל קיין האָט איך! 'I beg your pardon (formal)'. Model verb is חרטה האָבן [kharótə hobm] 'change one's mind' (lit. 'have regret / remorse').

SAMPLE ANALYTIC VERB WITH האָבן:
חרטה האָבן 'CHANGE ONE'S MIND'

present singular

I'm changing (/I've changed) my mind   איך האָב חרטה

You're changing (/You've changed) your mind   דו האָסט חרטה

You're changing (/You've changed) your mind (formal)   איר האָט חרטה

He's changing (/He has changed) his mind   ער האָט חרטה

She's changing (/She has changed) her mind   זי האָט חרטה

People are changing (have changed) their minds   מ'האָט חרטה

Change your mind! (familiar)   האָב חרטה!

Change your mind! (plural)   האָט חרטה!

present plural

We're changing (/We have changed) our minds   מיר האָבן חרטה

You're changing (/You've changed) your minds   איר האָט חרטה

They're changing (/They have changed) their minds   זיי האָבן חרטה

Change your mind!   האָט חרטה!

past singular

I changed my mind   איך האָב חרטה געהאַט

You (informal) changed your mind   דו האָסט חרטה געהאַט

You (formal) changed your mind   איר האָט חרטה געהאַט

He changed his mind   ער האָט חרטה געהאַט

She changed her mind   זי האָט חרטה געהאַט

People changed their minds   מ׳האָט חרטה געהאַט

past plural

We changed our minds   מיר האָבן חרטה געהאַט

You've changed your minds   איר האָט חרטה געהאַט

They've changed their minds   זיי האָבן חרטה געהאַט

future singular

I'll change my mind   איך וועל חרטה האָבן

You (informal) will change your mind   דו וועסט חרטה האָבן

You (formal) will change your mind   איר וועט חרטה האָבן

He will change his mind   ער וועט חרטה האָבן

She will change her mind   זי וועט חרטה האָבן

People will change their minds   מ׳וועט חרטה האָבן

future plural

We will change our minds   מיר וועלן חרטה האָבן

You will change your minds   איר וועט חרטה האָבן

They will change their minds   זיי וועלן חרטה האָבן

SAMPLES OF INHERENTLY ANALYTIC VERBS WITH האָבן

have pleasure   [hanóə hobm] הנאה האָבן

be eager; be in the mood   [khéyshək hobm] חשק האָבן

get married   [khásənə hobm] חתונה האָבן

love, like strongly   ליב האָבן   (var. האַלט האָבן)

be afraid; fear (with פֿאַר)   [móyrə hobm] מורא האָבן

hate   פֿײַנט האָבן

9.2.2   The inherently analytic verb with זײַן

The analytic verb with זײַן 'be' produces hundreds of verbs. Many are restricted to a traditional learned style, but quite a few have widespread use. In the present tense, the appropriate part of זײַן (→ §§7.7.1 – 7.7.2) must precede the main verb. In the future, װעלן precedes the main verb and infinitive זײַן follows. In the past, the analytic verb with זײַן, alone in the standard language, uses a mixed conjugation comprising the inflected part of האָבן plus the past participle of זײַן געװען [gəvén]), giving the characteristic 'האָט געװען' conjugation of analytic verbs with זײַן. Model verb is מסכים זײַן [máskəm zayn / máskim zayn] 'agree'.

SAMPLE ANALYTIC VERB WITH זײַן: מסכים זײַן 'AGREE'

present singular

I agree   איך בין מסכים

You (familiar) agree   דו ביסט מסכים

You (formal) agree   איר זײַט מסכים

He agrees   ער איז מסכים

She agrees   זי איז מסכים

Everybody agrees / We agree   מ'איז מסכים

Agree! (familiar)   זײַ מסכים!

Agree! (formal)   זײַט מסכים!

present plural

We agree   מיר זײַנען מסכים

You agree   איר זײַט מסכים

They agree   זײ זײַנען מסכים

Agree!   זײַט מסכים!

past singular

I agreed   איך האָב מסכים געווען

You (familiar) agreed   דו האָסט מסכים געווען

You (formal) agreed   איר האָט מסכים געווען

He agreed   ער האָט מסכים געווען

She agreed   זי האָט מסכים געווען

Everybody agreed / It was agreed   מ'האָט מסכים געווען

past plural

We agreed   מיר האָבן מסכים געווען

You agreed   איר האָט מסכים געווען

They agreed   זײ האָבן מסכים געווען

future singular

I will agree   איך וועל מסכים זײַן

You (familiar) will agree   דו וועסט מסכים זײַן

You (formal) will agree   איר וועט מסכים זײַן

He will agree   ער וועט מסכים זײַן

She will agree   זי וועט מסכים זײַן

Everybody will agree / We will agree   מ'וועט מסכים זײַן

future plural

We will agree   מיר וועלן מסכים זײַן

You will agree   איר וועט מסכים זײַן

They will agree זײ וועלן מסכים זײַן

SAMPLES OF ANALYTIC VERBS WITH זײַן (PAST TENSE WITH הָאבן)

suspect [khóyshəd zayn] חושד זײַן

distinguish; differentiate [máfkhn zayn] מבחין זײַן

concede (a point); confess [móydə zayn] מודה זײַן

trouble somebody for a favour [mátriəkh zayn] מטריח זײַן

take the trouble to do somebody a favour מטריח זײַן זיך (זיך)

offer hospitality [= food/drinks]; treat [to] [məkhábəd zayn] מכבד זײַן

continue [mámshəkh zayn] ממשיך זײַן

agree [máskim zayn] מסכים זײַן

succeed [mátsliəkh zayn] מצליח זײַן

receive / welcome [guest] [məkabl pónim zayn] מקבל פנים זײַן

presume / assume [məsháər zayn] משער זײַן (זיך)

sacrifice; give up [mákriv zayn] מקריב זײַן

9.2.2.1 Passives of the analytic verb with זײַן

A few analytic verbs with זײַן have passives using וערן (→ §9.1.7).

SAMPLES OF ANALYTIC VERBS WITH זײַן WITH PASSIVES

מציל זײַן [mátsl] 'rescue' → ניצול וערן [nítsl vern] 'be rescued'

מקיים זײַן [məkáyəm] 'fulfil' → מקוים וערן [məkúyəm vern] 'be fulfilled'

10 ADVERBS

10.0 OVERVIEW

Adverbs modify, specify or elaborate on verbs or the state and time in which the verb action occurs. Where they occur in the middle of a phrase, adverbs follow the inflected verb. Thus, adverb אפשר [éfshər] 'perhaps' follows the part of קומען 'come' inflected for third person singular in ער קומט אפשר 'He may come'. Adverbs usually precede uninflected verbs (i.e., infinitive and past participle), hence ער וועט אפשר קומען. There are however occasions where the adverb may follow the uninflected verb for emphasis (→ §14.10), e.g. ער וועט קומען אפשר. Adverbs may generally be used to begin a sentence. There are four major types of adverbs: true adverbs (§10.1); adverbs from adjectives and nouns (§10.2); relic adverbs(§10.3); adverbs from prepositional phrases (§10.4). Some adverbs have diminutives (§10.5). Psychoadverbial inserts are phrases inserted into a sentence that serve to betray the speaker's true emotional disposition toward the object of speech or writing (§10.6).

10.1 TRUE ADVERBS

True adverbs are not derived from any other part of speech. They have no comparative or superlative.

SAMPLES OF TRUE ADVERBS

now איצטער (var. איצט, אצינד, איצטערט; nonliterary var. יעצט}

once; someday   [amól] אַמאָל

maybe   [éfshər] אפֿשר

soon; soon after   באַלד

(deliberately) illogically; necessarily; exclusively   [dáfkə] דווקא

then   דעמאָלט (var. דאַמאָלס(ט), דענסטמאָל, דאַן, יעמאָלט)

really; in point of fact   טאַקע

really; in full; no kidding   [máməsh] ממש

suddenly   פּלוצלונג (var. פּלוצלינג, פּלוצעם)

early   פֿרי

earlier   פֿריער

barely; just   [kam] קוים

already   שוין

late   שפּעט

later   שפּעטער

10.2   ADVERBS FROM ADJECTIVES AND NOUNS

New adverbs arise continually from adjectives and nouns by way of the
following productive mechanisms.

10.2.1   Adverbs from adjective stems

Most adjective stems can double as adverbs. Unlike true adverbs, they may
attract comparative suffix -ער just as adjectives do (→ §5.10).

SAMPLES OF ADVERBS FROM ADJECTIVE STEMS

preferably   בעסער

well   גוט (better: בעסער; better still: נאָך בעסער)

quickly   גיך   (more quickly: גיכער)

slowly   פּאַמעלעך   (more slowly: פּאַמעלעכער)

calmly   רואיק [rúik]   (more calmly: רואיקער)

quietly   שטיל   (more quietly: שטילער)

badly   שלעכט   (worse: ערגער)

10.2.2   Adverbs from adjective stem plus ‑ערהייט

Adjectives may be adverbialized by suffixation of ‑ערהייט [ərhéyt] to the adjective stem.   Most frequently, the ‑ערהייט adverbs denote a general state of being rather than modifying a verb as directly as true adverbs (→ §10.1) and adverbs from adjective stems (→ §10.2.1).   געזונטערהייט [gəzuntərhéyt] 'in good health' is used with imperatives in the idiomatic sense of 'Enjoy (...)!', e.g. עס געזונטערהייט! 'Eat in good health' (= 'Bon appétit' or 'No need to feel bashful').   געזונטערהייט is also used ironically in the sense of 'Go ahead and (...) (but don't blame me)!', e.g. גיי געזונטערהייט! 'Well if you want to go, then go, but don't blame me!'.   ‑ערהייט may also be suffixed to present participles of verbs (→ §7.2), e.g. גייענדיק 'while going' → גייענדיקערהייט [gèyəndikərhéyt], שטייענדיק 'while standing' → שטייענדיקערהייט [shtèyəndikərhéyt].   The ‑ערהייט forms are more forceful.

SAMPLES OF ADVERBS WITH SUFFIX ‑ערהייט

angrily; while in an angry mood   [òngəbroygəstərhéyt]   אָנגעברויגזטערהייט

carefully; cautiously   [òpgəhitərhéyt]   אָפּגעהיטערהייט

while / when young   [yùngərhéyt]   יונגערהייט

while / when wet   [nàsərhéyt]   נאַסערהייט

without having been invited   [nìtfarbetnərhéyt]   ניט‑פֿאַרבעטנערהייט

while / when ill   [krànkərhéyt]   קראַנקערהייט

quietly   [shtìlərhéyt]   שטילערהייט

10.2.3   Adverbs from nouns by suffixation of ‑װײז

Nouns may be adverbialized by suffixation of ‑װײז. It is often the plural of the noun that serves as the base of the adverb. Frequently, the ‑װײז adverbs are partitive, denoting a delimitation of period of time, or a conceptual division into subparts.

SAMPLES OF ADVERBS FROM NOUNS WITH SUFFIX ‑װײז

one by one; one at a time   [éyntsigvayz] אײנציקװײז

before marriage (m.)   [bókhərvayz] בחורװײז

slowly   [bíslaghvayz] ביסלעכװײז

youthfully (m.); as a boy   ייִנגלװײז

in great numbers; in droves; massively   מאַסנװײז

before marriage (f.); youthfully (f.); as a girl   מײדלװײז

in pairs; by the couple; two by two   פּאָרלעכװײז

at times   צײטנװײז

10.3   RELIC ADVERBS

Relic adverbs are not 'relic' because of numerical scarcity. On the contrary, they are amply represented. The classification denotes rather that the relevant prefixes and suffixes are, generally speaking, no longer productive in the modern language. They cannot be used at will to create new adverbs.

10.3.1   Prefix ‑אַ

In addition to its function as a relic adverbial prefix used with a number of common adverbs, prefix אַ‑ is used systematically for telling time, e.g. — אײנס אַזײגער 'one o'clock', צװײ אַזײגער 'two o'clock' etc. (→ §13.2.2).

SAMPLES OF RELIC ADVERBS WITH PREFIX -אַ

certainly; of course   [avádə] אַוודאי

like this; so אַזוי

in short   [aklál] אַכלל   (cf. כלל (דער) 'rule; generalization')

apparently   [apónim] אַפּנים   (cf. פנים (דאָס) 'face')

all the more obvious   [apshítə] אַפּשיטא

beforehand   [afríər] אַ)פֿריער)

in short; to sum up; to get right to the point   [akítsər] אַקיצור

for example   אַשטײגער (cf. שטײגער (דער) 'manner; kind of')

10.3.2   Prefix -אַמ

Prefix -אַמ plus superlative adjective plus suffix -ן forms an adverbial superlative. Alternatively, these may be formed via preposition צו ($\rightarrow$ §10.4.1).

SAMPLES OF ADVERBS WITH PREFIX -אַמ

most preferably; at (his/her/its) best   אַמבעסטן

most undesirably; at (his/her/its) worst   אַמערגסטן

most beautifully; at (his/her/its) most beautiful   אַמשענסטן

10.3.3   Prefix -דער

-דער (often pronounced [da]) combines with a number of prepositions to form an adverb. Prefix -דער is unstressed. The preposition is stressed. A number of the -דער plus preposition adverbs have parallel forms comprising the preposition plus the dative article דעם, which *is* stressed, e.g. דערנאָך [danókh /dernókh] 'afterwards' = נאָך דעם [noghdém]. There are, however, instances where the meanings of the two constructions do not converge, e.g. דערפֿאַר [dafár/derfár] therefore vs. פֿאַר דעם [far dém] 'before that'.

SAMPLES OF ADVERBS WITH PREFIX דער-

present; nearby; [dabáy/derbáy] דערבײַ

in the vicinity [dálebm/derlébm] דערלעבן

afterwards [danókh/dernokh] דערנאָך (= [noghdém] נאָך דעם)

therefore [dafár/derfár] דערפֿאַר

of it; from this; therefrom; hereof [dafún/derfún] דערפֿון (= פֿון דעם)

in addition; moreover; on top of everything else [datsú/dertsú] דערצו

on the other hand; against it [dakégn/derkégn] דערקעגן (= קעגן דעם)

10.3.4 Prefix -ב

-ב [bə] occurs naturally only within the Semitic component.

SAMPLES OF ADVERBS WITH PREFIX ב-

somewhat drunk [bəgilúfn] בגילופֿין

retrospectively; after the fact; it now being too late [bədiévəd] בדיעבֿד

(if you) forgive me for saying so [bəm(ə)khílə] במחילה

anyway; in any case [bəméylə] במילא

explicitly; specially [bəféyrəsh] בפֿירוש

publicly; openly [bəfrésyə] בפֿרהסיא

10.3.5 Prefix -כ

Like -ב, -כ [kə] occurs naturally only within the Semitic component. Most words with prefix -כ are used in a learned style.

SAMPLES OF ADVERBS WITH PREFIX כ-

as agreed [kfihamdúbər] כפֿי־המדובר

extremely difficult   [kəkrìəs yám suf] **כקריעת ים-סוף**

(lit. 'like the parting of the Red Sea')

understood literally   [kəpshútoy] **כפשוטו**

according to plan; in good order   [kəshúrə] **כשורה**

10.3.6 Prefix -ל

Like -ב, and כ, -ל [lə] occurs naturally only within the Semitic component.

SAMPLES OF ADVERBS WITH PREFIX -ל

after the fact; too late   [l(ə)akhəramáysə] **לאחר-המעשה**

at first; in the first instance; initially   [ləkhatkhílə] **לכתחילה**

for example   [ləmóshl] **למשל**

at the present time   [ləsátə] **לעת-עתה**

10.3.7 Suffix ס-

The only systematic use of adverbial suffix ס- is in the numeric adverbs ערשטנס 'firstly', צווייטנס 'secondly' etc. (→ §12.2.2). The remaining surviving items generally have to do with time, space or direction. In some, suffix ס- is optional.

SAMPLES OF ADVERBS WITH SUFFIX ס-

Friday evening (eve of Sabbath) [fráytik tsə nákht(s)] **פֿרײַטיק-צו-נאַכט(ס)**

Saturday night [shàbəs tsu nákht(s)] **שבת-צו-נאַכט(ס)**

Saturday night (var.) [sh(a)béysə nakht(s)] **שבת נאַכט(ס)** (→ §13.3.2.1)

the next day; on the morrow **צומאָרגנס**

on the way [ahínveks] **אַהינוועגס**

on the way; en route [untərvégnz] **אונטערוועגנס**

at least **ווייניקסטנס**

מערסטנס mostly

פֿונדערווײַטנס [fundərváytnz] from far; looking at a distance

צוריקוועגס [tsuríkvegz] on the way back; while returning

לינקס (to the) left

רעכטס (to the) right

10.3.8 Suffix ‎ן‎-

SAMPLES OF ADVERBS WITH SUFFIX ‎ן‎-

אין גיכן‎ (also spelled ‎אינגיכן‎) in the near future

אינדערוואָכן during the week (days)

פֿאַראַכטאָגן last week (cf. ‎איבעראַכטאָג‎ 'next week')

פֿאַראַיאָרן last year (cf. ‎איבעראַיאָר‎ 'next year')

אין גאַנצן‎ (also spelled ‎אינגאַנצן‎) totally; altogether

אויף אַן אמת [afanémas] = ‎אין דער אמתן‎ [indərémasn] truthfully

פֿונדעסטוועגן [fundéstvegn] nevertheless

10.4   ADVERBS FROM PREPOSITIONAL PHRASES

A prepositional phrase is a preposition plus the noun phrase that is its object. At a higher level than the sum of its parts, a prepositional phrase can function as an adverb in the syntax of the language (→ §14.4.1). Some modern adverbs derive historically from prepositional phrases (e.g. from the classical Hebrew prefixed prepositions ‎ב-‎, ‎כ-‎ and ‎ל-‎ → §§10.3.4 – 10.3.6; from prepositional phrases with relic suffix ‎ן-‎ → §10.3.8). Many others derive from modern prepositions that double as adverb formers. Prepositional phrases tend to become fully adverbialized when they acquire 'stock phrase' status by regular use.

SAMPLES OF ADVERBS FROM PREPOSITIONAL PHRASES

to be spiteful; as a provocation [aftselókhəs] אויף צו להכעיס

to a certain extent אין אַ געוויסער מאָס

at home אין דער היים

after that [nogh dém] נאָך דעם (also spelled נאָכדעם)

before that פֿאַר דעם

on one hand פֿון איין זײַט

on the other hand פֿון דער אַנדערער זײַט

from nearby פֿון דער נאָענט

after all נאָך אַלעמען

10.4.1 Superlative adverbs from preposition צו

Preposition צו plus definite article דעם (conflating obligatorily to צום) plus adjective with superlative ending -סט plus suffix -ן forms an adverbial superlative.   Some adverbial superlatives with צו have alternate forms with the far less frequent -אַם ($\rightarrow$ §10.3.2).

SAMPLES OF ADVERBIAL SUPERLATIVES WITH צום

first of all צום אַלעם ערשטן

most easily צום גרינגסטן

at least צום ווינציקסטן \ ווייניקסטן

most difficult of all צום שווערסטן

at the very latest צום שפּעטסטן

10.4.2 'For the sake of' constructions from preposition פֿון

Preposition פֿון plus possessive pronoun or proper name plus וועגן

corresponds with 'for the sake / benefit of; as far as ___ is concerned'. Where a possessive pronoun is used, it is suffixed by -ט (optionally -עט for some). Proper names and other human nouns have possessive -ס.

singular

for my sake פֿון מײַנ(ע)ט װעגן

for your (familiar) sake פֿון דײַנ(ע)ט װעגן

for your (formal) sake פֿון אײַערט װעגן

for his sake פֿון זײַנ(ע)ט װעגן

for her sake פֿון איר(ע)ט װעגן

plural

for our sake פֿון אונדזערט װעגן

for your sake פֿון אײַערט װעגן

for their sake פֿון זײערט װעגן

SAMPLES OF THE USE OF פֿון — װעגן

זײַ אַזוי גוט, טו עס פֿון מײַנט װעגן

Please, do it for my sake

פֿון מײַנט װעגן קענסטו גײן אַפֿילו [afíle] הײַנט

As far as I'm concerned, you can even go today

לאָמיר בלײַבן [bláybm] פֿון לייזערס װעגן

Let's stay for Léyzər's sake

10.5   DIMINUTIVES OF ADVERBS

Monosyllabic adverbs may be diminutivized by suffixing -לעך ([ləkh] or [lakh]) to the adverb stem. There are no internal vowel shifts. The diminutivized adverb is pronounced slowly in falsetto. It is often accompanied by side-to-side movement of the head, horizontal movement of the hands and fingers up to 180°, and a slight smile. Cf. §5.13.1 on diminutives of adjectives.

SAMPLES OF DIMINUTIVES OF ADVERBS

גיכלעך 'quite fast (but not at top speed!)' (from גיך 'fast')

פֿרילעך 'sort of early (but not too early!)' (from פֿרי 'early')

קלוגלעך 'quite cleverly (but not exactly brilliantly!)' (from קלוג 'clever')

שיינלעך 'quite prettily (but not exactly beautifully!)' (from שיין 'beautiful')

שפּעטלעך 'sort of late (but not too late!)' (from שפּעט 'late')

10.6 PSYCHOADVERBIAL INSERTS

Psychoadverbial inserts are parenthetic interpolations in a sentence. They are uttered rapidly with clipped intonation (i.e. surrounded by split-second pauses, marked here by |). They serve to betray to the listener the speaker's attitude toward whatever it is he or she is speaking about. Virtually all can be used as self-contained sentences (i.e. interjections) in reply to a situation described by the interlocutor. Many psychoadverbial inserts may be used ironically. The following list represents a modest sampling.

10.6.1 אין אַ מזלדיקער שעה [inamázldikərshó]

gloss:	with my best wishes; all being well (lit. 'in a lucky hour')
attitude:	friendly hope for a positive outcome
sample:	מיר וועלן רעדן וועגן דעם ווען דו וועסט אין אַ

מזלדיקער שעה אָנקומען

transcription: [miln/mirn rédn vegn dem az du vest |inamázldikərshó|
ónkumən]

translation: We'll talk about it when you (all being well!) arrive. *or:*
We'll talk about it when you return. Have a good
journey back!

10.6.1.1 Use of אין אַ מזלדיקער שעה as reply

use as reply: — איך פאָר דינסטיק   I'm leaving on Tuesday.

אין אַ מזלדיקער שעה!   Every success!; Bon voyage!

10.6.1.2 Ironic use of אין אַ מזלדיקער שעה

ironic use: hope for positive outcome of a perceived stupidity

sample: דו ווילסט אין אַ מזלדיקער שעה אַראָפשפּרינגען פֿון
דאַך?

transcription: [du vilst |inamázldikərshó| arópshpringən fun dákh?]

translation: Do you want to jump off the roof? Well, have
fun!

10.6.1.3 Ironic use of אין אַ מזלדיקער שעה as reply

use as reply: — איך שפּרינג אַראָפּ פֿון דאַך   I'm jumping off the
roof.

אין אַ מזלדיקער שעה!   Well, go ahead! Don't come
crying to me!

10.6.2 אם ירצה השם [mírtsəshèm / mìrtsəshém]

gloss: hopefully (lit. 'if God wills it; God willing')

attitude:	looking forward to something
sample:	אִיך װעל קומען אם ירצה השם מאָרגן
transcription:	[khvel kúmən |mìrtsəshém| mórgn]
translation:	I look forward to coming tomorrow.

10.6.2.1 Use of אם ירצה השם as reply

use as reply:	קומסט דאָנערשטיק? You're coming on Thursday?
	אם ירצה השמו I certainly hope so; Yes, of course!

10.6.3 במחילה [bim(ə)khhílə]

gloss:	asking you to forgive me (for saying something potentially offensive, embarrassing, vulgar or unkind).
attitude:	aggressive state of mind toward interlocutor
sample:	דײַנע קליידער זעען אויס במחילה אַ ביסל לעכערלעך
transcription:	[daynə kléydər zeən óys |bəmekhílə| a bisl lekherləkh]
translation:	Your clothes, if you forgive me for saying so, do look a bit ridiculous.

10.6.3.1 Ironic use of במחילה

ironic use:	mitigating an insult by apologizing for it in the same sentence
sample:	דו ביסט במחילה אַן אידיאָט
transcription:	[du bist |bəmekhílə| anidyót]
translation:	Do forgive me for saying so, but you are an idiot.

10.6.4 גאָט צו דאַנקען [gotsədánkən]

gloss:	thank God

attitude: happiness at the way something has turned out

sample: איך בין שוין גאָט־צו־דאַנקען אַדורך דעם עקזאַמען

transcription: [khbin shoyn |gotsədánkən| adúrkh dem ekzámən]

translation: Thank God, I've passed the examination *or* I'm thrilled
that I passed the examination

10.6.4.1 Use of גאָט צו דאַנקען as reply

use as reply: — ס'איז געוחען אַ דערפאָלג   It was a success.

גאָט צו דאַנקען! [gót tsə dánkən] Thank God!

10.6.5 חלילא [kholílə]

gloss: Heaven forfend; God forbid

attitude: fear of worst scenario

sample: קענסט חלילא אַראָפפאַלן

transcription: [kénst |kholílə| arópfaln]

translation: You may (God forbid) fall down.

10.6.5.1 Use of חלילא as reply

use as reply: ביסט אויף [af] מיר אין כעס? [ka(ə)s]   Are you
angry with me?

חלילא!   Of course not!; God forbid!

10.6.5.2 Ironic use 1 of חלילא

ironic use 1:   'fear' that something will turn out well

sample: קום ניט, קענסט חלילא גוט פאַרברענגען

transcription: [kúm nit, kénst |kholílə| gut farbréyngən]

translation: Don't come, you might (God forbid) have a good time.

192

10.6.5.3 Ironic use 1 of חלילא as reply

use as reply: עֶר וויל ניט פָֿארן אויף וואַקאַציעֿ?   He doesn't want
to go on vacation?

חלילא!   No way!; God forbid!; How stupid of him!

10.6.5.4 Ironic use 2 of חלילא

ironic use 2:   satiric denial of something obviously correct

sample: איך הָאבּ געזָאגט אַז עֶר איז חלילא אַ ליגנער?

transcrpition: [ikho gəzókt az er iz |kholílə| a lígnər?]

translation: I said that he is (God forbid) a liar.

10.6.5.5 Ironic use 2 of חלילא as reply

use as reply: זֵיי געפֿעלן דיר ניט, אמת?   You don't like them,
right?

חלילא!   God forbid. When did I say that?

10.6.6 להבדיל [ləhávdl]

gloss: though one shouldn't mention them in the same breath
(lit. 'to differentiate [between sacred and profane]', i.e.
'not to say I don't differentiate although I mention them
together')

attitude: contempt for one of the two things or persons
mentioned

sample: דֵיין פֿרֵיינד און להבדיל זֵיין ברודער וועלן זֵיין דָארטן

transcription: [dayn fraynt un |ləhávdl| zayn brudər vein zayn dórtn]

translation: Your friend and his brother (whom I can't stand) will be
there.

10.6.6.1 Use of להַבֿדיל as reply

use as reply: דײַן פֿרײַנד און זײַן ברודער װעלן זײַן דאָרטן?

Will your friend and his brother be there?

להַבֿדיל!

Please don't mention them in the same breath.

10.6.7 נעבעך [nébakh]

gloss: sadly; pitifully; alas.

attitude: genuine sorrow for an unfortunate person

sample: דער זײדע איז נעבעך קראַנק

transcription: [der zéydə iz |nébakh| kránk]

translation: Grandfather is sadly ill.

10.6.7.1 Use of נעבעך as reply

use as reply: — דער זײדע איז קראַנק געװאָרן   Grandfather has become ill.

נעבעך   How very sad.

10.6.7.2 Ironic use of נעבעך

ironic use: feigned sympathy for somebody who is in fact very well off; pointing out caustically that too much is being made of a trifle

sample: ער האָט נעבעך קײן געלט ניט

transcription: [erót |nébakh| kin gélt nit]

translation: (e.g. of a millionaire): He has no money! How very sad!

10.6.7.3 Ironic use of נעבעך as reply

use as reply: — איך האָב פֿאַרלוירן מײַן פֿען   I've lost my pen.

נעבעך! [néebaakh *(with extra lengthening)*] Big tragedy! How awful!

10.6.8 טעלאדעג טינ םעניק ראַפֿ [farkéynəmni(t)gədákht]

gloss: it shouldn't happen to anybody

attitude: sorrow or shock over a calamity

sample: מ'האָט אים פֿאַר קײנעם ניט געדאַלט איבערגעפֿאָרן

transcription: [məhòtəm |farkéynəmnigədákht| íbərgəforn]

translation: He was (it shouldn't happen to anybody) run over.

10.6.8.1 **Use of** טעלאדעג טינ םעניק ראַפֿ **as reply**

use as reply: — די זײַנען זײער קראַנק They are very ill

פֿאַר קײנעם ניט געדאַלט! How dreadful!; Oh my God!

10.6.9 עין∗הרע קײן [kinaynhórə / kinəhórə]

gloss: no evil eye!; not to provoke the attention of 'the evil eye' by praising the good news too much (cf. 'knock on wood!')

attitude: gratification or pride concerning good news or an achievement

sample: די טאָכטער האָט קײן עין∗הרע חתונה געהאַט

transcription: [di tókhtər hot |kinaynhórə| khásənə gəhat]

translation: My daughter got married. I'm thrilled.

10.6.9.1 **Use of** קײן עין∗הרע **as reply**

use as reply: —די טאָלטער האָט חתונה געהאַט

קײן עין∗הרע! [kìn àyn hórə] Fantastic!

11 QUESTIONS

11.0 OVERVIEW

Questions can be formed from declarative sentences by change in intonation alone (§11.1). Explicitly structured questions are formed by inversion of subject and predicate (§11.2) or by combining inversion with an interrogative word (§11.3). Interrogative additives serve to add emotional force to questions (§11.4).

11.1 INTONATION

Declarative sentences may be turned into questions by the characteristic rising intonation at the end, marked in written usage by a question mark (?).

SAMPLES OF QUESTIONS VIA INTONATION ALONE

You're coming tomorrow	דו קומסט מאָרגן ←
Are you coming tomorrow?	?דו קומסט מאָרגן

They really know	זיי װײסן טאַקע ←
Do they really know?	?זיי װײסן טאַקע

It's true [émǝs]	ס׳איז אמת ←
Is it true?	?ס׳איז אמת

11.1.1 Sarcastic intonation questions

When a declarative sentence righteously purporting to state a mere fact is 'overquestionized' by invoking a rise-fall intonation pattern, it becomes a harshly satiric attack.

SAMPLES OF SARCASTIC INTONATION QUESTIONS

He's a doctor   ער איז אַ דאָקטער ←

You call him a doctor!?   ?ער איז אַ דאָקטער!

It's summer in Oxford   ס'איז זומער אין אָקספֿאָרד ←

You call this summer in Oxford?   ?ס'איז זומער אין אָקספֿאָרד

We're experts   מיר זײַנען עקספּערטן ←

You think we're experts?   ?מיר זײַנען עקספּערטן

11.1.1.1   Use of דען in sarcastic intonation questions

The use of 'doubtful דען' explicitly marks doubt or satire in sarcastic
intonation questions. It is inserted immediately after the inflected verb, e.g.
?ער איז דען אַ דאָקטער! 'You call him a doctor!?'.

11.2   INVERSION

Questions may be formed by inversion of subject and predicate. The predicate
consists of the inflected verb. Thus, דו קומסט מאָרגן 'You are coming
tomorrow?' → ?קומסטו מאָרגן 'Are you coming tomorrow?'. When
inversion results in the sequence of second person familiar verb ending -סט
+ pronoun דו, the two are obligatorily conflated to ending -סטו (or, less
formally, to -סט) which is suffixed to the verb. The ending -סטו is usually
pronounced [stə] or [st], unless stressed for contrast.

SAMPLES OF QUESTIONS BY INVERSION

Are you (formal) telling the truth?   [éməs] ?זאָגט איר דעם אמת

Are you (familiar) coming home?   קומסטו אַהײם?

Do you (familiar) want to see?   װילסטו זען?

Do they really want things to be different?   װילן זײ טאַקע אַנדערש?

Is the answer known?   מ' חײסט דעם ענטפֿערן?

11.3   INTERROGATIVE PLUS INVERSION

Interrogatives are explicit 'question words'. They automatically trigger inversion of subject and predicate (→ §§14.4 – 14.5).

11.3.1   Interrogatives

The interrogatives, most of which double as relative pronouns, are on the whole uninflecting.

INTERROGATIVES

where װאו (→ locative װאוהין 'where to; whither')

what װאָס

what kind of / what type of   װאָסער   (→ pl. װאָסערע)

what kind of a(n)   (often aggressive)   װאָס פֿאַר אַ(ן)

how (אַזױ) װי

how much / how many   װיפֿל   (– װיפֿיל)

who   װער   (→ object [vémən] װעמען 'whom')

whose   [vémənz] װעמענס

when   װען

for what reason (lit. 'because of what')   מחמת װאָס [makhməzvós]

why   פֿאַרװאָס (also spelled פֿאַר װאָס)

for whom   פֿאַר װעמען

for what reason (lit. 'because of what') [tsəlìbvós]   צוליב װאָס

is / are; does / do (in a yes or no question)   צי

SAMPLES OF THE USE OF INTERROGATIVES

Where are you ?   [vu bístə?]   װאו ביסטו?

Where are we going? / Where shall we go?   װאוהין גייט מען?

What are you thinking?   װאָס טראַכטסטו?

What kind of machine is this?   װאָסער מאַשין איז דאָס?

What kind of friend is that?   װאָס פֿאַר אַ פֿרײַנד [fraynt] איז דאָס?

How do you (familiar) do it?   [viazóy mákhstə dos?]   װי אַזױ מאַכסטו דאָס?

How many books do you (formal) have?   װיפֿל ביכער האָט איר?

Who's coming?   װער קומט?

Whom can you (formal) recommend?   װעמען קענט איר רעקאָמענדירן?

Whose house is this?   װעמענס הױז איז דאָס?

When do we see each other?   [vén zétmənzəkh?]   װען זעט מען זיך?

Why don't you say yes?   [farvóz zòkstnit yó?]   פֿאַרװאָס זאָגסטו ניט יאָ?

For whom do you work?   פֿאַר װעמען אַרבעטסטו?

Why don't they answer?   צוליב װאָס ענטפֿערן זײ ניט?

Are you (familiar) coming tomorrow?   צי קומסטו מאָרגן?

11.3.1.1   Inflecting interrogative װעלכער

װעלכער 'which' inflects for case, gender and number. The older separate neutral form װעלכעס can occasionally be encountered in the written language but it is rare in modern usage. Neutral usually aligns with feminine in nominative and with masculine in both objective cases.

װעלכער in nominative

which (masculine)   װעלכער

which (feminine)   װעלכע

which (neutral) וועלכע

SAMPLES OF THE USE OF וועלכער IN NOMINATIVE

Which coat (דער מאַנטל) is this? וועלכער מאַנטל איז דאָס?

Which ship (די שיף) is this? וועלכע שיף איז דאָס?

Which house (דאָס הויז) is this? וועלכע הויז איז דאָס?

וועלכער in accusative

which (masculine)   וועלכן ← וועלכער

which (feminine) וועלכע

which (neutral)   וועלכן ← וועלכע

SAMPLES OF THE USE OF וועלכער IN ACCUSATIVE

Which coat do you see? וועלכן מאַנטל זעסטו?

Which ship do you see? וועלכע שיף זעסטו?

Which house do you see? וועלכן הויז זעסטו?

וועלכער in dative

which (masculine)   וועלכן ← וועלכער

which (feminine)   וועלכער ← וועלכע

which (neutral) וועלכע ← וועלכן

SAMPLES OF THE USE OF וועלכער IN DATIVE

Of which coat are you speaking? פֿון וועלכן מאַנטל רעדסטו?

On which boat are you coming? מיט וועלכער שיף קומסטו?

Near which house will you stand? לעבן וועלכן הויז וועסטו שטיין?

plural
וועלכע

200

SAMPLES OF THE USE OF PLURAL וועלכע

Which ones do you have in mind?	וועלכע האָסטו אין זינען?
Which ones are you talking about?	וועגן וועלכע רעדסטו?

11.4   INTERROGATIVE ADDITIVES

The interrogative additives are טאָ and זשע. Their use parallels that of imperative additives טאָ and זשע (→ §7.5.6). טאָ [tə / to] immediately precedes the interrogative and זשע [zhə] immediately follows it. They can be used independently of each other or they may surround the interrogative for increased effect. Like their imperative counterparts, the interrogative additives טאָ and זשע may serve to invoke affection, love or familiarity in support of a request or demand for an answer to the question being asked. They may also have the force of 'then; so; in that case'. Interrogative טאָ and זשע also add forcefulness, seriousness, and occasionally annoyance, to the question. Their use is most frequent with וואָס 'what', פֿאַרוואָס 'why' and חי (אַזוי) 'how'.   Like their imperative counterparts, they may invoke feelings of guilt in support of the question or request laced with the additive.

SAMPLES OF INTERROGATIVE ADDITIVES טאָ and זשע

So why don't you tell me?	טאָ פֿאַרוואָס זאָגסטו מיר ניט?
Come on, why don't you tell me?	פֿאַרוואָס זשע זאָגסטו מיר ניט?
	טאָ פֿאַרוואָס זאָגסטו מיר ניט?

Come on then, why don't you tell me? (You owe it to me!)

12 NUMBERS

12.0 OVERVIEW

Alongside the international number system, used in everyday life, Yiddish retains the traditional Jewish alphabetic numbering system for culture-specific purposes.

12.1 CARDINAL NUMBERS

12.1.1 Basic cardinal numbers

1	אײנס
2	צװײ
3	דרײַ
4	פֿיר
5	פֿינף
6	זעקס
7	זיבן [zibm]
8	אַכט
9	נײַן
10	צען
11	עלף
12	צװעלף
13	דרײַצן

202

14	פֿערצן
15	פֿופֿצן
16	זעכצן
17	זיבעצן
18	אַכצן
19	נײַנצן
20	צוואַנציק
30	דרײַסיק
40	פֿערציק
50	פֿופֿציק
60	זעכציק
70	זיבעציק
80	אַכציק
90	נײַנציק
100	הונדערט
1,000	טויזנט
1,000,000	מיליאָן

12.1.1.1   איין and איינס

איינס is used for the number 'one' in isolation when counting and in clock time (→ §13.2.2). When used as an attributive adjective, and in double digit combinations (→ §12.1.2.1), איין occurs, e.g. איין מאַן 'one man', איין פֿרוי 'one woman'. איין does not inflect as an attributive adjective. As a predicative adjective (→ §5.7), איין inflects for gender, e.g. גאָט איז איינער 'God is one' (name of the Yiddish variant of a Passover song). In usage parallel to the possessive-indefinite construction (→ §6.2.1.5), איינער combines with indefinite article (אַ(ן), e.g. איינער אַ מאַן 'some fellow', איינע אַ פֿרוי 'some woman'. איינער with the indefinite article inflects for case and gender, e.g.

איך האָב געזען איינעם אַ סטודענט 'I saw some student or other'. Cf.
§6.4.1 on partitive pronoun איינער.

12.1.2 Combined cardinal numbers

12.1.2.1 Double digit combinations

Double digit combinations are ordered upward with conjunction און 'and'
(often rendered [n] or [ən] in speech) in between. איין (rather than איינס)
is used in combination.

SAMPLES OF DOUBLE DIGIT COMBINATIONS

21	[eynən tsvántsik]	איין און צוואַנציק
34	[firn dráysik]	פיר און דרייסיק
48	[akhtn fértsik]	אַכט און פערציק
56	[zeksn fúftsik]	זעקס און פופציק
67	[zibmən zékhtsik]	זיבן און זעכציק
71	[eynən zíbətsik]	איין און זיבעציק
89	[naynən ákhtsik]	ניין און אַכציק

12.1.2.2 Multiple digit combinations

Multiple digit combinations are ordered downward, as in English, but
upwardly ordered double digit combinations within them are retained, e.g.
432 = פיר הונדערט צווי און דרייסיק (lit. 'four hundred two-and-thirty').

SAMPLES OF MULTIPLE DIGIT COMBINATIONS

121	[húndərt eynən tsvántsik]	הונדערט איין און צוואַנציק
234	[tsvéy hundərt firn dráysik]	צווי הונדערט פיר און דרייסיק
348	[dráy hundərt akhtn fértsik]	דרי הונדערט אַכט און פערציק
1,056	[tóyznt zeksn fúftsik]	טויזנט זעקס און פופציק

טויזנט הונדערט זיבן און זעכציק

1,167[tóyznt | hundərt zibmən zékhtsik]

צען טויזנט, פיר הונדערט אײן און זיבעציק 10,471

[tsén tóyznt | fír hundərt eynen zíbətsik]

אַכט הונדערט אַכט טויזנט, אַכט הונדערט נײַן און אַכציק 808,889

[ákht hundərt ákht tóyznt | ákht hundərt nàynən ákhtsik]

12.2 ORDINAL NUMBERS

There are special ordinal forms for '1st' to '19th', all ending in ט-, to which usual adjective endings are suffixed. For '20th' to '100th' and in '1000th', a ס appears between the number (which has the same stem as both cardinal and ordinal) and the adjective ending. In higher numbers, it is the very last number in the sequence that determines the suffix — if it is betwen 20 and 100, or ends in the word 'thousand', ס appears. Note the anomalous ערשט for 'first'.

12.2.1 Basic ordinal numbers

first ערשט

second צווייט

third דריט

fourth פֿערט

fifth פֿינפֿט

sixth זעקסט

seventh זיבעט

אַכֿט eighth

נײַנט ninth

צענט tenth

עלפֿט eleventh

צוועלפֿט twelfth

thirteenth דרײַצענט (דרײַצנט .var)

fourteenth פֿערצענט (פֿערצנט .var)

fifteenth פֿופֿצענט (פֿופֿצנט .var)

sixteenth זעכֿצענט (זעכֿצנט .var)

seventeenth זיבעצענט (זיבעצנט .var)

eighteenth אַכֿצענט (אַכֿצנט .var)

nineteenth נײַנצענט (נײַנצנט .var)

twentieth צוואַנציקסט

thirtieth דרײַסיקסט

fortieth פֿערציקסט

fiftieth פֿופֿציקסט

sixtieth זעכֿציקסט

seventieth זיבעציקסט

eightieth אַכֿציקסט

ninetieth נײַנציקסט

hundredth הונדערטסט

thousandth טויזנטסט

ten thousandth צען טויזנטסט

hundred thousandth הונדערט טויזנטסט

millionth מיליאָנט

SAMPLES OF ORDINAL NUMBERS

Second Avenue צווייטע (\ 2טע) עוועניו

אויף דער צווייטער (\ 2טער) עוועניו   on Second Avenue

צווי און פֿערציקסטע (\ 42סטע) גאַס   42nd Street

אויף דער צווי און פֿערציקסטער (\ 42סטער) גאַס   on 42nd Street

צום טויזנטסטן (\ 1000סטן) מאָל   for the thousandth time

צום צען טויזנטסטן (\ 10,000סטן) מאָל   for the ten thousandth time

די ערשטע צווי ביכער   the first two books

12.2.2 Ordinal numbers as adverbs

Points made in discussion may be numbered by adverbializing ordinals by suffixing טנ-, usually [nz]. Where only two points are being made, Semitic component ראשית [réyshəs] 'firstly' and שנית [shéynəs] 'secondly' may be substituted for ערשטנס and צווייטנס. If extra emphasis is required, ראשית כל [réyshəskòl] 'first of all' and והשנית [vəhàshéynəs] 'and secondly' may be used.

ערשטנס [ershtnz] firstly

צווייטנס [tsveytnz] secondly

דריטנס [dritnz] thirdly

פֿערטנס [fertnz] fourthly

פֿינפֿטנס [finftnz] fifthly

זעקסטנס [zekstnz] sixthly

12.3   FRACTIONS

Fractions are formed by suffixing טל- or סטל-, generally along the lines of the ordinals (→ §12.2), to the unsuffixed form of the ordinal number. They are neutral in gender. Simple major-digit fractions with a numerator of one may alternatively be expressed with suffix חלק [khéylik / khéylǝk] 'part'. The חלק forms may be used in everyday situations but the -טל forms alone are used in arithmetic. Note the special form (די) העלפֿט 'half (n.)' and its adjective counterpart האַלב. האַלב inflects for case and gender as an attributive adjective.   Single digit number plus a half may alternatively be expressed by suffixing -האַלבן to the ordinal stem of the *following* full number, e.g. דריטהאַלבן = two and a half, פֿערטהאַלבן = three and a half. Note, however, אַנדערטהאַלבן for 'one and a half'.

12.3.1 Major fractions

העלפֿט half

דריט∹חלק [drít khèylik] / דריטל third

פֿערט∹חלק [fért khèylik] / פֿערטל fourth

פֿינפֿט∹חלק [fínft khèylik] / פֿינפֿטל fifth

זעקסט∹חלק [zékst khèylik] / זעקסטל sixth

זיבעט∹חלק [zíbǝt khèylik] / זיבעטל seventh

אַכט∹חלק [ákht khèylik] / אַכטל eighth

נײַנט∹חלק [náynt khèylik] / נײַנטל ninth

צענט∹חלק [tsént khèylik] / צענטל tenth

עלפֿט∹חלק [élft khèylik] / עלפֿטל eleventh

צוועלפֿט∹חלק [tsvélft khèylik] / צוועלפֿטל twelfth

(var. דרײַצענטל) דרײַצענטל thirteenth

(var. פֿערצענטל) פֿערצענטל fourteenth

(var. פֿופֿצענטל) פֿופֿצענטל fifteenth

(var. זעכצענטל) זעכצענטל sixteenth

(var. זיבעצענטל) זיבעצענטל seventeenth

(var. אַכצענטל) אַכצענטל eighteenth

nineteenth נײַנצנטל (var. נײַנצעטל)

twentieth צוואַנציקסטל

hundredth הונדערט־חלק [húndərt khèylik] / (var. הונדערטל) / הונדערטסטל

thousandth טויזנט־חלק [tóyznt khèylik] / (var. טויזנטל) / טויזנטסטל

millionth מיליאַנט־חלק [milyónt khèylik] / מיליאַנטל

SAMPLES OF FRACTIONS

an eighth אַן אַכטל

one eighth איין אַכטל

four fifths פיר פינפטל

three and a half דרײַ מיט אַ האַלב אַ (= פערטהאַלבן)

six nineteenths זעקס נײַנצנטל

nine twenty-fifths נײַן פינף־ און ־צוואַנציקסטל

12.4 THE ALPHABETIC NUMBERING SYSTEM

The traditional Jewish numbering system uses the letters of the alphabet.
Combined numbers are ordered downward. From 1,000 and upward, the
system recycles itself, separating the thousands from the small numbers by
an apostrophe and/or by use of larger or bold letters for the thousands).

12.4.1 The basic alphabetic numbers

1	א
2	ב
3	ג
4	ד
5	ה

6	ו
7	ז
8	ח
9	ט
10	י
11	יא
12	יב
13	יג
14	יד
15	טו
16	טז
17	יז
18	יח
19	יט
20	כ
30	ל
40	מ
50	נ
60	ס
70	ע
80	פ
90	צ
100	ק
200	ר
300	ש
400	ת
500	תק
600	תר
700	תש
800	תת

תתק 900

'א 1000

'ב 2000

'ג 3000

'ד 4000

'ה 5000

SAMPLES OF ALPHABETIC NUMBERS

יח 18

כח 28

לו 36

מ 40

עז 77

קכ 120

רמח 248

שסה 365

תתקסט 969

12.4.1.1 Anomalies

The anomalies in the system result from traditional cultural considerations. The combinations 10 (י) + 5 (ה) for 15 and 10 (י) + 6 (ו) would result, when written out, in variants of the sacred name of God. They are therefore subject to the traditional ban on using God's name in vain in an everyday context, even where reference to God is not intended. The combinations 9 (ט)+ 6 (ו) and 9 (ט) +7 (ז) are substituted, giving טו = 15 and טז = 16. Traditional sacred Hebrew and Aramaic books with extensive Jewish letter numbering also avoid combinations with negative overtones, e.g. 304 = דש, (4+300) rather than the expected שד (300+4,) because it spells the word שד [shed] 'evil spirit'.

12.4.2 Supplementary uses of the Jewish alphabet

12.4.2.1 Calendar

The Jewish calendar is outlined in §13.5.

12.4.2.2 Numerology

Traditional Jewish numerology, called גמטריא [gəmátriyə] 'gematria', adds up the numeric values of the letters of Hebrew words and names as a starting point for exegetical or mystical extrapolation. It is a practice prevalent in rabbinic lore and kabbalistic inquiry. Thus, for example, it has been noted in support of the rabbinic adage סוד יצא יין נכנס [nìkhnəs yáyin | yòtso sód] 'When wine goes in, a secret comes out', that the words for 'wine' and 'secret' both add up to 70 in gematria (wine = יין = 10+10+50 = 70; secret = סוד = 60+6+4 = 70). In a lighter vein, traditional wedding speeches often entertain guests by demonstrating the compatibility and good fortune of the bride and bridegroom via interlocking series of gematrias.

12.4.2.3 Acronyms

Traditional Jewish acronyms are called ראשי־תיבות [roshətéyvəs] '[abbreviations from the] heads [=first letters] of words'. Traditionally, words thus created are marked by the double apostrophe " before their final letter to mark their acronymity, but the apostrophe is frequently omitted for well established acronyms. A number of semantic classes are particularly inclined to acronyms. Great rabbinic figures are often known to Yiddish speakers by their acronyms. Most frequently, the vowel *a* is supplied to create syllables from the initials, except in final syllables ending in a vowel where *o* is supplied. Maimonides is traditionally known as רמב"ם דער [der rámbam] 'the Rambam', the acronym from his full traditional name

רֵבֵּנוּ מֹשֶׁה בֶּן מַימוֹן Rabéynu Móyshə ben Máymən. The great sixteenth-century Ashkenazic codifier Rabbi Moyshe Isserles is known as דער רמ"א [der ramó] 'the Ramo' from his initials. The tradition is on occasion continued in modern Yiddish cultural circles. Among the best known examples are leading Yiddish cultural institutions founded in pre-World War II Eastern Europe — ייוואָ [yívo / yivó] (from ייִדישער וויסנשאַפֿטעלעכער אינסטיטוט 'Yiddish Scientific Institute', now the Yivo Institute for Jewish Research in New York), צישאָ [tsísho] (from צענטראַלע ייִדישע שול אָרגאַניזאַציע 'Central Yiddish School Organization') and ציקאָ [tsíko / tsikó] (from צענטראַלע ייִדישע קולטור אָרגאַניזאַציע 'Central Yiddish Culture Organization'). A number of Jewish names are themselves רָאשֵׁי תֵּיבוֹת e.g. כ"ץ [kats] 'Katz' from כֹּהֵן צֶדֶק [kóyhən tsédək] 'righteous kohen (descendant of the Biblical priestly caste)'.

13 TIME

13.0 OVERVIEW

Alongside international units of time and the general calendar, Yiddish retains active use of the Jewish calendar and concepts of time associated with it.

13.1 LIFE

13.1.1 Age

עלטער age

ווי אַלט...? how old...?

__ יאָר (אַלט) __ years old

(געבורטסטאָג (var. נעבוירן-טאָג (דער) birthday

SAMPLES OF AGE

ווי אַלט ביסטו? How old are you (familiar)?

איך בין אַלט צוויי און צוואַנציק יאָר I'm twenty-two years old

13.1.2 Youthfulness

נײַ-געבוירן just-born

יונג young (comparative: ייִנגער; superlative: ייִנגסט—)

middle aged   מיטליעריק

quite young; youngish   יונגלעך

quite old; oldish   אַלטלעך

old   אַלט (comparative: עלטער; superlative: -עלטסט)

13.1.3 The age cycle

baby [éyfələ(kh)]   (דאָס) עופֿעלע(ך)

child   (דאָס) קינד(ער)

little boy   (דאָס) יינגעלע(ך)

little girl   (דאָס) מיידעלע(ך)

boy   (דער\דאָס) יינגל(עך)

bar-mitsvah boy (i.e. 13 year old) [bókhər(im)]   (דער) בר=מצווה בחור(ים)

girl   (די\דאָס) מיידל(עך)

young man (also: fellow; bachelor) [bókhər(im)]   (דער) בחור(ים)

young woman [bókhərtə(s)]   (די) בחורטע(ס)

(*rare:* מיידל is the usual female correspondent of בחור)

young fellow   [yungərmán]   (דער) יונגערמאַן

young woman   (די) יונגע פֿרוי(ען)

man   (דער) מאַן (מענער)

woman   (די) פֿרוי(ען)

old man   [zókn; skéynim]   (דער) זקן(ים)

old woman   [skéynə(s)]   (די) זקנה (זקנות)

13.1.4 Death

7 days of mourning upon a death   [shívə]   (די) שבֿעה

(end of) thirty-day mourning period   [shlóyshim] (pl.)   (די) שלושים

date of anniversary of a death   יאָרצײַט (דער\די)

13.2   TIME

13.2.1   Units of time

second   [səkúndə(s)]   (די) סעקונדע(ס)

minute   [minút(n)]   (די) מינוט(ן)

hour   [shó(ən)]   (די) שעה(ן)

day   (pl. טעג)   (דער) טאָג

period of twenty-four hours   [məslés(n)]   (דער) מעת‑לעת(ן)

week   (די) וואָך(ן)

month   [khóydesh]   (דער) חודש   (pl. חדשים [khadóshim])

year(s)   (דאָס) יאָר(ן)

decade   [yortséndlik(er)]   (דער) יאָרצענדליק(ער)

century   [yorhúndert(er)]   (דער) יאָרהונדערט(ער)

millennium   [yortóyznt(er)]   (דער) יאָרטויזנט(ער)

13.2.1.1   Plurals of יאָר and שעה, מינוט

When used with a specific number, מינוט 'minute', שעה 'hour' and יאָר 'year' themselves serve as plural forms, e.g. צען מינוט 'ten minutes', צוויי שעה 'two hours', צוואַנציק יאָר 'twenty years'. When used as conceptual time units with no specific number, the plural in ן- is used, e.g. מינוטן, ניט קיין שעהן 'minutes, not hours'; יאָרן לאַנג 'for many years'.

13.2.2   Clock time

Clock time is given without a preposition, e.g. מיר קומען צוויי אַזייגער

216

'We're coming at 2 o'clock'. Hours and minutes may be given consecutively
– 9:21 is read נײַן אײן און צוואַנציק. Note the alternative forms for
expressing half hours: דרײַסיק 'thirty' or האַלב נאָך 'half past' after the
preceding whole hour, and האַלב 'half (to)' *before* the *following* hour,
e.g. '8:30' = האַלב נײַן = האַלב נאָך אַכט = אַכט דרײַסיק.

אַזײגער   o'clock

אַ פערטל צו   a quarter to

אַ פערטל נאָך   a quarter past

דרײַסיק   –thirty

האַלב נאָך   half past

האַלב   half to

SAMPLES OF CLOCK TIME

12:30 האַלב אײנס – האַלב נאָך צוועלף – צוועלף דרײַסיק

1:15 אַ פערטל נאָך אײנס

3:25 פינף און צוואַנציק נאָך דרײַ

3:50 דרײַ פופֿציק – צען (מינוט) צו פיר

5:00 פינף אַזײגער

7:45 זיבן פינף און פערציק – אַ פערטל צו אַכט

8.26 אַכט זעקס און צוואַנציק

13.2.3 Parts of the day

פֿאַרטאָג   before dawn

(אין דער פֿרי   in the morning (also spelled אינדערפֿרי)

(נאָך מיטאָג, נאָכמיטאָג, נאָך מיטיק   in the afternoon; (also spelled נאָכמיטיק)

פֿאַרנאַכט   at dusk; in the early evening

(→ §13.3.2.1)   אויף דער נאַכט [avdərnákht]   in the evening

אין אָונט in the evening

בײַנאַכט [banákht] at night

SAMPLES OF CLOCK TIME AND DAY TIME

פיר פֿאַרטאָג 4 a.m.

צען אינדערפֿרי 10 a.m.

דרײַ נאָכמיטיק 3 p.m.

אַכט אין אָונט – אַכט אויך דער נאַכט 8 p.m.

עלף בײַנאַכט 11 p.m.

13.2.4 Conceptual time sequences

אַ מינוטקעלע [minútkələ] / אַ סעקונדע just a second!; in a jiffy!

אַ מאָמענט [momént] just one moment

אַ װײַלינקע a little while

אַ װײַלע a while

אַ היפּשע װײַלע quite a while

13.2.5 Idiomatic time sequences

פֿון כמעלניצקיס צײַטן a long long time ago

('of Chmielnitski's times', after Bogdan Chmielnitski, who led massacres of
Jews in the Ukraine in 1648 and 1649)

אײן מאָל אין אַ שמיטה [shmíta] seldom

('once in a sabbatical' after the Biblical sabbatical at seven-year intervals)

אײן מאָל אין אַ יובֿל [yóyvl] very seldom

('once in a jubilee' after the Biblical jubilee at fifty-year intervals) very long   [góləs] נלות דער װי לאַנג (→ §16.1)

('long as the diaspora' after the two-thousand-year Jewish diaspora)

very short [púrim] פורים ביז [estərtónəs] תענית־אסתר פֿון

('from the Fast of Esther to Purim', i.e. a timespan of one day)

in / until a ripe old age   [məsushélakhs yórn] יאָרן מתושלחס ביז \ אין

('Methuselah's years', after Methuselah who lived 969 years; cf. Genesis 5:27)

13.2.6   Relative time concepts

now   איצטער (var. איצט, אַצינד, איצטערט; nonliterary var. יעצט)

then; (= 'at that time')   דעמאָלט (var. דעמאָלס(ט), דאַמאָלס(ט), דעמאָלס, דעמאָל, דעמענסט, דאַן, יעמאָלט)

before (preposition requiring object)   פֿאַר

after (preposition requiring object)   נאָך

before, previously (adv.)   פֿריִער

later (adv.)   שפּעטער

during [méshəkh] פֿון משך אין / [bəshás/pshás] בשעת \ בעתֿ[b(ə)éys]

concurrent with   מיט גלײַכצײַטיק

at the same time   צײַט זעלביקער דער (אין \) צו

13.3   THE CALENDAR

13.3.1   Seasons

spring   פֿרילינג (דער)

summer   זומער (דער)

autumn   [harpst] (דער) הַאַרבסט

winter   (דער) ווינטער

13.3.2 Days

Sunday   זונטיק

Monday   מאָנטיק

Tuesday   דינסטיק

Wednesday   מיטוואָך

Thursday   דאָנערשטיק

Friday   פֿרײַטיק

Saturday   [shábəs] שבת

13.3.2.1 Friday and Saturday evening

Because the Jewish Sabbath, like all Jewish holidays, begins on the evening preceding the date of the holiday (→ §13.5.3), the preceding day has special cultural and linguistic status. In addition to פֿרײַטיק, Friday is also called ערב שבת [èrəv shábəs] 'eve of Sabbath'. The part of Friday afternoon immediately preceding the onset of the Sabbath celebration is known as פֿאַר⸗שבת [farshábəs]. Friday evening, upon and following the start of the Sabbath, is פֿרײַטיק⸗צו⸗נאַכט(ס). Saturday night, from the end of the Sabbath at sundown and onwards, is known as מוצאי שבת [motsə shábəs], שבת⸗צו⸗נאַכט(ס) [shàbəs tsu nákht(s)] or שבתע נאַכט(ס) [sh(a)béysə nakht(s)] 'Saturday night' (→ §10.3.7). The stock-phrase use of preposition צו is unique to these days. On other evenings of the week, אויף דער נאַכט [avdərnákht] is used, e.g. מיטוואָך אויף דער נאַכט 'Wednesday evening' (→ §13.2.3).

13.3.3 Months

January	יאַנואַר
February	פֿעברואַר
March	מערץ (var. מאַרץ)
April	אַפּריל
May	מײַ (var. spelling: מײ)
June	יוני
July	יולי
August	אויגוסט
September	סעפּטעמבער
October	אָקטאָבער
November	נאָוועמבער
December	דעצעמבער

13.3.4 Dates

Dates are formed with ordinal numbers (→ §12.2). They are masculine and traditionally given in dative with masculine definite article דעם.

SAMPLES OF DATES

October 3   (דעם דריטן אָקטאָבער = דעם 3טן אָקטאָבער)

April 12   (דעם צוועלפֿטן אַפּריל = דעם 12טן אַפּריל)

January 28   (דעם אַכט און צוואַנציקסטן יאַנואַר = דעם 28סטן יאַנואַר)

13.4 USE OF PREPOSITIONS WITH EXPRESSIONS OF TIME

In many cases where English uses 'at' 'on' or 'for' in expressions of time, there is no preposition at all. Preposition אויף [af] is used in the sense of intention with respect to a period of time, but no preposition appears in the factual recounting of the period of time. מיט — צוריק corresponds with 'ago'; אין — אַרום corresponds with 'in — time'.

SAMPLES OF THE USE AND NON-USE OF PREPOSITIONS

WITH EXPRESSIONS OF TIME

We'll meet at 4   מיר וועלן זיך טרעפֿן פֿיר אַזײגער

I'm coming on the 24th   איך קום דעם 24סטן

I came intending to stay three weeks   איך בין געקומען אויף [af] דרײ וואָכן

I stayed three weeks   איך בין געבליבן דרײ וואָכן

I saw them ten years ago   איך האָב זיי געזען מיט צען יאָר צוריק

I'll see them again in ten years   איך וועל זיי ווידער זען אין צען יאָר אַרום

13.5   THE JEWISH CALENDAR

13.5.1   The calendric system

The Jewish lunar calendar makes use of the alphabetic numbering system (→ §12.4). The calendar is calibrated to Biblical history as chronologized in Jewish tradition, and counts from the Biblical creation of the world. That event is placed in Jewish year 1, which corresponds with 3761/3760 BC. Thus, for example, 586 BC coincides with the Jewish years ג׳קעה (3,175) and ג׳קעו (3,176); 1492 AD coincides with ה׳רנב (5,252) and ה׳רנג (5,253). To simplify the system for everyday use, the ה׳ representing 5,000 is deleted where discussion is limited to years after ה׳ (i.e. AD 1239/1240). The abbreviated forms of years are usually written out using the traditional double apostrophe (״) before the final letter. Thus, 1900 is תרס״ט / תרס״א ([5,]661

/ [5,]662). To convert any Jewish year after 1240, add 1,240 to the abbreviated Jewish date (i.e. without the 'ה = 5,000). If the exact date is known and it falls between the Jewish new year in autumn and 1 January, add 1239 instead. If the exact date is not known, it is customary to add 1240 with the understood caution that the first few months of the Jewish year coincide with the preceding year. Jewish dates generally become 'words' via the insertion of an [a] vowel for years that end in a consonant, and an [o] vowel for years that end in a vowel, e.g. תשמ"ח [tashmákh] = 1987/1988, תשנ"א [tashnó] = 1990/1991. Many names of years are historical concepts, e.g. גזירות ת"ח ות"ט [gzéyrəs tákh vətát] 'the persecutions of [5,]408 and [5,]409', refers to the massacres of Ukranian Jewry in those years. Adding 1240 converts the years to AD 1648 and 1649.

13.5.2 Months

The Jewish lunar year has twelve months. Leap years, which occur seven times within a nineteen-year cycle, have thirteen months. The month added is ואדר [véyodər], also called 'אדר ב [òdər béyz].

תשרי [tíshrə] (September / October)

חשון [khéshvn] (October / November)

כסלו [kísləv] (November / December)

טבת [téyvəs] (December / January)

שבט [shvat] (January / February)

אדר [òdər] (February / March; called 'אדר א [òdər áləf] in leap years)

ואדר [véyodər] / 'אדר ב [òdər béyz] (in leap years only)

ניסן [nísn] (March / April)

אייר [íyər] (April / May)

סיון [sívn] (May / June)

תמוז [táməz] (June / July)

אב [ov] (July / August)

אלול [éləl] (August / September)

13.5.3. Dates of the month and of major holidays

Dates of the month are given using the Jewish alphabetic numbering system (→ §12.4). The Jewish day extends from dusk to dusk and the date therefore begins on the previous day in the general calendar. Jewish holidays therefore begin on the evening of the date before their counterparts in the general calendar.

MAJOR JEWISH HOLIDAYS AND THE DATES ON WHICH THEY BEGIN

Holiday	Transcription	Popular English name	Date
ראש השנה	[roshəshónə]	'Jewish New Year'	א' תשרי
יום כיפור	[yomkípər]	'Day of Atonement'	י' תשרי
סוכות	[súkəs]	'Feast of Tabernacles'	ט"ו תשרי
שמחת תורה	[sìmkhəs tóyrə]	'Simhath Torah'	כ"ג תשרי
חנוכה	[khánəkə]	'Hanukkah'	כ"ה כסלו
ט"ו בשבט (חמשה־עשר=)	[tu bishvát] ([kham(i)shósər])	'Tu biShevat'	ט"ו שבט
פורים	[púrim]	'Purim'	י"ד אדר
פסח	[péysakh]	'Passover'	ט"ו ניסן
לג בעמר	[lag bóymər]	'Lag baOmer'	י"ח אייר
שבועות	[shvúəs]	'Shavuoth'	ו' סיון
י"ז בתמוז	[shivósər bətámuz]	'Fast of Tamuz'	י"ז תמוז
תשעה באב	[tíshəbov]	'Fast of Av'	ט' אב

14 SYNTAX

14.0   OVERVIEW

Yiddish syntax is highly flexible. Because the three cases (→ §5.1) themselves
maintain clarity of subject and object, there is scope for extensive variation in
word order. Changes in word order empower the speaker and writer to
determine nuance and emphasis by transposing many of the parts of a
sentence at will with no loss of clarity. The major constraints are the placement of the inflected verb in second position within a sentence, the
application in certain conditions of obligatory inversion of subject and
predicate, and the position of verbal additive זיך and negator ניט.

14.1   THE INFLECTED-VERB-SECOND RULE

The inflected-verb-second rule stipulates that the inflected verb be placed in
second position within a sentence. Inflecting verbs are those that inflect for
person and number.   In the present tense, the main verb itself inflects (→
§7.5) and is therefore subject to the rule. In the past and future tenses, it is
the helping verbs that inflect (האָבן or זײַן in the past → §§7.6 – 7.7; װעלן
in the future → §7.9). The helping verbs in the past and future tenses must
adhere to the inflected-verb-second rule. The main verbs – the past
participle in the past and the infinitive in the future – do not inflect and are
therefore exempt from the rule.

14.2   BASIC SENTENCE ORDER: NOUN PLUS INFLECTED VERB

The primitive sentence type comprises a noun phrase followed by a verb phrase. Note from the samples provided that the inflected verb adheres to the inflected-verb-second rule in all three tenses. In the present, where the main verb itself inflects, it is simply placed after the subject. In the past, the appropriate part of the past tense helping verb – הָאבּן or זײַן – is second. In the future, the appropriate part of וועלן must be placed second.

SAMPLE SENTENCES IN BASIC SENTENCE ORDER

present
דו ביסט גערעכט

You are right

past
דער טאַטע האָט גערעדט מיט זײַן ייִנגעלע

Father spoke to his little boy

future
די נײַע לערערין וועט אָנקומען מאָנטיק

The new teacher (f.) will arrive on Monday

14.3   WORD PLACEMENT IN BASIC SENTENCE ORDER

14.3.1   זיך in basic sentence order

If a verb is accompanied by additive זיך (→ §7.3), זיך immediately follows the inflected verb in basic sentence order. The result is that in the past and future of synthetic verbs, and in the present of verbs with stressed prefixes, זיך is sandwiched between the inflected and uninflected verb.

SAMPLES OF זיך IN BASIC SENTENCE ORDER

present

איך פֿריי זיך מיט די גוטע נײַעס   I'm delighted to hear the good news

מ'שטופּט זיך אין יענער פֿירמע   People are pushy in that company

(inf. [shtupm] זיך שטופּן 'push oneself; be ambitious; sell oneself')

present of verbs with stressed prefixes

'fit in') אַרײַנפּאַסן זיך (inf.   איך פּאַס זיך דאָ אַרײַן   I fit in here

'stop אָפּטשעפּענען זיך (inf.   טשעפּע זיך אָפּ!   Stop bothering me!

bothering someone')

past

מ'האָט זיך געזעגנט פֿאַראַיאָרן   We said goodbye to each other last year

זיי האָבן זיך באַגריסט אין גאַס   They greeted each other on the street

future

מ'וועט זיך ווידער זען איבעראַיאָר   We'll see each other again next year

דאָס האַרץ וועט זיך פֿאַרבענקען   I will miss you (lit. 'The heart will yearn')

14.3.2   Object pronouns in basic sentence order

Accusative pronouns (→§6.1.2) immediately follow the inflected verb. Dative pronouns (→ §6.1.3) follow the preposition of which they are the object.

SAMPLES OF OBJECT PRONOUNS IN BASIC SENTENCE ORDER

present

Our friends can see us אונדזערע חברים [khavéyrim] קענען אונדז זען

He looks at you (familiar) all day ער קוקט אויף דיר אַ גאַנצן טאָג

present of verbs with stressed prefix

They are throwing us out (אַרויסטואַרפֿן .inf) מ'טשאַרפֿט אונדז אַרויס

They're taking everything away from us מ'נעמט פֿון אונדז אַוועק אַלצדינג

past

We were fooled (/cheated) מ'האָט אונדז אָפּגענאַרט

They spoke to us זיי האָבן מיט אונדז גערעדט

future

We'll see them tomorrow מיר וועלן זיי מאָרגן זען

They won't yell at us זיי וועלן אויף אונדז ניט שרײַען

14.3.3 ניט in basic sentence order

Negator ניט (→ §7.4) occurs somewhere after the inflected verb. In
sentences with helping (inflected) and main (uninflected) verbs, ניט occurs
somewhere between the two. This is applicable for all helping+main verb
combinations (past → §§7.6–7.7; future → §7.9; present of verbs with
stressed prefixes → §8.2; analytic verbs → §9). The scope for manoeuvre
within these constraints allows for considerable variation of sentence
emphasis (→ §14.10).

228

SAMPLES OF ניט IN BASIC SENTENCE ORDER

present

איך גיי ניט   I'm not going

זיי ווייסן ניט פֿון זייערע הענט און פֿיס

They don't know what they're talking about (lit. 'They don't know of their hands and feet')

present of verbs with stressed prefix

(אויפֿשטיין .inf) מיר שטייען ניט אויף [uf] פֿרי   We're not getting up early

(אַוועקוואַרפֿן .inf) איך וואַרף ניט אַוועק דעם מאַנטל

I'm not throwing away the coat

past

איך בין ניט געפֿאָרן אין ירושלים [yərusholáyim]   I didn't go to Jerusalem

ער האָט זיך ניט געפֿונען   He didn't find himself

future

מיר וועלן ניט פֿאָרן אין מאָנטרעאַל   We won't go to Montreal

מיר וועלן זיך ניט זען פֿרײַטיק   We won't see each other on Friday

14.3.3.1   ניט with זיך

Where verbs have additive זיך (→ §7.3), זיך always precedes ניט. Adverbs may intervene.

SAMPLES OF ניט WITH זיך

איך באַמי זיך ניט   I don't try

איך באַמי זיך שוין ניט   I don't try anymore

14.3.3.2 ניט with object pronouns

ניט follows an object personal pronoun (→ §§6.1.2 – 6.1.3). An adverb may appear between them. In analogous sentences with common or proper nouns, ניט may precede the noun.

SAMPLES OF ניט WITH OBJECT PRONOUNS

I don't see him upstairs איך זע אים ניט אויבן

I don't see him upstairs anymore איך זע אים שוין ניט אויבן

I don't see the people upstairs איך זע ניט די מענטשן אויבן

I don't see Zálmən upstairs איך זע ניט זלמנען [zálmənən] אויבן

14.3.3.3 ניט קיין

Where a transitive verb with an indefinite object is negated and ניט קיין (→ §7.4) is used, קיין [kin / ka] occurs immediately before the noun phrase that is its object. ניט קיין are often separated by the requirements of ניט placement.

SAMPLES OF THE POSITION OF ניט קיין

We don't have any time מיר האָבן ניט קיין צײַט

They didn't have any money זיי האָבן ניט געהאַט קיין געלט

You won't have any worries here וועסט ניט האָבן דאָ קיין דאגות [dáygəs]

Don't tell me any stories דערצייל מיר ניט קיין מעשיות [máysəs]

14.4 INVERTED SENTENCE ORDER: INFLECTED VERB PLUS NOUN

In inverted sentence order, the inflected verb is jumped forward so that it precedes the subject. The most frequent cause of inversion is the inflected-verb-second rule. Jumping the inflected verb forward places it in second position, in conformity with the rule. In past and future, this generally results in separation of the helping verb (הָאבן or זײַן in the past; וועלן in the future) from the main verb (past participle or infinitive). Main verbs, which are not subject to the inflected-verb-second rule, are unaffected by the jump.

14.4.1 Adverbial triggered compulsory inversion

Adverbials comprise adverbs, adverb phrases (phrases launched by an adverb) and prepositional phrases (functioning in effect as adverbs → §10.4). Adverbials at the beginning of a sentence would result in the inflected verb being in third position. This is averted by inversion, which jumps the inflected verb forward to second position. The samples provided illustrate the same sentence in basic sentence order and in inverted order triggered by placement of an adverbial at the beginning of the sentence. Subject and object are underlined; adverbials triggering inversion are outlined. The adverbs and prepositional phrases provided have similar meanings.

SAMPLES OF ADVERBS AND ADVERB PHRASES TRIGGERING INVERSION

present

מלכה קומט באַלד   Málkə is coming soon   →

באַלד קומט מלכה

past

מיר האָבן געטאַנצט שפּעט אין דער נאַכט   We danced late at night   →

שפּעט אין דער נאַכט האָבן מיר געטאַנצט

future

איך וועל אַװדאי [avádə] גײן   I will certainly go   →

אַװדאי וועל איך גײן

SAMPLES OF PREPOSITIONAL PHRASES TRIGGERING INVERSION

present

Málkə is coming in a little while   מלכה קומט אין אַ וויילינקע ←

אין אַ וויילינקע קומט מלכה

past

We danced until late at night ביז שפּעט אין דער נאַכט געטאַנצט האָבן מיר ←

ביז שפּעט אין דער נאַכט האָבן מיר געטאַנצט

future

I will certainly go   גיין [avzíkhər] זיכער אויף וועל איך ←

אויף זיכער וועל איך גיין

14.4.2   Midsentence adverb-triggered inversion

A sentence need only have a noun phrase and a verb phrase. A written sentence may comprise any number of true sentences tied by link words. Whether or not inversion is triggered in the middle of a sentence depends on the nature of the link word. If the link word is an adverbial, inversion is triggered. If it is a conjunction, there is no inversion. In the samples provided, subject and object are <u>underlined</u>; inversion triggers (adverbs, adverb phrases and prepositional phrases) are outlined. Conjunctions, which do not trigger inversion, are in **bold type**.

SAMPLES OF MIDSENTENCE ADVERBIALS TRIGGERING INVERSION

present

I'm coming on Thursday   איך קום דאָנערשטיק ←

I might be coming on Thursday   אפשר קום איך דאָנערשטיק

232

past

→ מיר זײַנען געפֿאָרן אין אײראָפּע   We went to Europe

פֿאַרן זומער זײַנען מיר געפֿאָרן אין אײראָפּע

We went to Europe before the summer

future

→ זי װעט ניט גײן [zít / zíət / zi vet]   She won't go

מסתּמא [mistámə] װעט זי [vetsi / vedzi] ניט גײן   She probably won't go

SAMPLES OF MIDSENTENCE CONJUNCTIONS *NOT* TRIGGERING INVERSION

present

→ איך קום דאָנערשטיק   I'm coming on Thursday

איך מײן אַז איך קום דאָנערשטיק   I think that I'm coming on Thursday

past

→ מיר זײַנען געפֿאָרן אין אײראָפּע   We went to Europe

דאָס איז געשען װען מיר זײַנען געװען אין אײראָפּע

It happened when we went to Europe

future

→ זי װעט ניט גײן   She won't go

דבֿורה קען אים ניט פֿאַרטראָגן און זי װעט ניט גײן

Dvóyrə can't stand him and she won't go

14.4.3 Distinguishing conjunctions from adverbs

By definition, adverbs trigger inversion while conjunctions do not. It is therefore important to know which link words are adverbs and which are conjunctions. There are hundreds of adverbs in the language used to describe states of time, place, feeling and situation. Adverbs (including adverbial and prepositional phrases) often represent the more complex logical relations (e.g. פֿונדעסטוועגן 'nevertheless', פֿון דער אַנדערער זײַט 'on the other hand'). Many conjunctions are the link words that express the basic linking concepts 'and', 'but', 'if', 'or' 'because' and 'that'. Some, however, do express time relations, and some have developed more sophisticated logical connotations. In stock phrases combining an adverb with a conjunction, it is the final word that determines status with respect to triggering inversion. װי 'as' concludes the stock phrase באַלד װי 'as soon as'. The entire phrase therefore functions as a conjunction and inversion is blocked (→ §5.10 on conjunctions vs. prepositions with comparative adjectives).

14.4.3.1 Major conjunctions

אָבער but

אױב if

אָדער or

און and

אַז that; when; if

איידער before (preceding subject; cf. adverb פֿריער)

באַלד װי as soon as

הגם although [hagám]

װאָס which / that

װען when / if

װי as / like

טאָמער if / in case / in the event

כאָטש although

after [nogh dém vi] נאָך דעם װי (preceding subject; cf. preposition נאָך)

notwithstanding that [nit gəkùkt av dém vos] ניט געקוקט אױף דעם װאָס

but / only נאָר

rather; it is rather the case that [nor vodén] נאָר װאָדען (= נאָר װאָס דען)

14.4.4 Present participle triggered compulsory inversion

Present participles (→ §7.2) trigger inversion. Inversion triggering present participles are outlined.

SAMPLES OF PRESENT PARTICIPLES TRIGGERING INVERSION

גײענדיק האָט חוה [khávə] באַטראַכט דעם ענין [ínyən]

While walking, Khávə thought about the matter

לױפֿנדיק האָט דער אַטלעט צעקלאַפּט אַ פֿוס

While running, the athlete injured his foot

14.4.5 If-then clause triggered compulsory inversion

If-then clauses trigger inversion in the then-clause. Inversion is triggered regardless of the type of word beginning the if-clause. Inversion here has the force of English 'then'. Noun phrases and inflected verb are underlined, inversion-triggering if-clauses are outlined.

SAMPLES OF IF-THEN CLAUSE TRIGGERED INVERSION

→ מיר װעלן קומען צו דיר צו גאַסט We will come to visit you

אַז דו װעסט אונדז פֿאַרבעטן, װעלן מיר קומען צו דיר צו גאַסט

If you invite us, we'll come to visit you

→ איך ווייס ניט [khvéysnit]   I don't know

אַזז, ווייס איך ניט [tòmərnít | véysikhnit]
If not, then I don't know

→ ס'טויג ניט [stóygnit]   It's no good

און אַז יאָ, טויג עס במילא ניט [unazyó | toygəs bəméylə nit]
And if so (/if yes), it's no good anyway

14.4.5.1   Inversion in the if-clause

Where there is no word (adverb, prepositional phrase or conjunction) to
signify the concept 'if' in the if-clause, inversion is invoked in the if-clause.
Inversion in the if-clause itself serves to supply the concept 'if'.

SAMPLES OF INVERSION IN THE IF-CLAUSE

קומט זי, קום איך אויכעט [kumdzí | kum ìkh óykhət]
If she comes, then I'll come too

וויל מען גיין, טאָ לאָמיר גיין [vílmən géyn | təlómir géyn]
If we want to go, then let's go

גיי איך ביסטו אין כעס, גיי איך ניט ביסטו אויך אין כעס [inkás]
If I go, you're angry;   If I don't go, you're also angry

14.4.6   Interrogative inversion

Interrogatives trigger inversion (→ §§11.2 – 11.3).

14.4.7   Fronting inversion

Any word that is fronted (brought forward) to the beginning of a sentence for emphasis (→ §14.10) triggers inversion. In the samples provided, inversion-triggering fronted words are **outlined**.

SAMPLES OF OBJECT-FRONTING INVERSION

I really needed *this!* [dóz dafikh nòkh] דאָס דאַרף איך נאָך

I have enough *apples* עפּל האָב איך גענוג

We didn't need *him* yesterday [em] האָבן מיר נעלטן ניט געדאַרפֿט עים

I have too many *problems* already פּראָבלעמען האָב איך שוין צופֿיל

14.4.8 Stylistic inversion

Unless it is subject to obligatory inversion, the first sentence in a spoken or written text exhibits basic sentence order (noun phrase followed by verb phrase). Follow-on sentences may, however, be inverted to avert monotony. Such inversion often has the additional force of 'so', 'then' or 'and' in a continuous text, serving to provide continuity the way an adverb, prepositional phrase or conjunction might do. In many traditional styles of discourse and narrative, only the first sentence in any paragraph is in basic word order. The rest may be processed by stylistic inversion.

SAMPLES OF STYLISTIC INVERSION

איך בין אַרײַן אין צימער. איז עס געוען פֿינצטער.

I entered the room. It was dark.

איך האָב ניט פֿאַרשטאַנען. האָב איך געלייענט ווײַטער.

I didn't understand. So I continued reading.

איך האָב געוואָלט מיט אײַך רעדן. בין איך געקומען.

I wanted to speak with you (formal). So I came.

14.5   WORD PLACEMENT IN INVERTED SENTENCE ORDER

14.5.1   זיך in inverted sentence order

זיך follows the nominative in inverted sentence order if the nominative is a
personal pronoun. זיך follows the inflected verb where the nominative is a
common or proper noun.

SAMPLES OF זיך IN INVERTED SENTENCE ORDER

present

That is why he is delighted   צוליב דעם פֿרייט ער זיך

That is why the boss is delighted   צוליב דעם פֿרייט זיך דער באַלעבאָס

present of verbs with stressed prefixes

Why do you (familiar) refuse?   ?אָפּזאָגן זיך (inf.)   פֿאַרוואָס זאָגסטו זיך אָפּ?

Why does Esther refuse?   ?אָפּ   פֿאַרוואָס זאָגט זיך אסתּר [éstər]

past

They became friends in Peru   [bafráynt]   אין פּערו האָבן זיי זיך באַפֿרײַנדט

Those two became friends in Peru   אין פּערו האָבן זיך די צוויי באַפֿרײַנדט

future

We will meet next year   איבעראַיאָר וועט מען זיך טרעפֿן

The sons will meet next year   איבעראַיאָר וועלן זיך טרעפֿן די זין

14.5.2   Object pronouns in inverted sentence order

Accusative pronouns (→§6.1.2) immediately follow the subject. Dative pronouns (→ §6.1.3) follow the preposition of which they are the object, as they do in basic sentence order (→ §14.3.2).

SAMPLES OF OBJECT PRONOUNS IN INVERTED SENTENCE ORDER

present

While listening , he paints you (formal)   צוהערנדיק דיך מאָלט ער אײַך

He looks at you (familiar) all day   אַ גאַנצן טאָג קוקט ער אויף דיר

present of verbs with stressed prefix

Why are they throwing us out?   פֿאַרוואָס וואַרפֿט מען אונדז אַרויס?

פֿאַרוואָס נעמט מען פֿון אונדז אַוועק אַלצדינג?
Why are they taking everything away from us?

past

We were cheated on Thursday   דאָנערשטיק האָט מען אונדז אָפּגענאַרט

They spoke to us later   שפּעטער האָבן זײ מיט אונדז גערעדט

future

Will we see them tomorrow?   צי וועלן מיר זײ מאָרגן זען?

Of course they won't yell at us   זיכער וועלן זײ אויף אונדז ניט שרײַען

14.5.3 ניט in inverted sentence order

As in basic sentence order (→ §14.3.3), ניט occurs somewhere after the inflected verb, and, in verbs comprising helping plus main verb, somewhere between the two.

SAMPLES OF ניט IN INVERTED WORD ORDER

present

Nevertheless, I'm not going   דאָך גײ איך ניט

פֿאַרוואָס ווייסן זיי ניט פֿון זייערע הענט און פֿיס?

Why don't they know what they're doing? (lit. 'Why don't they know of
their hands and feet?')

present of verbs with stressed prefix

מאָנטיק שטייען מיר ניט אויף פֿרי   We're not getting up early on Monday

דערווײַל וואַרף איך ניט אַרויס דעם מאַנטל

In the meantime, I'm not throwing away the coat

past

פֿאַראַיאָרן בין איך ניט געפֿאָרן אין ירושלים [yərusholáyim]

Last year I didn't go to Jerusalem

future

אויב זיי קומען וועלן מיר ניט פֿאָרן אין מאָנטרעאַל

If they come, we won't go to Montreal

פֿאַרוואָס וועלן מיר זיך ניט זען פֿרײַטיק?

Why won't we see each other on Friday?

14.5.3.1   ניט with זיך   in inverted sentence order

As in basic sentence order (→ §14.3.3.1), זיך   always precedes ניט. Adverbs
and the subject may appear between them.

SAMPLES OF ניט WITH זיך IN INVERTED SENTENCE ORDER

איצט באַמי איך זיך ניט   I don't try now

איצט באַמי איך זיך שוין ניט   Now I don't try anymore

איצט באַמיט זיך שוין שמעון [shímən] ניט   Now Shímən doesn't try anymore

240

14.5.3.2 נ׳ט with personal pronoun as subject in inverted sentence order

Where the subject that has been transposed by inversion is a personal pronoun, נ׳ט must appear after the pronoun. An adverb may appear between them. Where the subject is a proper or common noun, נ׳ט may precede the object noun.

SAMPLES OF נ׳ט WITH SUBJECT NOUNS IN INVERTED SENTENCE ORDER

If you come, he won't come   אַז דו קומסט וועט ער ניט קומען

אַז דו קומסט וועלן ניט קומען די מענטשן = וועלן די מענטשן ניט קומען

If you come, the people won't come

אַז דו קומסט וועט ניט קומען בריַינדל = וועט בריַינדל ניט קומען

If you come, Bráyndl won't come

14.5.3.3 נ׳ט with object pronoun

As in basic sentence order (→ §14.3.3.2), נ׳ט follows an object personal pronoun. An adverb may appear between them. In analogous sentences with common or proper nouns, נ׳ט may (and usually does) precede the object noun.

SAMPLES OF ניט WITH OBJECT NOUNS IN INVERTED SENTENCE ORDER

Today, I don't see him upstairs   הײַנט זע איך אים [em] ניט אויבן

Today, I don't see him upstairs anymore   הײַנט זע איך אים שוין ניט אויבן

Today, I don't see the people upstairs   הײַנט זע איך ניט די מענטשן אויבן

Today, I don't see Zálmən upstairs   הײַנט זע איך ניט זלמנען[zálmənən] אויבן

14.5.3.4 נ׳ט קיין in inverted sentence order

As in basic sentence order (→ §14.3.3.3), קיין [kin / ka] occurs immediately before the noun phrase that is its object. נ׳ט קיין are often separated by the requirements of נ׳ט placement.

SAMPLES OF THE POSITION OF קײן ניט IN INVERTED SENTENCE ORDER

We don't have any time on Sunday   זונטיק האָבן מיר ניט קײן צײַט

האָסט מיר ניט דערצײלט קײן באָבע־מעשה? [bóbə màysə]

You didn't tell me a tall story?

14.5.3.5 ניט jumped to end during fronting

When a negative sentence undergoes object fronting for emphasis ($\rightarrow$ §§14.4.7, 14.10), ניט is jumped to the end of the sentence for emphasis.

SAMPLES OF ניט IN OBJECT FRONTING INVERSION

I'm not Rothschild   ראָטשילד בין איך ניט

She did not kill him   [derhárgət] האָט זי אים ניט דערהרגעט

You don't have any sense   [séykhl] האָסטו ניט שׂכל

She is no fool   [kinár] איז זי ניט קײן נאַר

14.6   PREDICATIVES

14.6.1   Positive predicatives

The positive predicatives are singular ס'איז דאָ 'there is', plural ס'זײַנען דאָ 'there are'. In the past and future, דאָ disappears. It is replaced by past participle געװען in the past and the appropriate part of װעלן זײַן in the future. When applied in the present tense to humans, the predicative can have the sense of 'just arrived'. Where דאָ '(over) here' occurs alongside ס'איז דאָ or ס'זײַנען דאָ, the resulting sequences ס'איז דאָ דאָ 'there is (over) here' and ס'זײַנען דאָ דאָ 'there are (over) here', are retained.

present singular

there is   [sidó / sizdó] ס'איז דאָ

SAMPLES OF THE PRESENT SINGULAR PREDICATIVE

There's a theatre in town   ס'איז דאָ אַ טעאַטער אין שטאָט

Shlóymə is here / Shlóymə has just arrived   שלמה [sido dó] ס'איז דאָ דאָ

present plural

there are   [(s)záynən dó] ס'זײַנען דאָ

SAMPLES OF THE PRESENT PLURAL PREDICATIVE

There are many students here   ס'זײַנען דאָ אַ סך סטודענטן דאָ

Are the guys here yet?   [khévrə] ס'זײַנען שוין דאָ די חברה?

past singular

(there / it) was   [sigəvén / səìz gəvén] ס'איז געװען

SAMPLES OF THE PAST SINGULAR PREDICATIVE

It was a nice day   ס'איז געװען אַ שײנער טאָג

Was Símə here?   ס'איז דאָ געװען סימע?

past plural

there were   [(s)záynən gəvén] ס'זײַנען געװען

SAMPLES OF THE PAST PLURAL PREDICATIVE

There were many robbers   [asákh] ס'זײַנען געװען אַ סך רױבער

Were Símə and Zálmən there?   ס'זײַנען געװען סימע און זלמן?

future singular

there will be   [sitzáyn / səvet záyn]   ס׳וועט זײַן

SAMPLES OF THE FUTURE SINGULAR PREDICATIVE

It will turn out well   ס׳וועט זײַן גוט

Kháne will be there   ס׳וועט זײַן דאָרטן חנה

future plural

there will be   [səln záyn / sveln záyn]   ס׳וועלן זײַן

SAMPLES OF THE FUTURE PLURAL PREDICATIVE

There will be students there   ס׳וועלן זײַן דאָרטן סטודענטן

Kháne and Shmúəl will be there   ס׳וועלן זײַן דאָרטן חנה און שמואל

14.6.2 Negative predicatives

In the present tense, the negative predicatives are ס׳איז ניטאָ (or ניטאָ)
ס׳איז ניט געווען 'there isn't' and ס׳זײַנען ניטאָ 'there aren't'. In the past – ס׳איז ניט געווען
'there wasn't' and ס׳זײַנען ניט געווען 'there weren't'. Future forms are
ס׳וועט ניט זײַן 'there won't be', plural ס׳וועלן ניט זײַן. In colloquial
speech it is common to use the singular forms for both singular and plural. If
the negative predicative has an indefinite object, the indefinite article
disappears and is replaced by קיין. When the object is a personal name, קיין is
omitted unless the proper name is being treated as a common noun, for
identification of a stranger or humorously for a familiar individual (cf. 'Isn't
there a Joe around?'). When the object has a definite article, the definite
article is retained in the negative and no קיין appears, unless the sense of

'any' or 'none at all' is required, in which case קײן replaces the definite article.

present singular

there is no   [sinitó / siz nitó /səlz nitó] ס׳איז ניטאָ

SAMPLES OF THE PRESENT SINGULAR NEGATIVE PREDICATIVE

There isn't a theatre in town   ס׳איז ניטאָ קײן טעאַטער אין שטאָט

The theatre doesn't exist any more   ס׳איז ניטאָ מער דער טעאַטער

Shlóymə is not here / Shlóymə hasn't arrived   ס׳איז ניטאָ דאָ שלמה

There is no Shloyme here   ס׳איז ניטאָ דאָ קײן שלמה

present plural

there are no   [(s)záynən nitó] ס׳זײנען ניטאָ

SAMPLES OF THE PRESENT PLURAL NEGATIVE PREDICATIVE

There aren't many students here   ס׳זײנען ניטאָ דאָ קײן סך סטודענטן

Our friends aren't here yet? [khavéyrim]   ס׳זײנען נאָך ניטאָ די חבֿרים?

past singular

there wasn't any [sinigəvén / s(ə)iz nít gəvén] ס׳איז ניט געװען

SAMPLES OF THE PAST SINGULAR NEGATIVE PREDICATIVE

It wasn't a nice day   ס׳איז ניט געװען קײן שײנער טאָג

Wasn't Símə here?   ס׳איז ניט געװען דאָ סימע?

past plural

there were no   [(s)záynən nigəvén / nit gəvén] ס׳זײנען ניט געװען

SAMPLES OF THE PAST PLURAL NEGATIVE PREDICATIVE

There weren't many robbers ס'זײנען ניט געוחען קײן סך [kinsákh] רױבער

Were Símə and Zálmən not there? ?ס'זײנען ניט געוחען סימע און זלמן

future singular

There won't be [sətnitzáyn / səvet nit záyn] ס'חעט ניט זײן

SAMPLES OF THE FUTURE SINGULAR NEGATIVE PREDICATIVE

It won't turn out well ס'חעט ניט זײן גוט

Khánə won't be there חנה חעט ניט זײן דאָרטן

future plural

there won't be [səin ni(t)záyn / svein nít záyn] ס'חעלן ניט זײן

SAMPLES OF THE FUTURE PLURAL NEGATIVE PREDICATIVE

There won't be any students there ס'חעלן ניט זײן דאָרטן קײן סטודענטן

Khánə and Shmúəl won't be there ס'חעלן ניט זײן דאָרטן חנה און שמואל

14.7   RELATIVES

Relatives 'who' and 'that/which' replace the subject they refer to. The inflected verb usually follows the relative and is thus maintained in second position within the relative phrase (the subsentence launched by the relative), in conformity with the inflected-verb-second rule. The relatives are uninflecting חאָס and inflecting חעלכער. Its inflection follows the same anomalous pattern of interrogative חעלכער (→ §11.3.1.1). חאָס and חעלכער are frequently but not always interchangeable. While חעלכער occurs in all three cases, וואָס is limited to nominative and accusative. When referring to people, both וואָס and וועלכער may be replaced in either object case by וועמען 'whom', which does not inflect for number or gender.

SAMPLES OF RELATIVES IN NOMINATIVE

דער טיש וואָס\וועלכער שטייט דאָ איז אַ שיינער

The table that stands here is a pretty one

די פֿרוי וואָס\וועלכע זיצט דאָרטן איז מײַן פּראָפֿעסאָרשע [profesórshə]

The woman sitting over there is my professor (f.)

דאָס ליד וואָס\וועלכע איז זייער שיין איז צו לאַנג אויף איצטער

The poem, which is very beautiful, is too long for now

די מענטשן וואָס\וועלכע קומען זײַנען מײַנע גוטע פֿרײַנד

The people who are coming are my good friends

SAMPLES OF RELATIVES IN ACCUSATIVE

דעם טיש וואָס\וועלכן איך האָב געקויפֿט איז אַ שיינער

The table I bought is a pretty one

די פֿרוי וואָס\וועלכע איך זע דאָרטן איז מײַן פּראָפֿעסאָרשע

The woman I see over there is my professor (f.)

דאָס ליד וואָס\וועלכע די פּאָעטעסע האָט אָנגעשריבן איז זייער שיין

The poem, which the poetess wrote is very beautiful

די מענטשן וואָס\וועלכע\וועמען איך זע זײַנען מײַנע גוטע פֿרײַנד

The people whom I see are my good friends

SAMPLES OF RELATIVES IN DATIVE

דער טיש פֿון וֹועלכן איך האָב גערעדט שטײט דאָ

The table of which I was speaking is standing over here

די פֿרוי מיט וֹועלכער\וֹועמען איך רעד איז מײַן פּראָפֿעסאָרשע

The woman with whom I am speaking is my professor (f.)

דאָס ליד וֹועגן וֹועלכן דו האָסט געליֿיענט איז זיֿיער שיֿין

The poem of which you read is very beautiful

די מענטשן צו וֹועלכע\וֹועמען איך גיֿי זײַנען מײַנע גוטע פֿרײַנד

The people to whom I am going are my good friends

14.7.1 וואָס as subordinate phrase launcher

Unlike its English counterpart, relative וואָס can launch a subordinate sentence.

SAMPLES OF וואָס AS A SUBORDINATE PHRASE LAUNCHER

די מענטשן וואָס מיט זיֿי קען מען ניט רעדן זײַנען וֹוידער דאָ

The people with whom one cannot communicate (lit. 'the people that with them one cannot talk') are here again

דער דאָקטער וואָס איך קען אים איז הײַנט אָנגעקומען

The doctor whom I know (lit. 'that I know him') arrived today

14.8 REFLEXIVE CONSTRUCTIONS

Reflexive verbs are formed by putting the subject, usually human, with all its articles and adjectives into dative (→ §§5.1.3, 5.3.3, 5.5.3). As it happens, the minority of Yiddish nouns that do inflect (→ §5.14) are human designators — intimate nouns (→ §5.14.1), proper names (→ §5.14.2) and personal pronouns (→ §6.1.3). The noun phrase, appropriately inflected for dative, is linked to the verb via the third person singular of זיך (→ §7.7.1): איז in the present, (זײַנען געװען) איז געװען (plural) in the past, and װעט זיך (plural וועלן זיך) in the future. The literal sense of reflexivity is therefore 'it is / was / will be something to somebody'. Many verbs just happen historically to take the reflexive. They denote states of being or feeling rather than actions per se. A number of reflexives are formed with װערן 'become' (→ §9.1.7) rather than זיך. Note that the passively constructed געפֿעלן װערן 'like' (→ §15.5.6) takes the reflexive.

SAMPLES OF USE OF THE REFLEXIVE

I'm o.k.; all is well with me; I've got it good   מיר איז גוט

She's feeling cold   איר איז קאַלט

Martin is feeling hot   מאַרטינען איז הייס

Father is feeling cool outside   דעם טאַטן איז קיל אין דרויסן

Grandmother is feeling warm today   דער באָבען [bóbm] איז היַנט װאַרעם

She likes him [er gəféltir]   ער געפֿעלט איר

She once liked him more   אַמאָל איז ער איר מער געפֿעלן געװען

Blúmkə likes Nósn [nósn]   בלומקען געפֿעלט נתן

He likes her [zi gəféltəm]   זי געפֿעלט אים

He once liked her more [em]   אַמאָל איז זי אים מער געפֿעלן געװען

Séndər likes Kháykə   סענדערן געפֿעלט חיהקע

You don't know how good you had it   װייסט ניט װי גוט ס'איז דיר געװען

It will be difficult for us next year   איבעראַיאָר װעט אונדז זיַן שװער

Are you getting fed up? [níməs]   ס'װערט דיר שוין נמאס?

Here you'll find it better   דאָ װעט דיר בעסער װערן

14.9 THE DOUBLE VERB CONSTRUCTION

The use of the infinitive followed by the same verb in its appropriately inflected form, with inversion, is a popular device for denoting contrast or habitual activity. For the small minority of verbs where the first person plural differs from the infinitive, the double verb construction follows the first person plural (e.g. װײסן rather than װיסן, ניבן rather than געבן).

SAMPLES OF THE DOUBLE VERB CONSTRUCTION

טראַכטן טראַכט ער אָבער אַרבעטן אַרבעט ער ניט

He does think, but he certainly doesn't do any work (lit. 'but work he doesn't')

לאַכן לאַכן מיר אָבער קאָמיש איז עס ניט

We do laugh but it's not funny (lit. 'but funny it's not')

קומען קומט די יעדע נאַכט אַזײגער עלף

She comes every night at eleven o'clock

14.9.1 The discontinued double verb construction

A double verb construction with no follow-on tends to imply dissatisfaction, or to provide implicit criticism or irony, the nature of which is evident from context.

SAMPLES OF THE DISCONTINUED DOUBLE VERB CONSTRUCTION

קומען קומט ער... [kúmən | kúmt er]

He will most certainly come (but...)

לאַכן לאַכט זי... [lákhn | lákhtzi]

She certainly is laughing (but...)

14.9.2 The double infinitive construction

An infinitive fronted to the beginning of the sentence for emphasis ($\rightarrow$ §§14.4.7, 14.10) may be repeated in an inverted phrase following upon it. The construction has implicit but powerful comparative force.

SAMPLES OF THE REPEATED INFINITIVE

One can certainly laugh (but.....) לאַכן קען מען לאַכן

They will certainly try (but...) פרואוון וועלן זיי פרואוון

14.10 VARIABILITY OF WORD ORDER

Subject to the constraints outlined in this chapter, word order can vary dramatically depending both on rhythmic factors and the speaker's wish to lay greater stress on one of the several parts. Most frequently, the part of the sentence brought up to the front marks its semantic prominence. Apart from inflected verbs which are assigned to second position, nearly anything can be brought up to the front. And even inflected verbs may be brought up front to create a dramatic exclamation. The item at the end may also carry greater or greatest stress, depending on intonation (or, in written texts, context). Items in the middle generally have less emphasis.

SAMPLES OF VARIABILITY OF WORD ORDER

I have enough apples איך האָב גענוג עפל

I have *enough* apples גענוג עפל האָב איך

I have *enough apples* גענוג האָב איך עפל

I have enough *apples* עפל האָב איך גענוג

Do I have enough apples! האָב איך גענוג עפלו

We can't come now מיר קענען ניט קומען איצטער

We can't come *now* איצטער קענען מיר ניט קומען

We can't actually *come* *now*   איצטער קומען קענען מיר ניט

We can't actually *come* now   קומען קענען מיר ניט איצטער

We *can't* come now   קומען איצטער קענען מיר ניט

We just *can't* come now!   קענען מיר איצטער ניט קומען!

We just *can't* come *now*!   קענען מיר ניט קומען איצטער!

15 SEMANTICS

15.0   OVERVIEW

The notes in this chapter provide acquaintance with a number of semantic distinctions that have no direct correlates in English.

15.1   'AT'

The most frequent equivalent of 'at' is בײַ [ba]. בײַ also translates 'from' that ascribes learning something from somebody or studying with or under somebody. בײַ has a number of additional uses which must be mastered case by case. בײַ regularly conflates with the dative definite article דעם, giving בײַם [bam] (→ §5.3.3.1).

SAMPLES OF THE USE OF בײַ

דאָס האָט ער געלערנט בײַם [bam] זײדן

He learned this from his grandfather

מיר האָט שטודירדט בײַ אַ גרויטן פּראָפֿעסאָר

We studied under a great professor

בײַ זײ איז אַנדערש

Things are different with them

איך האָב געוואוינט בײַ אים [ba em] צוויי יאָר

I lived at his place for two years

בײַ זײ אין דער הײם איז וואַרעם

It's warm in their house

ביסט געװען בײַם דאָקטער?

Have you been to see the doctor?

15.2 'FROM'

פֿון translates most instances of 'of', hence טייל פֿון דעם 'part of it'; most instances of 'from', hence איך בין אַנטלאָפֿן פֿון אַלקאַטראַז 'I escaped from Alcatraz'; 'by' that ascribes authorship, hence אַ נײַ בוך פֿונעם זעלביקן שרײַבער 'a new book by the same author'.

15.3 'GO'

To walk or to go a conceptually short distance is גײן; to go by vehicle is פֿאָרן. Cf. איך גײ אַהײם 'I'm going home' (on the assumption that home is nearby) vs. איך פֿאָר קײן אויסטראַליע 'I'm going to Australia'.

15.4 'KNOW'

קענען is used for knowledge acquired by study, knowledge of languages, and acquaintanceship with humans or objects. װיסן, on the other hand, is used with reference to more general empirical knowledge of the world and in cases where there is no object (→ §9.1.16 on קענען as an analytic verb former).

SAMPLES OF קענען .VS וויסן

She knows geometry well	זי קען גוט גיאָמעטריע
She knows a little Turkish	זי קען אַ ביסל טערקיש
He knows Bob well	ער קען באָבן גוט
He doesn't know the street very well	ער קען ניט די גאַס זייער גוט
I don't know	איך ווייס ניט
I know how to answer	איך ווייס ווי אַזוי מ'דאַרף ענטפֿערן
Do you know that man's name?	צי ווייסט איר ווי ס'הייסט יענער מאַן?

15.5 'LOVE'

15.5.1 'Friend'

The neutral terms are פֿרײַנד (usually pronounced and occasionally spelled
פֿרײַנט) 'friend (m.)' and פֿרײַנדינע [frayndínə] 'friend (f.)'. Both refer to
platonic friendship. In addition, they may be used disingenuously about a
romantic relationship which one is reluctant to divulge. Thus, when a woman
says מײַן פֿרײַנד she implicitly claims not to be involved romantically with
the male friend referred to. Analogously, when a man says מײַן פֿרײַנדינע of
a woman, he does so to stress the nonromantic nature of the friendship. To
convey the general notion 'friend' of a person of the opposite sex, with no
romantic undertones or implicit denials, the predicative possessive pronoun
with indefinite article may be used, e.g. ער איז מײַנער אַ פֿרײַנד 'He is a
friend of mine', זי איז מײַנע אַ פֿרײַנדינע 'She is a friend of mine' (→

§§5.7, 6.2.1.5).

15.5.2 'Boyfriend' and 'Girlfriend'

חבֿר [khávər] 'friend (m.)' and חבֿרטע [khávərtə] 'friend (f.)' (occasionally חבֿרטאָרן [khávərtorn]) are synonymous with פֿרײַנד and פֿרײַנדינע when referring to persons of the same sex. Thus for a woman speaking of her woman friend, מײַן פֿרײַנדינע and מײַן חבֿרטע are synonymous, as are מײַן פֿרײַנד and מײַן חבֿר to a man. For opposite sexes, however, חבֿר and חבֿרטע have the sense of 'boyfriend' and 'girlfriend' respectively, most unequivocally so when used with possessive pronouns, e.g. איר חבֿר 'her boyfriend', דײַן חבֿרטע 'your girlfriend'.

15.5.3 'Going out'

A traditional expression is אַרומגײן מיט (lit. 'go around with'), e.g. זי גײט אַרום מיט אים [em] פֿיר יאָר 'She's been seeing him for four years'. In English-speaking countries, the anglicism אַרויסגײן מיט [aróyzgeyn] (lit. 'go out with') is very popular. Its near-homophony with אויסגײן [óyzgeyn] 'die' is often exploited in jokes. The most universal phrase in use is simply גײן מיט (lit. 'go with').

15.5.4 'Lover'

'Beloved' or 'lover' is an inflecting nominalized adjective —געליבט, hence געליבטער [gəlíptər] 'beloved (m.)'; געליבטע [gəlíptə] 'beloved (f.)'; pl. געליבטע 'lovers'. They are often used in Yiddish where English would have 'boyfriend' or 'girlfriend' although the semantic content of the Yiddish denotes a level of intimacy higher than חבֿר and חבֿרטע. There are a number of other terms which may be used for special effects, e.g. ליבהאָבער (f. ליבהאָבערין) in lighthearted jest (referring also to lovers of or dabblers in the arts); ליבסטער (f. ליבסטע), technically a superlative meaning 'most beloved', in folkloristic and poetic usage; ליובאָווניק (f. ליובאָווניצע) and ליובעניו, now archaic and used only to make fun of somebody else's relationship.

15.5.5   'Love affair'

שטילן אַ ליבע, פֿירן אַ ליבע or [román] פֿירן אַ ראָמאַן may be used for 'have a romantic relationship / love affair'.

15.5.6   'Like' and 'love'

'Like' is expressed via a reflexive construction (→ §14.8). Subject 'likee' + געפֿעלן (וועדן) + dative 'liker' combine, e.g. ער געפֿעלט איר 'She likes him', זי געפֿעלט אים [em] 'He likes her'. 'Love' is an analytic verb with האָבן (→ §9.2.1), ליב האָבן [líb hobm], which imposes accusative, e.g. זי האָט אים ליב 'She loves him', ער האָט זי ליב 'He loves her'. An alternative to ליב האָבן is האַלט האָבן.

15.6   'PAPER'

A piece of paper is אַ שטיקל פּאַפּיר [a shtíkl papír], pl. שטיקלעך פּאַפּיר. צײַטונג (די) is 'newspaper' (pl. צײַטונגען). רעפּעראַט (דער) refers to a learned or academic paper delivered before a conference or symposium (pl. רעפֿעראַטן). A leaf of a book is בלאַט; a single page is זײַט or זײַטל when not prefixing a specific number, e.g. אויף - אויף וועלכער זײַט איז דאָס? 'On which page is it?'. When a page number is included, only זײַט occurs, e.g. אויף זײַט 92 'on page 92'. Its abbreviated form is 'ז' 'p.' but older ז. is still encountered).

15.7 'PARTY'

Traditional Jewish celebrations, most notably weddings, bar-mitsvahs, and circumcisions, are called שׂמחות [símkhəs]. Some speakers expand the range of שׂמחה to cover a party of any type. Others Yiddishize the Israeli Hebrew מסיבה [məsibá] to [məsíbə], but neither option has gained much ground outside limited circles. A party characterized by the presence of single people and alcohol is a הוליאַנקע [hulyánkə] (pl. הוליאַנקעס). One that gets out of hand is a וואַקכאַנאַליע [vakkhanáiyə], lit. 'orgy' but usually used humorously of any 'wildish party'. A traditional and universally acceptable way of expressing the modern notion of 'party' is a prepositional phrase rather than a noun — קומען אויף לחיים [ləkháyəms] 'come for (alcoholic) drinks'.

15.8 'QUESTION'

A simple question of fact that is swiftly answerable, e.g. 'Which way is Delancey Street?' is most frequently rendered by the analytic אַ פֿרעג טאָן (→ §9.1.9) lit. 'give an ask'. The most universal and middle-of-the-road question is פֿראַגעס 'question' (→ §4.2.2.1 on the semantic nuances of variant plural endings of פֿראַגעס). An intellectually contentious question, implicitly or explicitly challenging a premise or argument, is a קשיא [káshə]. Finally, a traditional Jewish legal question asked of an appropriate (usually rabbinic) authority, most often on a matter requiring a yes or no answer, is a שאלה [sháylə]. Note the popular proverb אַז מ'פֿרעגט אַ שאלה איז טרייף [amə frékt a sháylə iz tréyf] lit. 'When one asks a question (of the rabbi as to whether certain food is kosher), the answer is that it is not kosher'. The proverb has the sense of 'If you ask permission the answer will be no (so go ahead and do what you please without asking)'.

15.9   'RIGHT'

For a human to 'be right' is דו ביסט גערעכט, e.g. האָבן רעכט or זײַן גערעכט - דו האָסט רעכט 'you are right'. For a thing (e.g. a statement, idea, book) to 'be right' is adjective ריכטיק, e.g. דאָס איז ריכטיק 'that's right'. The noun 'right' is רעכט (דאָס), which has no plural. It is often used as a collective abstract concept, e.g. מענטשלעכע רעכט 'human rights'.

15.10   'SENSE'

'Sense' meaning 'logic' is שׂכל [séykhl], e.g. אין דעם איז ניטאָ קיין שׂכל [indém initó kin séykhl] 'There's no sense in it'. 'Sense' meaning 'one of the possible meanings of a word or thing' is זין, e.g. אין וועלכן זין מיינסטו דאָס? 'In what sense do you mean it?'. Sense as a specific human faculty, or one of the five senses, is חוש [khush] (pl. חושים [khúshim]), e.g. די האָט אַ גוטן

חוֹש הוּמָאָר 'She has a good sense of humour'.

15.11 'SOLUTION'

Solution to an intellectual question (e.g. קְשִׁיא → §15.8) is a תירוץ [térəts], but note that in everyday use תירוץ may mean 'excuse'. אויסוועג [óyzveg] may be used for a solution that is a 'way out' of a problem. בּאַשייד [bashéyd] usually refers to the solution of a riddle or mystery in the world of ideas, and סגולה [zgúlə] (also 'remedy') to the solving of a more practical problem. The most generally applicable term is לייזונג. In popular usage, פּאַטענט [patént], lit. 'patent' is used approvingly of a promising or successful solution to a problem.

15.12 'TELL'

זאָגן is the most frequent correlate of 'tell', e.g. זאָג מירו 'Tell me!'. To 'tell (a story)' is דערצײלן, e.g. דערצײל מיר אַ מעשׂה [máysə] 'Tell me a story'. To 'tell' in the sense of 'convey information' is איבערגעבן, e.g. קענסט מיר איבערגעבן וואָס מ'האָט געזאָגט? 'Can you tell me what was said?'.

15.13 'THE'

The definite article substitutes for possessive pronouns (→ §6.2) where possession is known, understood, or can be inferred from context. Thus, in a conversation with someone about his or her father, one would say דער טאַטע

rather than מײן טאַטע (which is reserved for cases where there might be ambiguity). Analogously, the article is used with inanimate objects, e.g. דער אויטאָמאָביל איז קאַליע געװאָרן 'My car has broken down' where possession is clear.

15.14   'THINK'

טראַכטן is the most general verb for 'think'. It may be modified by unstressed prefixes -באַ, giving באַטראַכטן 'think (about something specific); consider', and -דער, giving דערטראַכטן זיך 'think until a solution is found'. It also attracts stressed prefix -צו, giving צוטראַכטן 'devise; come with (a solution)'. מיינען is to think in the sense of 'be of the opinion' and corresponds with its noun (די) מיינונג 'opinion'. רעכענען and קלערן may overlap with both טראַכטן and מיינען. קלערן has a more ponderous, considered mood about it. אַרײנקלערן generally has the sense of 'contemplate'. דענקען is rarely encountered in literary Yiddish. In journalistic prose and colloquial use, however, it is frequently used for מיינען.

SAMPLES OF THE USE OF VERBS FOR 'THINK'

I think a lot about the problem   איך טראַכט אַ סך װעגן דער פּראָבלעם

Man thinks and God laughs (proverb)   דער מענטש טראַכט און גאָט לאַכט

Well, what are you thinking about? [nu | vos trákhstə?]   נו, װאָס טראַכסטו?

I have to think about it   איך דאַרף עס באַטראַכטן

I've come up with an answer   איך האָב זיך דערטראַכט צו אַן ענטפֿער

Have you come up with anything?   האָסט עמעס צוגעטראַכט?

Well, what do you think?   נו, װאָס מיינסטו?

I have a different opinion   איך מיין אַנדערש

I thought about it a lot   איך האָב אַ סך געקלערט װעגן דעם

15.15   'TIME'

צײַט (די) covers time in the general sense only. The sense of 'occasion; event; occurrence' is מאָל (דאָס), hence דאָס) לעצטע מאָל '(the) last time'. The equivalent of 'a good time' is the verbal phrase גוט פֿאַרברענגען [farbréyngən] lit. 'spend the time well'.

15.16   'TO'

The usages covered by English 'to' correspond with a number of prepositions, depending on the nature of the prepositional object.

15.16.1   'To (a person)' = צו

Hence צו דבֿורהן [dvóyrən] 'to Dvoyre', צו שלמהן [shlóymən] 'to Shloyme', צו דער מאַמען 'to mother'. צום לערער 'to the teacher', צו is frequently omitted where it is the understood preposition in dative. Verbs concerned with human communication usually do not take צו, e.g. איך האָב איר געזאָגט 'I told her', איך האָב געזאָגט דער לערערין 'I told the teacher (f.)'.

15.16.2   'To (a physical object)' = צו

Hence, צום טיש 'to the table', צום בוים 'to the tree', צום בנין [bínyən] 'to the building'.

15.16.3   'To (a geopolitical concept)' = קיין [kin] or אין

Hence קיין אָקסטאָרד or אין אָקסטאָרד 'to Oxford', קיין סאַן פֿראַנציסקאָ or

אין סאַן פֿראַנציסקאָ 'to San Francisco', אין פּאַריז קיין or קיין פּאַריז 'to Paris'. If the place name happens to be a plural, or happens to include the feminine definite article די, only אין is used, hence אין די פֿאַראייניקטע שטאַטן 'to the United States', אין דער ליטע 'to Lithuania', אין דער שווייץ 'to Switzerland'.

15.16.4 'To (a place that is not a geopolitical concept)' = אין

Hence אין באַנק 'to the bank', אין פֿאַבריק [fabrík] 'to the factory', אין וואַלד 'to the forest', אין שטאָט 'to the city'. Cf. §5.3.3.2

15.16.5 'To (an event)' = אויף [af]

Hence אויף דער חתונה [av dər khásənə] 'to the wedding', אויף דער לוויה [av dər ləváyə] 'to the funeral', אויף דער זיצונג 'to the meeting', אויפֿן קאָנגרעס 'to the congress / conference'.

15.17 JEWISH VS. GENERAL

Yiddish evolved as the language of Ashkenazic Jewish civilization over a millennium, coterritorially with the cultures of Christian Europe. The language has a huge lexicon for traditional Jewish concepts, institutions and realia. All of these survive in full in traditional communities. There are, however, large numbers of items that survive both in literal and in metaphoric senses, in all varieties of Yiddish. There is also vocabulary to cover the civilization of Christian Europe specifically. Since the Westernizing movements of the nineteenth century, the language has been enriched by large numbers of borrowings from German, Russian and the international 'Western repertoire' of secular internationalisms. The result is a two or three tier semantics. The following is a modest sampling.

15.17.1 'Bible'

תנ"ך [tanákh] 'Jewish Bible (i.e. the Old Testament)'

vs.

ביבל [bíbl] 'Bible (in general)'

15.17.2 'Book'

ספֿר [séyfər] (pl. ספֿרים [sfórim]) 'traditional sacred book'

vs.

בוך [bukh] (pl. ביכֿער) 'book (in general)'

15.17.3 'Conference'

אסיפֿה [asífə] (pl. אסיפֿות [asífəs]) '(traditional) assembly / conference'

vs.

פֿאַרזאַמלונג (pl. פֿאַרזאַמלונגען) 'assembly / conference (in general)'

15.17.4 'Expert'

בקי [bóki] '(be) expert / proficient (in Talmudic studies)'

vs.

מומחה [múmkhə] 'expert / specialist (in anything)'

vs.

עקספּערט [ekspért] 'expert (in anything)'

15.17.5 'Fool'

שוטה [shóytə] (pl. שוטים [shóytim]) '(Jewish) fool'

vs.

טיפּש [típəsh] (pl. טיפּשים [típshim]) '(esp. Jewish) fool'

vs.

נאַר [nar] (pl. נאַראָנים [narónim]) '(any) fool'

15.17.6 'Genius'

גאון [góən] (pl. גאונים [gəóynim]) 'genius (esp. in Talmudic studies)'

vs.

עלוי [ílə] (pl. עלוים [ilúim]) 'young genius (esp. in Talmudic studies)'

vs.

געניע [gényə] (pl. גענ יעס) 'genius (in general)'

15.17.7 'God'

(דער) רבונו-של-עולם [dər rəbóynə shəlóyləm] 'God (viewed traditionally)'

vs.

(דער) רבונו-דעלמא [dər rəbóynə dəálmə] 'God (viewed traditionally)'
(used in learned style)

vs.

(דער) אײבערשטער [dər éybərshtər] 'God (viewed intimately)'

vs.

טאַטע זיסער (lit. 'Sweet father' →§5.8.1) 'God (viewed very intimately)'

vs.

גאָט 'God (as universal concept)'

15.17.8 'Justice'

יושר [yóyshər] '(traditional sense of) justice (in a specific case)'

vs.

נערעכטיקײַט '(modern / universal sense of) justice'

15.17.9 'Pray'

דאַווענען [dávənən] 'say the traditional Jewish prayers'

vs.

תפֿילה טאָן [tfílə ton] 'pray (in general)'

15.17.10 'Prayer'

תפֿילה [tfílə] '(traditional Jewish) prayer'

vs.

געבעט [gəbét] 'prayer (in general)'

15.17.11 'Rabbi'

רבֿ [rov] (pl. רבנים [rabónim]) 'traditional rabbi'

vs.

רבי [rébə] (pl. רביים [rabéyim]) 'Chassidic rebbe'

vs.

ראַבינער [rabíner] (pl. — or ס-; f. ראַבינערין, pl. ס-) 'modern rabbi'

vs.

רֵאבֵײ (pl. רֵאבֵײס) 'modern rabbi (in English-speaking countries)'

vs.

גלח [gáləkh] (pl. גלחים [galókhim]) 'priest'

vs.

גײסטלעכער (pl. –) 'clergyperson (of any faith)'

15.17.12 'Religious'

פֿרום 'observant of traditional Judaism'

vs.

אָרטאָדאָקסיש 'neo-Orthodox; observant of (quasi-)traditional Judaism'
(used especially of 'modern' Orthodox groups)

vs.

רעליגיעז [religyéz] 'religious (in any faith)'

15.17.13 'School'

חדר [khéydər] (pl. חדרים [khadórim]) 'traditional primary school'

vs.

שול(=עלעמענטאַר) (pl. שולן) 'primary school (in general)'

15.17.14 'Synagogue'

שול (pl. שולן) 'traditional synagogue'

vs.

סינאַגאָגן (pl. סינאַגאָגעס or סינאַגאָגע) 'modern synagogue'

vs.

קלויסטער (pl. -ס) '(specific) church'

vs.

קירך קידך (pl. ‎ן-) '(specific) church; the church in general (as an institution)'

vs.

מקום‌תפֿילה [mòkəm tfílə] (pl. מקום‌תפֿילות) 'house of prayer (in general)'

15.17.15 'Talmud'

גמרא [gəmórə] 'Talmud (looked at from the traditional point of view)'
(technically גמרא refers only to the later Aramaic portions comprising the
bulk of the Talmud but in traditional Yiddish usage, the term may refer to the
whole of the Talmud → §§4.3.2.2, 7.3.2.1)

vs.

תלמוד [tálmud] 'Talmud (looked at from a modern scientific or secular
point of view)'

15.17.16 'Teacher'

מלמד [məláməd] (pl. מלמדים [məlámdim]) 'traditional
primary school teacher'

vs.

רבי [rébə] (pl. רביס [rébəs]) 'traditional school / yeshiva teacher'

vs.

לערער (pl. — or ס-; f. לערערין, pl. ס-) 'teacher in general'

16 PHRASEOLOGY

16.0   OVERVIEW

The chapter provides introductory acquaintance with common idiomatic devices and a modest sampling of each. The categories are chosen to exemplify more general underlying strategies of Yiddish phraseology and idiomatic structure.

16.1   SIMILES

Stock similes with וי 'like; as', are frequently used in both speech and writing. They are drawn from everyday life or from Jewish history.

SAMPLES OF SIMILES

געזונט וי אָן אײַזן [gəzúnt vi an áyzn]

'healthy (/strong) as (a piece of) iron' (= 'very healthy / strong')

וי גאָט אין פּאַריז [vi gót in paríz]

'as God finds it in Paris' (= 'has it really good')

וי גאָט אין אָדעס (var.

'as God finds it in Odessa')

טויב וי די וואַנט [tóyb vi di vánt]

'deaf as the wall' (= 'very deaf')

מיאוס װי דער טױט [mֿ[əs vi der tóyt]

'ugly as death' (= 'very ugly')

נאָס װי אַ קאַץ [nás vi a káts]

'wet as a cat' (= 'very wet; drenched')

ס'װעט העלפֿן װי אַ טױטן באַנקעס [svət hèlfn vi a tòytn bánkəs]

'it will help as much as cupping glasses (once used to draw blood to the
skin as an alleged cure for numerous maladies) will help a dead
person' (= 'hopelessly useless')

פֿײַנט האָבן װי אַ שפּין [fàynt hobm vi a shpín]

'hate like a spider' (= 'hate intensely')

שײן װי די װעלט [shéyn vi di véit]

'beautiful as the world' (= 'very beautiful')

SAMPLES OF SIMILES FROM JEWISH HISTORY

גרױס װי עוג מלך הבשן [gróys vi óyg méylekh habóshn]

'tall as Og King of Bashan' (= 'very tall'; cf. Deuteronomy 3:11)

געזונט װי שמשון הגיבער [gəzúnt vi shìmshən hagíbər]

'healthy (/strong) as Samson' (= 'very strong'; → §5.8.1)

לאַנג װי דער גלות [láng vi der góləs]

'long as the Jewish diaspora' (= 'very long'; → §13.2.5)

קלוג חי שלמה המלך [klúg vi shlòymaméyləkh]

'wise as King Solomon' (= 'very wise'; often satiric; → §5.8.1)

ריַיך חי קורח [ráykh vi kóyrakh]

'wealthy as Korah' (cf. Pesaḥim 119a; Numbers 16; the Yiddish simile refers to the postbiblical legends of Korah's wealth rather than to the biblical account of his rebellion)

שיכור חי לוט [shíkər vi lót]

'drunk as Lot' (= 'very drunk'; Cf. Genesis 19: 30-35)

שלעכט חי ירבעם בן נבט [shlékht vi yəróvəm ben nəvót]

'evil as Jeroboam' (= 'very evil'; cf. Kings I 11:26-14:20)

16.2   REJOINDERS

Stock rejoinders are drawn from a variety of sources.

SAMPLES OF REJOINDERS

אדרבא [ádərabə]

'Of course!' (lit. 'to the contrary (I agree!)', i.e. 'Why shouldn't I agree?', hence 'Of course!')

אז די באָבע וואָלט געהאַט אַ באָרד וואָלט זי געוועַן אַ זיַידע

[adi bóbə volt gəhàt a bórd | voldzi gəvèn a zéydə]

'Stop saying *if* all the time!' (lit. 'If grandmother had a beard she would have been a grandfather')

מהילא תיתי [makh(ə)téysə / mékhə téysə]

'O.K!' (used to indicate agreeableness to a suggestion or proposal)

א נעכטיקער טאָג! [a nékhtikər tóg]

'No way it could be true!' (lit. 'yesterday's day')

קעלבערנע התםעלות! [kélbərnə hispáyləs]

'What naive enthusiasm!' (lit. 'enthusiasm of a calf / fool')

א קשיא אויף א מעשה! [akáshəf a máysə]

'Well, anything is possible!' (lit. 'a question on the veracity of a (made-up) story'; used to retract incredulity and concede a point; cf. §15.8 on קשיא)

16.3   SATIRIC CHARACTERIZATIONS

Anything in the language is capable of being turned around via the satiric rise-fall intonation (→ §11.1.1). Still, a number of characterizations have become part of a stock repertoire of ready-to-use epithets. They are often accompanied by raising of the head and eyebrows, and/or shaking of the head and upper part of the body.

SAMPLES OF SATIRIC CHARACTERIZATIONS

אַן איינפֿאַל! [an áynfal]

'What a stupid idea!' (lit. 'an idea / notion / novel proposal'; has the meaning of 'what a brilliant idea' when uttered loudly with falling intonation)

אַנטדעקט אַמעריקע! [andékt amérikə]

'Discovered America!' (used to mock a purported 'discovery' or 'innovation' or the purported 'importance' of the information offered)

א גרויסער קנאָקער! [a gróysər knákər]

'Big talker!' (lit. 'big knocker'; used to debunk a show-off, big-shot or person who has failed to pull something off)

זייער אַ גוטער חבֿר! [zéyər a gútər khávər]

'Some friend you are (/he is, etc.)!' (lit. 'a very good friend')

אַ חכם! [à khókhəm]

'What a fool (m.)!' (lit. 'a wise man')

אַ חכמתטע! [à khakhéym<code>ə</code>stə]

'What a fool (f.)!' (lit. 'a wise woman')

אַ חכמה! [à khókhmə]

'What a stupid thing to say!' (lit. '(a piece of) wisdom')

אַ ניַע מעשׂה! [a náyə màysə]

'We've heard that one before!' (lit. 'a new story'; used to debunk the alleged novelty of a statement or discovery)

אַ פֿיַנער מאַן! [á fáynər mán]

'What a nasty fellow!' (lit. 'a nice guy')

אַ קליַן ביסעלע טראָגעדיק! [á kléyn bísalə trógədik]

'Very slightly pregnant!' (used to reply to an attempted mitigation of a situation that is in fact a yes or no issue)

איין קליײניקײט! [éyn | kléynikayt]

'That's one little thing!' (used to debunk the allegedly minor importance of something and to argue that the point in question is in fact the heart of the matter)

א קראַסאַװיק! [á krasávits]

'Not a very good looking man/boy!' (lit. 'a handsome man')

א קראַסאַװיצע! [á krasávitsə]

'Not a very good looking woman/girl!' (lit. 'a beautiful woman')

16.4   PROVERBS

Proverbs are frequently used in both speech and writing.

SAMPLES OF PROVERBS

אַז מ'דאַרף דעם גנב נעמט מען אים אַראָפּ פֿון דער תליה

[amən dàf dem gánəv | nèmtmən em aróp fun der tíʃə]

'When the thief is needed, he is taken off the gallows' (i.e. it is permissible to associate with an undesirable person if necessity dictates)

אַז מ'קען ניט שרײבן זאָגט מען אַז די פּען איז אַ שלעכטע

[aməkènit shráybm | zoktmən adi pèn iza shiékhtə]

'People who can't write say the pen is no good'

אַליין גייט דער שוסטער באָרװעס [aléyn geyt der shùstər bórvəs]

'The shoemaker goes barefoot himself'

אַמאָל איז די רפֿואה ערגער פֿון דער מכה

[amòl idi rəfúə | èrgər fun der mákə]

'Sometimes the cure is worse than the malady'

וואו מ'האָט דיך ליב גיי ווייניק, וואו מ'האָט דיך ניט ליב גיי אין גאַנצן ניט

[vu məhot dəkh lìb gey véynik | vù məhot dəkh nìt lìb gey ingántsn nit]

'Where you are liked, go seldom; where you are not liked do not go at all' (i.e. don't rush to accept invitations)

ווער ס'האָט די מאה האָט די דעה [ver səhòt diméyə | hoti déyə]

'Wealth is power' (lit. 'whoever has the hundred has the authority')

די מלאכים גייען ניט אַרום אויף דער ערד

[di malókhim gèyən nit arùm af der érd]

'The angels don't walk about on earth' (used to allay disappointment in other people)

אַ נאַר בלײַבט אַ נאַר [a nár | bláypt a nár]

'A fool remains a fool'

פֿרעגט ניט דעם רופֿא פֿרעג דעם חולה [frègnit dəm róyfə | frèg dem khóylə]

'Don't ask the doctor, ask the patient'

אַ קללה איז ניט קיין טעלעגראַמע [a klólə | iz nit kin teləgrámə]

'A curse isn't a telegram' (used to allay the anxiety of a victim of verbal abuse)

16.5   REDUNDANT INTENSIFIERS

In addition to adding emphasis, redundant intensifiers convey a rather
humorous and happy mood, even in situations where the subject is one of
gravity.

SAMPLES OF REDUNDANT INTENSIFIERS

אַוועקגײן אין גאַנצן   [avèggeyn ingántsn]
'leave entirely'

דערהרגנען אויף טויט   [dahàrgənən af tóyt]
'kill completely' (lit. 'kill to death'; by overuse the phrase has also come to
mean 'beat up badly' and can be used to tease
lovingly as a facetious threat)

משוגע אויפֿן גאַנצן קאָפּ   [məshúgə | afn gántsn | kóp]
'completely crazy' (lit. 'crazy in the entire head')

פֿאַרפּלאָנטערט אין גאַנצן   [farplóntərt ingántsn]
'completely confused; inextricably entangled'

זיך צוהערן מיט ביידע אויערן   [zikh tsúhern mit béydə óyərn]
'listen with both ears' (= 'listen attentively')

16.6   HISTORICAL METAPHORS

Historical metaphors are used both as complete sentences on their own, in
reaction to a situation described, and as metaphors within a sentence.

SAMPLES OF HISTORICAL METAPHORS

איובֿס צרות [íəvs tsórəs]

'Job's troubles' (= 'grave personal difficulties')

חושך מצרים [khóyshəkh mitsráyim]

'the darkness of Egypt (during the Plague of Darkness)' (= 'very dark')

טעם גן־עדן [tám ganéydn]

'the taste of the Garden of Eden' (= 'delicious')

יתרוס נעמען [yísroys némən]

'Jethro's names' (said of a person or place with many names; cf. Rashi's commentary at Exodus 18:1)

מ'פֿירט שטרוי קיין מצרים [məfírt shtróy kin mitsráyim]

'They're carrying straw to Egypt' (after the Israelites escaped their former slave labour which included carrying straw)

(= 'wasted energy'; cf. 'carrying coals to Newcastle')

משה רבינוס שטעקן [móyshə rabéynuz shtékn]

'the rod of Moses' (said of something apparently miraculous; also to mock something allegedly impressive or to question the authenticity of a feat)

SELECT BIBLIOGRAPHY

DICTIONARIES

Aaron Bergman, **Student's Dictionary. English-Yiddish and Yiddish-English. A Popular Dictionary for School and Home**. Kinderbuch Publishers: New York 1968.

Alexander Harkavy, **Yiddish—English—Hebrew Dictionary**. Hebrew Publishing Company: New York 1925, 1928 and numerous reprints. Photomechanical reprint with introduction by Dovid Katz, Schocken and Yivo: New York 1987.

Judah A. Joffe and Yudel Mark, eds., **Great Dictionary of the Yiddish Language**, vols. I-IV only (vols III-IV by Mark). Yiddish Dictionary Committee: New York 1961, 1966, 1971, 1980.

M. Tsanin, **Complete Hebrew—Yiddish Dictionary**. Letste nayes: Tel Aviv 1960; **Complete Yiddish—Hebrew Dictionary**, H. Leyvik farlag: Tel Aviv 1982.

Uriel Weinreich, **Modern English-Yiddish Yiddish-English Dictionary**. Yivo & McGraw-Hill: New York 1968.

GRAMMARS

Yudel Mark, **A Grammar of Standard Yiddish** [in Yiddish]. Congress for Jewish Culture: New York 1978.

Mordkhe Schaechter, **Yiddish II. A Textbook for Intermediate Courses** [in Yiddish]. Institute for the Study of Human Issues: Philadelphia 1986.

Uriel Weinreich, **College Yiddish. An Introduction to the Yiddish Language and Jewish Life and Culture.** Yivo: New York 1949 and numerous revised reprints.

ANTHOLOGIES IN THE ORIGINAL YIDDISH

M. Basin, **Anthology: Five Hundred Years of Yiddish Poetry** [in Yiddish], II vols. Literarisher farlag: New York 1917.

H. Bass, **Yiddish Drama of the Twentieth Century**, II vols [in Yiddish]. Congress for Jewish Culture: New York 1977.

Nachmen Mayzel, **America in Yiddish Literature** [in Yiddish]. An Anthology. Yiddisher Kultur Farband: New York 1955.

Joseph and Eleanor Mlotek, **Pearls of Yiddish Poetry** [in Yiddish]. I. L. Peretz Publishing House: Tel Aviv 1974.

Chone Shmeruk, **An Anthology of Poetry and Prose by Twelve Soviet Yiddish Writers** [in Yiddish]. Di Goldene Keyt & I. L. Peretz Publishing House: Tel Aviv 1964.

Chava Turniansky, **From our Yiddish Literature. Textbook**

for the Study of Yiddish [with partial glossary] [in Yiddish]. World Council for Yiddish and Jewish Culture: Tel Aviv 1980.

S. Yefroikin and H. Bass, **The Yiddish Word** [in Yiddish]. Workmen's Circle: New York 1947 and further reprints.

Aaron Zeitlin and J. J. Trunk, **An Anthology of Yiddish Prose in Poland Between Two World Wars (1914–1939)** [in Yiddish]. Central Yiddish Culture Organization: New York 1946.

Y. Zilberberg and Yudel Mark, **Anthology of Yiddish Literature. Part I** [in Yiddish]. Congress for Jewish Culture: New York 1969; H. Bass, **Anthology of Yiddish Literature. Part II** [in Yiddish]. Congress for Jewish Culture: New York 1976.

FOLKSONGS

Menke Katz, **Yiddish Folksong and Poetry** [in Yiddish]. Oxford Programme in Yiddish: Oxford 1985.

Eleanor Gordon Mlotek, **Favorite Yiddish Songs of our Generation**. Educational Workmen's Circle: New York 1977.

Ruth Rubin, **Jewish Folk Songs in Yiddish and English**. Oak Publications: New York 1965.

Ruth Rubin, **Voices of a People. The Story of Yiddish**

Folksong. Jewish Publication Society of America: Philadelphia 1979.

Aharon Vinkovetzky and Abba Kovner and Sinai Leichter, **Anthology of Yiddish Folksongs**, IV vols [in Yiddish, Hebrew and English]. Mount Scopus Publications by the Magnes Press: Jerusalem 1983–1986.

PHRASEOLOGY

Ignaz Bernstein, **Yiddish Proverbs and Sayings** [in Yiddish and German]. J. Kauffmann: Warsaw 1908. Photomechanical reprint by Georg Olms Verlagsbuchhandlung: Hildesheim 1969. Yiddish language edition by Congress for Jewish Culture: New York 1983.

James A. Matisoff, **Blessings, Curses, Hopes, and Fears**. **Psycho-Ostensive Expressions in Yiddish**. Institute for the Study of Human Issues: Philadelphia 1979.

Nahum Stutchkoff, **Thesaurus of the Yiddish Language** [in Yiddish]. Yivo: New York 1950.

HISTORY OF YIDDISH

Solomon A. Birnbaum, **Yiddish. A Survey and a Grammar**. Manchester University and University of Toronto: Manchester & Toronto 1979.

Marvin I. Herzog et al., eds., **The Field of Yiddish. Studies in Language, Folklore, and Literature**. Fourth Collection. Institute for the Study of Human Issues: Philadelphia 1980.

Dovid Katz, ed., **Origins of the Yiddish Language** [Papers from the First Annual Oxford Winter Symposium in Yiddish Language and Literature]. Pergamon Press: Oxford 1987.

Max Weinreich, **History of the Yiddish Language**. University of Chicago: Chicago & London 1980 [= partial translation of the original Yiddish edition, **History of the Yiddish Language. Concepts, Facts, Methods**, IV vols. Yivo: New York 1973].

Uriel Weinreich, **'Yiddish Language'** in **Encyclopaedia Judaica**, Vol. XVI, pp.789–798. Keter Publishing House: Jerusalem 1972.

HISTORY OF YIDDISH LITERATURE

Max Erik, **A History of Yiddish Literature from its Beginnings until the Haskalah Period** [in Yiddish]. Kultur-lige: Warsaw 1928 [photo-mechanical reprint by Congress for Jewish Culture: New York 1979].

Charles Madison, **Yiddish Literature. Its Scope and Major Writers**. Schocken Books: New York 1971.

Chone Shmeruk, **'Yiddish Literature'** in **Encyclopaedia**

Judaica, Vol. XVI, pp.798–833. Keter Publishing House: Jerusalem 1972.

Chone Shmeruk, **Yiddish Literature: Aspects of its History** [in Hebrew]. Porter Institute for Poetics and Semiotics, Tel Aviv University: Tel Aviv 1978.

Ruth R. Wisse, **A Shtetl and other Yiddish Novellas**. Behrman House: New York 1973.

Israel Zinberg, **Old Yiddish Literature from its Origins to the Haskalah Period**. Hebrew Union College Press & Ktav Publishing House: Cincinnati & New York 1975.

SOCIOLOGY OF YIDDISH

Joshua A. Fishman, ed., **Never Say Die! A Thousand Years of Yiddish in Jewish Life and Letters**. Mouton: The Hague & Paris & New York 1981.

Emanuel S. Goldsmith, **Architects of Yiddishism at the Beginning of the Twentieth Century. A Study in Jewish Cultural History**. Fairleigh Dickinson University Press and Associated University Presses: Rutherford & London 1976.

STUDIES IN YIDDISH CULTURE

Nathan Ausubel, **A Treasury of Jewish Humour**. Doubleday & Company:

New York 1951.

Lucy S. Dawidowicz, **The Golden Tradition. Jewish Life and Thought in Eastern Europe**. Schocken Books: New York 1984.

Irving Howe, **The Immigrant Jews of New York. 1881 to the Present** [published in the United States as **World of Our Fathers**]. Routledge & Kegan Paul: London & Boston.

Maurice Samuel, **In Praise of Yiddish**. Cowles Book Company: New York 1971.

MAJOR DISTRIBUTORS OF YIDDISH BOOKS

CYCO Books, 25 East 21st St, New York, NY 10010, USA.

National Yiddish Book Center, Old East Street School, PO Box 969, Amherst, Massachusetts 01004, USA.

I. L. Peretz Publishing House, 14 Brenner St, Tel Aviv, Israel.

Workmen's Circle, Education Department, 45 East 33rd St., New York, NY 10016, USA.

Yivo Institute for Jewish Research, 1048 Fifth Avenue, New York, NY 10028, USA.

GENERAL INDEX

GRAMMATICAL INDEX

INDEX OF SELECTED YIDDISH ITEMS